The Case for District-Based Reform

Leading, Building, and Sustaining
School Improvement

The Case for District-Based Reform

Leading, Building, and Sustaining
School Improvement

JONATHAN A. SUPOVITZ

HARVARD EDUCATION PRESS
CAMBRIDGE, MASSACHUSETTS

Library of Congress Control Number 2006930072

Paperback 10-digit ISBN 1-891792-27-X
Library Edition 10-digit ISBN 1-891792-28-8

Paperback 13-digit ISBN 978-1-891792-27-4
Library Edition 13-digit ISBN 978-1-891792-28-1

Published by Harvard Education Press,
an imprint of the Harvard Education Publishing Group

Harvard Education Press
8 Story Street
Cambridge, MA 02138

Cover Design: Anne Carter

The typeface used in this book is Adobe Minion Pro.

Dedicated to my heart and soul,
Isabela and Lukas,
who embody the children of the future,
whose lives I hope this book
in some small way improves.

Contents

Acknowledgments

There are many people who contributed, either directly or indirectly, to making this book possible. First, I'd like to thank the district leaders, school leaders, and teachers of the Duval County Public Schools, who so graciously welcomed me into their professional homes every time I returned to Jacksonville with ever more inquiries about what they were doing and why. These include, but are not limited to, Tim Ballentine, Mary Brown, Jill Budd, Charles Cline, Marita Eng, John Fryer, Steve Hite, Donna Hulsey, Janice Hunter, Selinda Keys, Barbara Langley, Elaine Mann, Levi Mcintosh, Leila Mousa, Ed Pratt-Dannals, Ruth Sentflebber, Terri Stahlman, Nancy Snyder, John Thompson, Barbara Vandervort, and Peggy Willliams. I'd also like to thank my colleagues a the Consortium for Policy Research in Education at the University of Pennsylvania, Susan Fuhrman, Peg Goertz, Tom Corcoran, Henry May, Elliot Weinbaum, and Kate Hovde, who provided me with an engaging and supportive environment within which to incubate this work. Thanks also to Marjory Jacobson for her love and backing throughout the process. Finally, thanks to Patricia, whose support I probably did not understand and appreciate enough. Thank you all for the countless hours you spent helping me to understand and communicate this complicated thing called district-based reform.

Prologue

From the start, there was something exciting percolating in the air. My first meeting with retired Air Force major general John Fryer, the new superintendent of the Duval County, Florida, Public Schools, the nation's twentieth largest school district, took place on a sultry September morning in 1999. As I entered the school board building for that 7 A.M. meeting, I was met with the pungent aroma of freshly ground coffee wafting across the St. John's River from the Maxwell House Coffee roasting plant on the opposite bank.

Superintendent Fryer ushered me into his sixth-floor office and laid out his ambition to use a national comprehensive school reform program called America's Choice—for which I was directing the national evaluation—as the fulcrum for his efforts to improve not just a few but *all* of the district's 150 schools. My notes from that first meeting quote Fryer as calling the original set of Duval County's America's Choice schools his "vanguard of schools" and talking about using the school reform design to build capacity across the district to expand and sustain broad instructional reform. In the years since, I have been following the scale-up of standards-based reform in Duval County, which has produced significant improvements in student learning.

From 1999 through 2005 I chronicled the uneven progress of the district's landmark reform process and the sometimes volatile political environment within which it incubated. This included major reform initiatives in standards, curriculum, assessment, professional development, and data use, as well as firestorms over school busing, school board relations, and community perceptions of America's Choice. My long-running work in the district has given me unprecedented access to the key players and inner workings of the system. Thus the research that informs this study includes well over one hundred interviews with teachers, school leaders, and district officials; annual survey data of school principals; site visits and classroom observations in a representative sample of district schools; annual analyses of student performance results; and an examination of district policy documents and newspaper reports.

The greatest challenge that education leaders face today is the wide-scale improvement of teaching and learning. If the core mission of schooling is to build the knowledge and thinking skills of students, then raising the quality of teaching and learning across school systems is the central goal. To reach this goal, we need examples of how school systems can raise the quality of their teaching and learning, along with distillations of lessons learned from those who have embarked on this quest. The story of Duval County is central to education reform in the United States precisely because the school district is currently the prevailing organizing unit supporting school improvement. It is hard to imagine broad-scale educational improvements today that do not run directly through school districts.

This book has two central purposes. First, it closely chronicles the long and winding journey of one district and its efforts to improve teaching and learning systemwide. Through longitudinal case study research I examine the implications, tensions, and tradeoffs for district leaders who seek to enact a particular vision of instructional quality. School and district leaders can learn a tremendous amount from this account of another district's journey.

The second purpose is more ambitious. I seek to redefine the role of the school district in the twenty-first century. By leading instructional improvement efforts with a vision of commitment, capacity, and sustainability, and by reorienting relationships within both the district and the larger educational environment, school districts can play a central role in improving the quality of public education in the years to come. The future of public education depends on developing new ways to support instructional improvement in large numbers of schools. I offer some important possibilities in this book.

Introduction

Local control of education is a distinctly American ideal. In virtually no other country does the local community maintain so much influence over the form, function, and funding of schooling. As a result, there are almost sixteen thousand school districts in the United States (Hoffman & Sable, 2006), and their diversity is astonishing. The vast majority of these districts are tiny; almost two-thirds of them have fewer than fifteen hundred students—the enrollment of a fair-sized urban middle school. Only about 3 percent of U.S. school districts have enrollments of more than fifteen thousand, yet this 3 percent educates nearly 45 percent of America's public school students!

Along with local control comes local responsibility for results. If you look at the achievement within any of these midsize to large (i.e., over fifteen thousand students) districts, you will likely find marked disparities in student performance that cannot be explained solely by differences in socioeconomic status. In other words, even within the same school district, there are schools performing well and others faring poorly. How can we explain these differences? What is happening in some schools that is not happening in others? These differences are in substantial part due to variations in instructional emphasis and in the quality of teaching across schools. So, whose job is it to ensure that the quality of instruction is uniformly high in all schools within a system? This is the job of the school district.

My overarching argument in this book is that school district leaders who wish to improve the performance of *all* students within their system must make a concerted effort to employ the central lever that is in their power to improve student learning—the fulcrum of instructional improvement. This approach is distinguishable from the more common scenario in which district leaders, for all intents and purposes, cede instructional authority to school leaders, who in turn may pass it on to individual teachers. The result of this vacuum of instructional leadership at the district level is huge variability in the quality of learning opportunities children receive from school to school and from classroom to classroom. Hence the inequities in student opportunities to learn.

Now make no mistake, the problem of variable instructional quality is complex, and not readily solvable by simple remedies or top-down solutions. If it were easy to correct, then smart, goodhearted people would have done so already. But American education is a peculiar institution, with its own distinctive history, particular organizational characteristics, and singular culture. In such an environment, the influence of a central authority on dispersed classrooms is tenuous. Strong-arm efforts have traditionally failed to improve teaching and learning and would likely fail if tried again. So, are there viable alternative approaches that help district leaders have a strong influence on instructional practice in classrooms across school systems?

District leaders approach the task of wide-scale instructional improvement in many ways. Perhaps the most common approach is to adopt a range of curricula across different subject areas and then provide training and support for those materials. In another popular approach, district leaders require schools to choose from a set of external school reform models. Some district leaders may attempt to guide teachers' inquiry into their own instructional practice and its relationship to their students' learning. Still others develop their own particular vision of instructional quality and focus their efforts around that vision. This is by no means an exhaustive list of strong district support strategies, but it provides some examples of how district leaders attempt to improve teaching and learning across a school system.

All of these theories of action have been the subjects of natural experiments in education. The first approach of curricular adoption has been criticized because of weak district influence and lack of coherence across grades and content areas (Fuhrman, 1993). Supported by New American Schools, several urban districts, including Memphis, San Antonio, and Cincinnati, pursued the second approach by encouraging all schools to adopt comprehensive school reform models. Evaluations of these efforts indicated large variability in the effectiveness of the approaches and raised questions about the district's ability to support such widely differing philosophical approaches to school improvement (Berends, Bodilly, & Kirby, 2002). The third approach, fostering more intimate inquires into instructional improvement, is being undertaken in Trenton, New Jersey, by superintendent James Lytle (2002). While this approach has the advantages of encouraging reform to grow deeper roots and teachers and school leaders to take more ownership, it raises questions about the pace of reform and the districts' ability to support diverse approaches.

In this book I examine the implications of the fourth approach—the articulation and enactment of a unifying vision of instructional quality while maintaining some level of local flexibility. I explore the promises and pitfalls for district leaders who seek to infuse a distinct conception of what instruction should look like within classrooms and across a system, even as they encourage local choice and commitment. With this book I also intend to add to and build upon the tradition of researchers who have shined a spotlight on effective districts. This work focuses on one site—Duval County, Florida—that has achieved notable success. A critical examination of that site's experience may provide insights from which other district leaders might profit.

More specifically, this book has two layers of purpose. At one level my intentions are to tell the story of how Duval County leaders developed their vision and system of instructional improvement that produced districtwide learning gains. Like most such stories, Duval County's is a meandering one, full of promising ideas and false starts, strokes of genius and folly, and both intended and unintended consequences. An analysis of the implications of some key decisions of Duval County leaders reveals some of the tensions and tradeoffs implicit in their choices. Therefore, if other education leaders are to learn from this story, they must hear about not just the ultimate shape of the system but also the process and decisions that contributed to molding it into its current form.

My second purpose in writing this book is to extrapolate beyond Duval County's experience and use these lessons to consider new ways of conceiving of the school district as a stronger support organization for widespread instructional improvement in schools. I believe that if the school district is to have a future in American education, we must rethink its role and responsibilities within the present educational environment and re-conceptualize its tasks and functions to provide stronger support for teaching and learning in schools. Districts can play a powerful role in supporting school improvement if they reposition themselves both internally to the schools they serve and externally to the greater educational environment. Internally, districts must develop a reciprocal relationship with schools, exchanging a commitment to capacity-building for accountability. Externally, districts must develop the capacity to scan the broader educational environment and negotiate relationships with external providers in order to enhance the expertise within their systems. Perhaps most important, districts must evolve into organizations that explore instructional problems more systematically in order to build their own knowledge base, and thus to improve teaching across their systems.

My familiarity with education reform in Duval County comes from many years working in the district. Since 1999 I have been the principal investigator of the Consortium for Policy Research in Education's (CPRE) national evaluation of the America's Choice comprehensive school reform model, and it is through that evaluation that I first began to do fieldwork in Duval County. In 2000, district leaders asked CPRE to conduct a separate, more intensive evaluation of their standards-based reform efforts because the America's Choice evaluation was not providing them with sufficient feedback on either implementation or performance in their schools. Even while CPRE conducted more concentrated fieldwork in Duval County, we continued to include the district's schools in our America's Choice evaluation reports, including those on instructional leadership (Supovitz & Poglinco, 2001), literacy workshop implementation (Bach & Supovitz, 2003; Supovitz, Poglinco, & Bach, 2002), instructional coaching (Poglinco et al., 2003), data use (Supovitz & Klein, 2003), and student impact studies (Supovitz, Poglinco, & Snyder, 2001; Supovitz, Taylor, & May, 2002).

Beginning in 2002, it gradually became clear that Duval County leaders were developing something special in the district that transcended the implementation of America's Choice. At that point the idea for this book began to take shape, and I became more systematic in my efforts to study the district's standards-based reform efforts. In that year I conducted fieldwork in a representative sample of ten schools in the district and continued my extensive interviews with district leaders and documentation of their work. I also continued to provide technical assistance to the district in its development of an instructional implementation monitoring system and conducted research on the influences of the system (Supovitz & Weathers, 2004).

This book is unlike other district research in several important respects. First, rather than just identifying key components of district support, I consider the merits and constraints of each component within a broader framework. Second, rather than identifying a district that has performed better than its peers and then looking back to understand why its results were different, this research follows a district throughout its reform implementation. Consequently, I am able to capture the uneven process of implementation rather than just the ultimate destination. This longitudinal method allows me to discuss the decisions, dilemmas, tensions, and uncertainties that are part of the journey. In this sense, I think this work breaks new ground in exploring the decisions of an effective district's sojourn and the implications of those decisions. Third, my ambition is to use Duval County's experience to consider a reconfiguration of the district role in supporting systemwide improvement in the twenty-first century. While districts have long handled the managerial functions of supporting schools—delivering textbooks to classrooms, getting the buses to run on schedule, maintaining school buildings—supporting the improvement of teaching and learning has been a thornier challenge.

The chapters of this book are loosely organized around the four central components of a theory of action for strong district support for systemwide improvement of teaching and learning. These are:

1. Developing a specific vision of what high-quality instruction should look like inside classrooms.
2. Building both the commitment and the capacity of employees across the system to enact and support the instructional vision.
3. Constructing mechanisms to provide data at all levels of the system that will be used both to provide people with information that informs their practices and to monitor the implementation of the instructional vision.
4. Developing a means to help people continually deepen their implementation and to help the district continually refine this vision and understand its implications.

These four central ideas are explored throughout this book. In chapter 1 I review the historical district role, as well as more recent district efforts to improve instructional quality. I then introduce Duval County's reform efforts and review the impacts its efforts have had on student performance. Chapter 2 establishes the central importance of district leaders developing a vision of instructional quality as a way to focus attention on the organizational mission of improving teaching and learning and providing a focal point for reform efforts. Chapter 3 explores the twin challenges of spurring commitment and developing capacity to enact an instructional vision. Chapter 4 examines how teachers and schools reacted to and implemented the instructional practices advocated by Duval County leaders and explores the rationale behind peoples' choices. Chapter 5 conceptualizes a system of districtwide data use and examines Duval County's use of various forms of data. Chapter 6 focuses on the challenge of sustaining reform and the utility of organizational learning mechanisms to do so. Chapter 7 extrapolates beyond the experiences of Duval County to examine the utility of districts in today's educational constellation and to reconsider how the school district can most effectively support the improvement of teaching and learning across its school system. In chapter 8 I propose a reconceptualization of the school district for the twenty-first century.

Sustained instructional emphasis and its systematic support is a tall order, one not easily achieved. Yet if districts are not willing and able to rise to the challenge of supporting systemwide improvements in teaching and expanding learning opportunities for all students, then perhaps it is time to think of other types and/or combinations of educational support organizations that can do this job more effectively. If we are to improve the quality of education for our citizenry in the twenty-first century, the capacity to do this must come from local educational support organizations.

1

The Challenge for School Districts

Historically, districts have not been considered very effective at facilitating the improvement of teaching and learning across their schools. Weak central office attention to teaching and learning is a well-documented pattern identified by educational researchers. Rowan (1982), for example, surveyed local district staffing patterns in California between 1930 and 1970 and showed that as district central office staff increased and job titles grew more specialized, specialization did not result in more personnel attending to issues of curriculum and instruction. A 1978 study by Hannaway and Sproull found that less than 10 percent of district work over a given time period had anything to do with schools, and less than 3 percent had to do with curriculum. Crowson and Morris (1985) analyzed how districts conducted their business and found that 80 percent of districtwide interactions focused on budget, personnel, scheduling, pupil behavior, facilities, and parent complaints, while less than 20 percent had to do with curriculum and instruction. Floden and his colleagues (1988) studied district influences on curriculum and teaching in fourth-grade mathematics classes in more than a hundred districts and five states and concluded that "the picture that emerges is one of districts with a vague intention to direct instructional content, but without any considered strategy to do so" (p. 98).

There are several challenges that may prevent district leaders from focusing on their core mission of improving teaching and learning. First, as the Crowson and Morris study suggests, there is a dizzying array of district functions and responsibilities that are more about managing the systems around schooling than attending to the improvement of teaching and learning. Districts serve a number of purposes. They manage numerous contracts and provide economies of scale for educational goods and services that can be purchased and distributed more efficiently by a centralized authority. They manage transportation systems that shuttle students between home and school. They maintain numerous facilities, including schools, training sites, and central office buildings. They administer federal programs that have a multitude of data collection and reporting requirements. Through school board elections and decisionmaking processes, they act as laboratories for local democracy and a means for mobilizing political support for public schools at the level where their impact is most immediate. But most of these purposes have little, if anything, directly to do with the teaching and learning of young people, which is the main purpose of schooling. Stanford education professor Larry Cuban, in his 1988 book *The Managerial Imperative and the Practice of Leadership in Schools*, argues that education leaders are caught in a crucible of managerial, political, and instructional demands and that instructional attention inevitably loses out.

A second challenge district leaders face is developing coherence across different elements and components within an education system. More recent theories of systemic educational reform hold that powerful improvements in teaching and learning can come from developing coherence and alignment across the complex and different elements and components of an educational system, including challenging standards for students, the alignment of the policy components of educational governance (curriculum, assessments, accountability systems, teacher certification requirements, preservice and in-service professional development), and school flexibility to develop the strategies that best suit the needs of their students (Cohen, 1995; Fuhrman, 1993; Smith & O'Day, 1991). Newmann, Smith, Allensworth, and Bryk (2001) define the problem of school improvement as one of program coherence. They argue that "instructional program coherence," or the development of a "set of interrelated programs for students and staff that are guided by a common framework for curriculum, instruction, assessment, and learning climate that are pursued over a sustained period of time" (p. 297), will lead to improved student outcomes. Using data from Chicago from 1994 to 1997, Newmann et al. (2001) found that schools with greater instructional program coherence had greater gains in student learning than schools that did not.

A third challenge district leaders face when trying to change the instructional practice of large numbers of teachers is the deeply rooted culture of teacher autonomy over instructional decisionmaking. Research suggests that teachers generally oppose the imposition of external constraints on their decisions about the teaching of students (Tyler, 1988; Wilson, Herriott, & Firestone, 1991). Teachers have the most intimate knowledge about the social development and learning needs of their students, the argument goes, and therefore are in the best position to make appropriate decisions about them. Impingement on faculty influence and teacher autonomy has been known to increase school conflict (Ingersoll, 1996), and policies that attempt to influence instructional practice by outside regulations, mandates, and incentives often get in the way of teachers' efforts to do their jobs in their own way. Cohen (1982) argues that educational policy has had little influence on instructional practices precisely because of the traditional autonomy teachers have in classrooms and their latitude to interpret policy to fit their own circumstances and proclivities.

A fourth impediment to district leaders' support for instructional changes is that they may lack incentives to persevere with instructional initiatives that may take many years to unfold. Hess (1999) examined the frequency that reforms were begun and sustained in fifty-seven districts across the United States. He found that the overwhelming majority of districts were initiating reforms at a dizzying pace and that reform was the status quo. He concluded that incentives for local policymakers are heavily stacked toward introducing reforms but that there are few incentives to encourage the more difficult work of supporting and maintaining reforms over the longer periods of time necessary for them to influence instructional practice in schools.

Beyond incentives, several researchers have framed the task of district-wide improvement as one of district capacity to support the more ambitious instructional reforms that characterize today's educational improvement efforts. Elmore and Fuhrman (1994) argue that current reforms that feature more ambitious standards, require deeper knowledge of subject matter, and rely on more complex pedagogical practices are even more dependent on local capacity than were previous reform efforts. Several authors have framed the task of ambitious policy implementation as one of leader learning (Cohen & Barnes, 1993; Spillane & Thompson, 1997). According to this line of reasoning, district capacity to promote and support ambitious instruction hinges on leaders' abilities both to learn themselves and to help others learn new ideas. In other words, leaders' beliefs about learning predicated the way they conceived of and structured learning opportunities within their organizations (Spillane, 2002).

A final challenge for district leaders is to develop systems to support a practice—instruction—that is inherently nonroutine, complex, and therefore difficult to manage and support. Elmore (1993), for example, explained district leaders' tendency to focus on district management and governance rather than on instruction by noting that actively managing teaching and learning is a far more complex and difficult task: "The basic work of teaching and learning is highly uncertain . . . so higher-level administrators tend to withdraw from it to focus their energies on mobilizing support in the community and actively managing the flow of people and money, rather than teaching and learning" (p. 113). Put simply, instructional change on a large scale is a tough nut for system leaders to crack.

RECENT DEVELOPMENTS IN DISTRICT SUPPORT
FOR INSTRUCTIONAL IMPROVEMENT

Despite these obstacles, there is perhaps more reason for optimism as we enter the twenty-first century. Recent educational research has chronicled several promising district improvement efforts and articulated their strategies. Elmore and Burney (1997) raised considerable interest and attention with their examination of the professional development strategies of New York City's Community District #2, led by Superintendent Anthony Alvarado. Elmore and Burney described Alvarado's strategy of focusing a range of professional development strategies on support for systemwide literacy improvement. The strategy featured a series of professional development models, including a professional development laboratory, instructional consulting, intervisitations and peer networks, and principal oversight.

Togneri and Anderson (2003) examined the traits of five high-poverty districts (Aldine, Texas; Chula Vista, California; Kent County, Maryland; Minneapolis, Minnesota; and Providence, Rhode Island) that were improving student achievement. They found that these districts had "a strikingly similar set of strategies to improve instruction" (p. 4), which included (1) the courage to acknowledge poor performance and the will to seek solutions;

(2) a vision that focused on student learning and guided instructional improvement; (3) a systemwide approach to improving instruction, including systemwide curricula and instructional supports; (4) data-based decisionmaking; (5) new approaches to professional development; (5) redefined leadership roles, and (6) commitment to sustaining reform over the long haul.

A highly publicized report from MDRC (Snipes, Doolittle, & Herlihy, 2002) presented case studies of four urban systems that were improving student achievement. The researchers selected four districts (Houston, Texas; Sacramento, California; Charlotte-Mecklenberg, North Carolina; and the Chancellor's District in New York City) based upon trends of improvement in reading and mathematics from 1995 to 2001. Their report highlighted the need for a prolonged period of political and organizational stability and consensus on educational reform strategies. They found that the improving districts had several things in common. First, they focused on student achievement and specific achievement goals, aligned curricula with state standards, and translated standards into instructional practices. Second, they complemented their state accountability system with a more specific system for holding district leaders and building staff responsible for producing results. Third, they focused on the lowest-performing schools. Fourth, they developed districtwide curricula and instructional approaches rather than allowing each school to choose its own strategies. Fifth, they focused on professional development and support for consistent implementation across their districts. Sixth, they drove reform by clearly defining the central office role of guiding, supporting, and improving instruction in schools. Seventh, they committed themselves to data-driven decisionmaking and instruction. Eighth, they initially focused on the elementary grades instead of trying to fix everything. Finally, in middle school and high school, they emphasized reading and mathematics.

WHAT IS THE DISTRICT'S ROLE IN INSTRUCTIONAL IMPROVEMENT TODAY?

Districts, whether improving or not, are at the crux of our American system of education. The district sits at the intersection of state policy and the work of schools. They are the classic middle in education policy, residing between federal and state policies above and local school practice below. State poli-

cies early in the twenty-first century are increasingly focused on the concepts of systemic (later standards-based) reform. The concept of systemic
reform, as articulated by Stanford researchers Marshall Smith and Jenni-
fer O'Day (1991) in their groundbreaking work on state relationships to districts and schools, expressed the state role in supporting the improvement
of teaching and learning in schools. According to Smith (who would later become assistant education secretary in the first Clinton administration)
and O'Day's conception, states were to develop a clear and coherent set of
education policies to improve classroom instruction and student learning.
Chief among these polices are clear and challenging standards for student
learning, an aligned assessment system to measure student progress, and an
accountability system to provide incentives and disincentives for improvement. States to a lesser degree articulate the curricula, professional development (in-service), and instructional programs necessary for students to
meet state standards, as measured by state assessments. An important component of this theory is that schools are to have the flexibility to determine
for themselves how best to increase student performance. Many of the core
concepts of systemic reform have taken root across America. Standards for
student performance, although variable in quality (Cross, Rebarber, Torres,
& Finn, 2004; Skinner & Staresina, 2004), are ubiquitous. Both the federal
government and states have cranked up their assessment and accountability
systems (Fuhrman & Elmore, 2004).

Many districts took this guidance as a cue locally to adopt a more refined
version of the standards, assessment, and accountability triumvirate. In an
important natural experiment, in 1996 the Pew Charitable Trusts gave four-
year grants to seven urban school districts to assist in their implementation
of standards-based systemic reform. Jane David and Patrick Shields (2001) of
SRI international evaluated this effort. They found that the core components
of standards-based reform—standards, assessments, and accountability—
"do not do a very good job of communicating high expectations for students,
providing information to guide instructional improvement, or motivating
widespread instructional change beyond test preparation" (p. ii). They concluded that "clear expectations for instruction are as critical as clear expectations for student learning" (p. iii), essentially calling for greater instructional
guidance on the part of district leaders. However, they warn, "creating an infrastructure to support teacher learning . . . and finding the right balance of

authority and discretion present significant challenges to district leaders (p. iii). Thus within the useful framework of standards-based systemic reform, district leaders must provide greater guidance and support balanced against the traditional autonomy that teachers have learned to expect.

Many alternative systems have also arisen in the form of attempts to provide stronger instructional support for students, teachers, and schools. A number of these are important as precursors to the external assistance/district relationship that is one focus of this book. A range of assistance providers have long offered a vast assortment of products and services to schools and districts. Teacher and school networks, often operating on the boundaries of district-sanctioned strategies, informally help teachers and schools adopt new practices and techniques. Subject-matter networks, often led by grassroots advocates or university faculty, create a web of resources for teachers and schools. But over the past decade, more purposeful partnerships have been formed between districts and other education organizations that are intended to build school and/or district capacity and provide models for district instructional support.

Two important efforts of the 1990s formalized external assistance to schools and districts as an important source of knowledge and ideas for improvement. These efforts revealed both the value of district-provider partnerships and the limitations of external assistance. The first trend toward formal external assistance started with the formation of New American Schools (NAS) in 1991, and the subsequent popularization of comprehensive school reform (CSR). NAS sponsored a variety of school reform model developers, including Accelerated Schools, America's Choice, the Comer School Development Program, Seymour Hirsch's Core Knowledge, Direct Instruction, and Success for All, to develop and/or refine "break the mold" comprehensive school-reform models. These models, focusing on whole school change, have been implemented in thousands of schools over the past decade (Datnow, Borman, Stringfield, Overman, & Castellano, 2003).

CSR represents an alternative way to think about providing instructional support to large networks of schools that transcended geographic boundaries. The CSR providers offered a set of instructional expertise, school reorganization techniques, curriculum materials, and improvement strategies that promised to build school capacity and improve student learning. In doing so, the reform model replaced the district as the central source of guidance for school improvement. Most of the CSR models even provided national gatherings for member schools to simulate the camaraderie traditionally offered by geographic proximity.

The second important movement of the 1990s came from the largesse of one wealthy individual and led to the formation of a series of intermediary organizations as informal partners in large system support. In 1993, Ambassador Walter Annenberg gave half a billion dollars to public education, largely in the form of challenge grants in sixteen major urban centers, including Boston, Chicago, Los Angeles, New York, and Philadelphia. To leverage change in these urban centers, intermediary organizations were set up both as the fiscal agents of the reforms and as places that could provide assistance without operating under the constraints of local bureaucracies and politics. The reform organizations were designed as "boundary crossing organizations" that "represent a coalition of interests supporting reform, neither 'of' the system nor wholly outside it. It enjoys license ... to cross the organizational boundaries dividing the various parties whose actions affect children in schools, and to serve as the catalyst for some kind of change" (McDonald, McLaughlin, & Corcoran, 2000, p. 6).

The intermediary organizations funded by Annenberg, including the Los Angeles Annenberg Metropolitan Project (LAAMP), the Bay Area School Reform Collaborative (BASRC), the Boston Plan for Excellence (BPE), and the New York Networks for School Renewal (NYNSR), represented an alternative conceptualization to the traditional school district as a system of support for school improvement. Like the CSR model developers, they provided instructional improvement expertise and delivery systems that were not readily available from districts and provided cross-district networks that connected schools in different configurations. Like CSR networks, the Annenberg intermediaries provided an alternative vision for supporting the improvement of teaching and learning across systems of schools and revealed the inadequate expertise and support contained within districts.

Despite their promise, both the CSR movement and the Annenberg challenge grants have met with mixed success. On the one hand, several of the CSR models, including America's Choice, the Comer School Development Program, Direct Instruction, and Success for All have developed substantial evidence of effectiveness (Borman, Hewes, Overman, & Brown, 2003; also see the National Center for Comprehensive School Reform website for a compilation of the research and evaluation studies on CSR models). Annenberg's evaluation of the challenge reported reaching thousands of teachers and 1.5 million children and creating new organizations that launched new community partnerships and provided ways for citizens reluctant to participate in school reform to get involved (Annenberg Institute for School Reform, 2003).

On the other hand, external reforms have proved difficult to sustain. In the most high-profile case, the Memphis Tennessee school district adopted seventeen different CSR models across the district in 1996, Gerry House became the national superintendent of the year in 1999, only to have her successor abandon all of the designs two years later (Franceschini, 2002). In another example, Datnow, Hubbard, and Mehan (2002) conducted a longitudinal study of thirteen schools using CSR models. After six years, only four of the thirteen were still implementing their chosen model. The Annenberg sites also met with mixed and complicated success. Charles Kerchner (2001), in reviewing the Los Angeles Annenberg project, found its legacy "much more in its contribution to the city's social capital infrastructure than in its discrete projects." An analysis of the Annenberg Challenge by the conservative Fordham Foundation found that intermediary organizations ultimately left shallow footprints, because of their weak leverage on the formal and entrenched educational institutions they sought to influence (Domanico, Finn, Innerst, Kanstoroom, & Russo, 2000).

Two unresolved problems seem to be at the root of the uneven success of these reform efforts. First, the external support providers were not positioned to supply the persistent, long-term support to schools that was necessary for deep-rooted and sustained change (Berends et al., 2002). Second, the efforts of external support providers were often disconnected, or even incompatible, with other district and state reforms. Because they operated outside of district and/or state boundaries, it was difficult for external supporters to tailor and align their efforts with district and state policies (Datnow, 2002). Thus, experiments in alternative formulations for districts have only served to reinforce the central role of districts in supporting sustainable school reform.

THE COMMUNITY AND SCHOOLS OF DUVAL COUNTY, FLORIDA

Jacksonville lies in the northeasternmost part of Florida, just one hour south of the Georgia border. Duval County, which includes Jacksonville, contains a diverse geography. Several swanky beach communities line the easternmost stretches of Duval County, overlooking the Atlantic Ocean. The St. John's River, the only North American river that flows from south to north, wends its way through the middle of the county. The river and its tributaries make Jacksonville a city of more than ten bridges, many of them majestically arching across the landscape. On the western bank of the St. John's sits downtown Jacksonville. The downtown area has seen better days, although city leaders are trying to put it on the comeback trail with the development of a commercial riverwalk, a new football stadium to house a professional football team, and luxury riverfront condominiums. The county has been home to a large naval air station since the 1940s. Jacksonville has a rich cultural tradition, including an annual Riverdance Festival, a symphony orchestra, and several notable museums.

The schools of Duval County are a study in contrasts. All school systems in Florida are countywide. Unlike the situation in other states, whereby poor urban school districts are ringed by more wealthy suburban systems, the school system of Duval County is a marble cake of black and white, rich and poor. Just over half of the schools in the district (82 out of 149) are majority minority, with more than 50 percent minority, largely black, students. Twenty-three of the district's schools have less than 30 percent minority populations. Unlike most other Florida urban areas, Duval County has only a small Hispanic population, with fewer than 5 percent Latino students in the district.

The minority student population in Duval County closely follows the patterns of poverty within the district. Federal lunch assistance, which either pays for or subsidizes school lunch for students, is commonly used in educational research as a measure of student poverty because family income must be below the federal poverty level ($14,810 for a family with one child in 2003) in order for students to qualify. Of the 104 elementary schools in the district, just under half, or 48, have more than two-thirds of their students receiving federal assistance for lunch, while 11 schools in the district have fewer than a quarter of their students receiving lunch assistance. Lunch assistance is considered to be most accurate at the elementary grade levels, because students tend not to avoid reporting family poverty because of social stigma.

Like all other urban areas in America, poverty in Duval County is highly correlated with skin color and inversely related to school performance. Just as the city is a picture of both wealth and poverty, black and white, so Duval County contains some of the highest-performing and lowest-performing schools in the state and even the nation. Stanton College Preparatory High School and Paxon School for Advanced Studies were ranked the second- and third-best high schools in the nation in 2003 by *Newsweek* magazine (Matthews, 2003). Darnell-Cookman and James Johnson middle schools were amongst the best-performing middle schools in the state on the Florida Comprehensive Assessment Test (FCAT) in 2003. Forty-five Duval County schools received an A on the state accountability system, which grades schools like children, on an A, B, C, D, or F scale. On the underside, Duval County has some of the lowest-performing schools in Florida. In 2003 the county had six failing schools, as measured by the state accountability system.

Like most stories of reform, this one begins with a troubled prologue. In 1997, the school board and mayor jointly appointed a commission to study the future of education in Duval County, aptly titled the New Century Commission on Education. Some of the interim commission findings—unclear roles and boundaries of authority for the school board, superintendent, and school system staff; lack of high-quality academic standards for all students in the system; and "a lot of fingerpointing and blame—pointed to the need for a new vision and direction for the Jacksonville public schools" (Mitchell, 1997).

The commission sought to make its recommendations within a period of leadership uncertainty for the district. In December 1996, the school board had bought out the contract of superintendent Larry Zenke amidst a scandal in which an assistant superintendent, Joe Seager, was accused and later convicted of rigging bids and getting kickbacks from businesses seeking school contracts. Zenke was replaced by interim superintendent Don Van Fleet, who made it clear he was a temporary custodian of the job.

It was not until June 1998, eighteen months after Zenke's dismissal, that the school board selected a new superintendent to lead it into the twenty-first century. The new superintendent was an unlikely choice. John Fryer was a retired two-star Air Force major general who had no formal experience in leading K–12 education systems. Arguing that "leadership is transferable," Fryer campaigned hard for the job, declaring, "It's a big district and it's a big challenge and it just struck me right in the heart" (Mitchell, 1998). Fryer had recently retired from a distinguished military career that included being a participant in 161 tactical fighter combat missions in Southeast Asia; commander of an F16 fighter wing; senior military advisor to the U.S. ambassador to NATO; commander of the U.S. Air Force Center for Aerospace Doctrine, Research, and Education; a White House fellow; and the commandant of the National War College in Washington, DC. Before seeking the superintendency in Jacksonville, Fryer spent two years as the vice president and general manager of an educational technology division of a hi-tech firm in Lacey, Washington. Fryer took the job immediately after receiving treatment for prostate cancer.

In being chosen to lead the nation's twentieth-largest school district, Fryer joined a select company of noncareer educators to lead major urban schools systems. In 1995, the Seattle public schools hired a retired Army general, John Stanford, who grew to be revered for his strong educational leadership before his tragically premature death from leukemia in 1998. Alan Bersin, a former U.S. attorney, was hired in 1998 to lead the San Diego public schools, and, despite a rocky relationship with the school board, he earned national renown for his efforts to improve literacy instruction in the district, with the assistance of his chancellor Anthony Alvarado. Other outsiders have fared less well. Julius Becton, a retired Army lieutenant general, retired in 1998 after less than two years as the chief executive of the Washington, D.C., school system.

Just as Fryer was taking office, important legal developments helped to energize the community for school improvement. In early 1999, after more than thirty-five years, the U.S. district court finally declared the school system unitary, meaning it was considered legally desegregated. Since 1962, the school system has been under court-ordered desegregation plans, which gave the court oversight of plans for student assignment, teacher placement, school construction, and other parts of the education system. Despite numerous attempts, the district was not able to shake free of court-ordered busing and oversight. In 1990, the school system and the NAACP reached an agreement that created magnet schools, a voluntary program designed to draw black and white students outside their neighborhoods. The magnet schools were a voluntary replacement for nearly two decades of forced busing. The agreement also established steps for racially balancing the public schools through student assignment, teacher and staff assignment, school buildings, extracurricular activities, and transportation. The 1999 desegregation order symbolically freed the district from its inequitable past and made it eligible to borrow hundreds of millions of dollars for capital improvements. While difficult racial issues continued to play out in the district, an important vestige of the past was exorcised.

During the tenure of Superintendent Fryer, Duval County put into place a coherent array of reforms. The district developed a strong partnership with an external provider, the National Center on Education and the Economy (NCEE) and, with some important enhancements, has embraced NCEE's standards-based reform principles and the model of NCEE's America's Choice comprehensive school reform design as the core of its reforms. In particular, Duval County embraced NCEE's conception of the centrality of standards, the scrutiny of student work as demonstrations of students' understanding of standards, and NCEE's literacy strategies for developing reading and writing skills. Simultaneously, the district's mathematics and science leaders were reconstructing the district's mathematics and science curriculum. They were guided by the findings of the Third International Mathematics and Science Study (TIMSS), which argued that American curriculum across grade levels was unnecessarily repetitive and disconnected. They sought to impose coherence and parsimony upon these two subjects.

District leaders also developed better mechanisms to build teachers' capacity to deliver literacy, mathematics, and science instruction and school leaders' capacity to support teachers in their efforts. Early on, Superintendent Fryer became convinced that teacher professional development should be embedded within schools, and he pursued a strategy of funding a full-time coach in each school. Efforts to build principals' capacity to support wider implementation in their schools led to the exploration of different techniques of leadership development. Over time, district leaders came to realize the importance of developing a network of capacity-building mechanisms for professionals at all levels of the system, including teachers, coaches, principals, and district administrators. As we shall see, the evolution of a thoughtful system to mutually support the professional development of all of these actors is both one of the secrets of Duval County's success and the source of some of its greatest uncertainty.

The Duval County leadership also believes strongly in the importance of data and evidence to inform its actions. Throughout its journey, Duval County has constantly struggled to develop data systems that will provide useful, timely feedback to monitor its efforts and inform its progress, and to build the capacity of actors throughout the system to interpret data appropriately.

Exploitation of data occurs at several levels and in different forms. The district has moved from a kludgy system of providing schools with state test results in Excel files to an adroit interface that allows school leaders to easily get an array of test data, grades, and attendance and referral data on any subgroup of students within a school. Recognizing the absence of systematic feedback on the implementation of district reform efforts, district leaders have also developed an innovative system to monitor the implementation of the district's major standards-based reform initiatives. The system, called the Standards Implementation Snapshot System, has turned into a mechanism to articulate the district's reform efforts to teachers and school and district leaders, a large-scale training device, as well as a way of gauging the depth of implementation of elements of the district's frameworks. The district has also refined the Schools Improvement Planning (SIP) process so that it is more meaningful and realistic for school leaders. Thus, while the district has not yet developed a systemwide perspective on the interplay between these data components, data do play an increasingly important dual role of formative feedback for school and district leaders and an accountability check on actors across the system.

Beneath all of these efforts lies a sense of the fragility of reform in Duval County. Why should this reform be any more resilient than the countless efforts that have come and gone before it? It is in this conundrum of how not only to enact a set of ideas but to make them self-sustaining and recursively deeper that district leaders latched onto the idea of fostering professional learning communities as a way for both schools and the district to continually burrow deeper and develop understanding that will withstand the inevitable backwash of educational faddism. Thus embedding a culture of learning into the ethos of the organization is the strategy for sustaining the reforms beyond their initial introduction. This effort is in its infancy and is proving a hard concept to instill, despite some notable progress.

EVIDENCE OF THE IMPACT OF DUVAL COUNTY'S REFORMS ON STUDENT LEARNING

Duval County's strategy is intriguing in its own right, but would not be worthy of investigation if there were not hard evidence that the strategy is

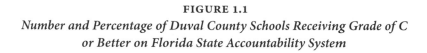

FIGURE 1.1

Number and Percentage of Duval County Schools Receiving Grade of C
or Better on Florida State Accountability System

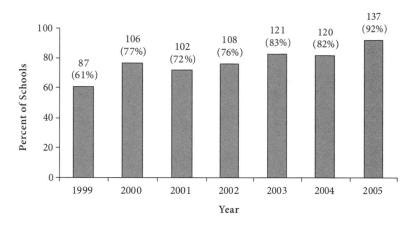

producing educationally significant improvements in the learning of the County's students. There are many ways to assess student learning. State accountability measures are usually considered the benchmarks by which the public assesses the quality of local schools. In Florida, the state uses Florida's A+ school accountability system, which has been in place since 1999. The system assesses schools based upon student performance in both reading and mathematics on the Florida Comprehensive Assessment Test, or FCAT. Florida's model measures student achievement through both the status of student performance and student growth from year to year. Special attention is paid to the students who are in the lowest 25 percent of performance.

One of the simplest ways to assess Duval County's performance is to look at trends in performance on the state grading system over time. Looking at the number of schools meeting the state standard is one of the simplest measures of district effectiveness. The data in figure 1.1 show the number of schools in the district scoring a C or better on the state accountability system. In 1999, 87 of the 142 schools that received state accountability grades that year received a C or better. In 2000, the number jumped to 106 of the 138 schools that were graded. Schools performing at a C level or better plateaued until 2003, when 121 of the 146 district schools received grades of C or bet-

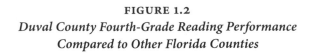

FIGURE 1.2

Duval County Fourth-Grade Reading Performance
Compared to Other Florida Counties

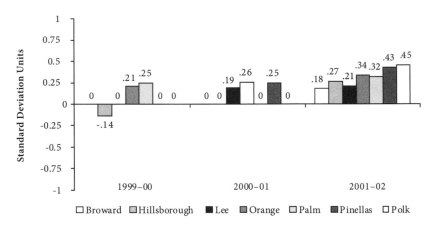

□ Broward ▦ Hillsborough ■ Lee ▨ Orange □ Palm ■ Pinellas □ Polk

ter. In 2005, Fryer's last year with the district, 137 of the districts 149 schools received a C. Also in 2005, for the first time over the seven-year period, no school in the district received an F on the state accountability system.

Of course, districts across a state could be improving on the state accountability system at the same rate. This could be a result of increasing familiarity and better preparation for the state test and not have anything in particular having to do with improved student learning (Linn, 2000). For this reason, it is important to compare Duval County to other Florida districts to see if its performance is any different from that of similar districts. In 2002, researchers at the Consortium for Policy Research in Education investigated the impact of Duval County's standards-based reform efforts by comparing the annual gains in school-average student performance for the county to other demographically similar counties in Florida (Supovitz & Snyder, 2002). Using regression analyses to control for the prior year's performance and demographic differences between schools (school size, proportion of students receiving financial assistance to purchase school lunch, proportion of minority students, proportion of students with limited English proficiency, mobility rates, etc.), the study examined changes in Duval County's test performance relative to the changes in test performance in seven compara-

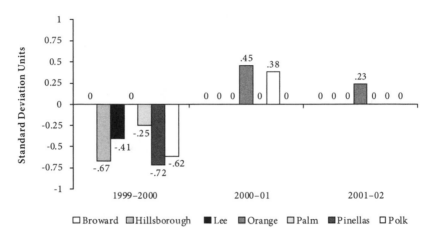

FIGURE 1.3

*Duval County Fourth-Grade Writing Performance
Compared to Other Florida Counties*

ble Florida counties. It was hypothesized that Duval County's schools would be gaining more than schools in similar counties if its strategies were improving student learning.

The patterns were remarkably persistent across grades and subject areas. In reading, writing, and mathematics in the elementary grades, Duval County schools gained more than schools in the seven comparison counties. In reading in 1999, as shown in figure 1.2, Duval County schools were performing significantly better than two other Florida counties, significantly worse than one county, and no different than four other counties. From 2000 to 2001, Duval County schools began to improve significantly more than most other counties in the sample. From 2001 to 2002, Duval County schools were gaining more in reading than schools in all of the seven other Florida counties.

The trends in writing performance in Duval County relative to comparable Florida counties are shown in figure 1.3. In writing in 1999, Duval County schools were performing significantly worse than five of their counterparts and no different than two others. By 2002, Duval County schools had caught up with the comparable Florida counties and were performing either better or at the same level as their peers.

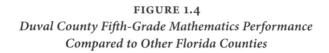

FIGURE 1.4
*Duval County Fifth-Grade Mathematics Performance
Compared to Other Florida Counties*

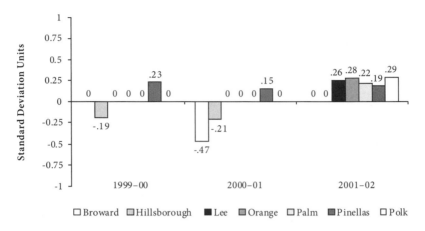

The story in mathematics was similar to that in reading and writing. The trends in mathematics performance are shown in figure 1.4. Duval County elementary schools began performing similarly to schools in the other counties, as shown by the negligible difference in performance from 1999 to 2000. By 2002, Duval County was performing significantly better than five of the seven comparison counties and no different from two of the others.

Interestingly, none of these effects were visible in Duval County middle schools, where there appeared to be no significant differences in performance between the Duval County middle schools and middle schools in the other Florida counties. High school performance was not examined, as the reforms were not seen as reaching deeply enough into high schools to decidedly influence student performance on state tests.

The results presented here and other even more sophisticated student performance analyses (see Supovitz & Taylor, 2005) suggest that Duval County elementary students were learning significantly more than students in other counties in the state. The overall trends in student performance in Duval County suggest that something distinctive was occurring in the district that is worthy of a closer examination.

2

Developing a Vision of Instructional Quality

Exceptional organizational leaders have a clear vision for the future and can describe what a dynamic and potent rendition of their organization would look like. With that vision in mind, they persistently mold the qualities and conditions of their institution to reflect that future state. This is a well-known strategy for improvement in the business world. According to Harvard Business School professor John Kotter, "In every successful transformation effort that I have seen, the guiding coalition develops a picture of the future that is relatively easy to communicate" (1998, p. 9). Peter Senge, in his influential book *The Fifth Discipline*, contends that leaders of successful organizations develop mental models, or "internal pictures of how the world works" (1990, p. 175). These mental models provide a clear way to depict a leader's vision. A crucial feature of such a vision is that it must be centered on the organization's core mission. In their book *Built to Last,* which describes how extraordinary businesses excelled over sustained periods of time, Jim Collins and Jerry Porras concluded that "a well conceived vision centers around two major components: core ideology and envisioned future. A vision builds on the interplay between these two complementary forces that define 'what we stand for and why we exist' and 'what we aspire to become, to achieve, to create,' that will require significant change and progress to attain" (1994, pp. 220–221). A powerful vision, therefore, not only frames a picture of the future state of an organization, but also focuses that image on its core mission, thus allowing leaders to convey where they are heading and sharpening their focus on the primary purpose of the organization.

Educational leaders, like business leaders, must have a vision of what their school or system of schools should look like that focuses on the core mission of schooling: high-quality instruction that produces demonstrable student learning. Therefore, at the heart of all efforts to improve education across a school system there must be a vision of what powerful teaching and learning looks like inside classrooms. Absent that vision, there is no focus for the efforts of the organization's members. Therefore, while there may and should be ample room for debate about what excellent instruction might look like and entail, an educational organization cannot be silent about the need for a concrete vision of instructional quality. It is therefore incumbent upon educational leaders who seek to improve the quality of teaching and learning to envision what powerful instruction should look like inside classrooms, and then to strive to convince, prepare, and support teachers and school leaders throughout their system to enact that instructional vision. This is the very definition of instructional leadership.

What exactly does it mean to specify an instructional vision? It means partly to spell out the content that teachers should cover, which is usually articulated in content standards, curriculum materials, and pacing charts. Another, more contested, part of an instructional vision is which pedagogical strategies teachers ought to use to convey content to students. A third piece is the alignment of instructional philosophies across content areas. Imagine how confusing it would be for students to try to learn by one paradigm in one subject area and then to encounter a distinctly different approach in another.

An instructional vision must be specific enough to provide guidance for teachers and school leaders while allowing them some room for local interpretation and enactment. In this sense, the enacted vision within classrooms is mutually constructed by district leaders, teachers, and school leaders. This is inevitable for two reasons. First, teachers must be able to incorporate their specific knowledge about their students into their enactment of the organization's instructional vision. If teachers are not allowed to do this, then their instruction will not be matched to student needs, and therefore will not be challenging to some students and will be beyond the understanding of others. Second, coconstruction is necessary because it allows teachers to take ownership of the general forms of instructional approach and to stay engaged with them long enough to influence their teaching practices.

An instructional vision is a growing and evolving idea. It is a myth to think that a vision arises fully formed and ready to be disseminated across an organization, like Athena springing fully battle-garbed from the head of her father, Zeus. No matter where a vision comes from and how robust it is, it needs to be incorporated into the local landscape, which has its own history, ways of doing things, and myriad other contextual factors. Thus a vision is dynamic, always changing, growing, and being refined.

One central hypothesis of this book is that if district leaders do not articulate a coherent vision of good instruction, they will cede instructional leadership either to individual schools or outside providers, or some unmanageable combination of the two. The consequences of this will be uniform mediocrity at worst and far-flung variation at best.

Many districts today have schools with similar student populations, some of which are high-performing, while others are run-of-the-mill. This is because district leaders too frequently relinquish instructional leadership to individual schools, which results in broad variation in the quality of education that children within that district receive. Some school leaders fill this vacuum with their own instructional vision, while others pass on that authority to teachers who work with little guidance. From a leadership perspective, this is neither a recipe for quality control nor a formula to encourage coherence across grades and/or subject areas. If district leaders leave instructional decisions entirely up to the schools, then some faculties will quite naturally thrive and others will founder.

In another common scenario, individual schools may have the latitude to develop relationships with external instructional support providers, but the implications of this for the quality of education across the system are similar. In some schools the external improvement ideas will take root and instruction will improve, but in others the match will not be good and the schools will struggle. Whatever the case may be, the ability of a district of any size to monitor and provide support to individual schools that work with a wide range of providers will be hampered by the complexity of the different instructional approaches. As a result, it will become all but impossible for the district to provide any reasonable semblance of quality support to schools that are pursuing markedly different instructional philosophies, and the district's role in instructional design will become increasingly unclear.

While it is possible to reenvision the district role in systemwide instructional leadership, an issue I will return to in chapter 7, it seems clear that the district—or at least some type of educational support organization—must play a central role in developing an instructional vision for schools across the system. Therefore, the central job of leaders of such an organization is to develop, communicate, and support a coherent vision of excellent instruction.

This view of instructional leadership has at least four important implications. First, it requires district leaders to choose a particular instructional path and move their organization down that path. This means clarifying the range of instructional interventions that the district will support. Second, it raises questions about the necessary specificity of an instructional vision. From the district perspective, the reform must be specific enough—and therefore constrain the autonomy of teachers to some extent—so the district can support teachers and school leaders in improving the quality of instruction. This need not be highly constraining for teachers, and the extent of specificity is one important area for debate (which I discuss later), but it must be specific enough to provide guidance, incentives, and accountability for teachers, and to enable them to give up ineffective practices and adopt more effective ones. This raises important questions about the boundaries of, and latitude around, district leaders' instructional vision. School systems are unique organizations with long traditions of autonomy and the need for a certain amount of teacher judgment and professionalism. Attempts to enact strong instructional visions will require leaders to confront these legitimate issues.

Third, constraining instructional practice will almost inevitably lead to challenges from those with alternative instructional visions that have probably long existed within a heretofore unconstrained environment. Both individual teachers and advocates of alternative instructional regimes will seek license to continue their work, and district leaders must contend with these approaches.

Finally, keeping focused on an instructional vision requires tremendous discipline on the part of district leaders. School districts are wonderlands of distraction, and countless issues will arise to sap the energy and resources from instructional attention. While addressing managerial and political issues are integral parts of the job of a district leader, leaders must not lose sight of their instructional vision.

In the rest of this chapter I describe the roots and evolution of the instructional vision of the leaders of Duval County, Florida. First, I examine what that instructional vision looks like, how it was developed, and how it manifests itself in different subject areas within the district. Second, I show what the vision looks like from the perspective of schools within the county five years into the district's reform efforts. Third, I explore the inevitable implications of a district's attempts to impose a distinct vision of instruction on a loosely coupled system. This includes competing instructional visions and the inevitable noninstructional but important issues that drain attention away from an instructional vision. This chapter sets the stage for the next, in which I explore the strategies that district leaders used to communicate and build teachers' and school leaders' capacity to enact the district's instructional vision.

DUVAL COUNTY'S INSTRUCTIONAL VISION

What did the instructional vision of the leadership team in Duval County look like? In a March 2001 speech, Superintendent John Fryer laid out his vision for the school system as follows:

> I have a vision for a school system in which every teacher and every principal truly believes that most of our children can qualify to go to college without remediation; a school system in which we have internationally benchmarked standards against which we measure the performance of all of our children; a school system in which student work is the focus, because, after all, it is the product. I have a vision of a school system in which every classroom teacher is a guide for their students so that learning is organized [such] that every minute of every day, students are surrounded by the guideposts and the roadmaps of better understanding. I have a vision of a system in which there are multiple layers of assessment which informs instruction and allows us to make it better all the way down to the student level. I have a vision of a system . . . in which we use time so carefully that we don't waste a minute in the day, . . . [and] that we know from the best of research that we use [our time] strategically. I have a vision of a system in which all children read a lot and love to read. I have a vision of a system in which we have in-school professional development in every school, supporting teachers every day and helping them grow, . . . a system in which collaboration is the norm, [and] teachers [are] talking to each

other and growing every day in what is called a true learning community. That system is not just a vision, but one that we are working toward and are well along in creating here in Jacksonville.

Fryer's speech captured many of the core components of the Duval County leadership team's vision for instructional change, including high expectations for student performance, clear standards that elucidate those expectations, a focus on student work as a meaningful representation of student mastery of the standards, instruction designed to develop deeper levels of student understanding, reorganization of school structures to use instructional time and resources more effectively, multiple forms and layers of assessment, school-based professional development, and the development of collaborative learning communities for ongoing improvement. This vision grew out of an evolutionary process of discovery and learning shared by the superintendent, his leadership team, and external assistance.

Fryer arrived in Jacksonville in the summer of 1998 believing that the district did not have a coherent vision of instructional quality. In one of his early interviews with the *Florida Times-Union*, Fryer told a local reporter, "What I see now is a lot of individual programs and efforts. But I don't see a system, and I don't see a coherence to it at all" (Mitchell, 1998). Even before going to Jacksonville, Fryer had become interested in standards-based reform as a way to articulate the knowledge and skills necessary to achieve high levels of performance and to communicate high expectations for student performance. Before going deeper into the elements of Duval County's instructional vision, it is important to understand the national context for instructional reform.

RIDING THE STANDARDS MOVEMENT IN EDUCATIONAL REFORM

In the mid-1990s, standards-based reform was just coalescing around the country as a promising strategy for broad-scale improvement in education. Standards-based reform was an outgrowth of Smith and O'Day's (1991) earlier conception of systemic reform. Systemic reform called for the development and alignment of a constellation of policies, including standards, curricula, assessments, accountability systems, teacher certification requirements, preservice, and in-service professional development. Standards-based reform increased the emphasis on clear, challenging standards for student performance at the core of federal and state policy, while envisioning the other policies in support. The difference between the two approaches was more in emphasis than philosophy.

Fervid promoters of standards in the 1990s argued that in order for our nation to meet the global economic challenges of the twenty-first century, our youth need to be prepared to compete globally for knowledge-based jobs (Marshall & Tucker, 1992; Thurow, 1999). Clear, ambitious standards for student performance were seen as the foundation for better systemwide performance, as they would provide both teachers and students with commonly understood expectations for student learning. One of the leading organizational advocates of the standards movement in education was the National Center on Education and the Economy (NCEE), whose founder, Marc Tucker, and vice president Judy Codding wrote *Standards for Our Schools* (1998), which laid out the rationale, purpose, and promise of standards.

Also in 1991, a privately financed foundation called New American Schools (NAS) began to provide seed money to a select group of school reformers to develop comprehensive "break-the-mold" school reform packages for schools. The comprehensive school reform (CSR) model developers were encouraged to create designs that would deal with world-class standards, curriculum, teacher training, student motivation, parental and community involvement, school finance, governance, and administration, and school relations with other parts of the education system. The whole ball of wax. NCEE's reform model, called America's Choice, was one of the programs supported by NAS.

The evolution of NCEE is in itself a fascinating story. NCEE started out in Rochester, New York, in the 1980s as an organization dedicated to district organizational reform. Over the past twenty-five years, Marc Tucker has had a profound influence on American education. In 1990 Tucker served on the Commission on the Skills of the American Workforce, a national commission funded by the Carnegie Corporation to explore the relationship between education and economic performance. The panel's subsequent report, "America's Choice: Low Skills or High Wages" (Commission on the Skills of the American Workforce, 1990), presented the argument that America's declining economic fortunes of the 1980s were tied to its lack of workers prepared to compete in the global economy. The report title also became the inspiration for NCEE's school reform model, America's Choice.

In 1991, Tucker and Lauren Resnick of the University of Pittsburgh co-founded the New Standards Project. This ambitious partnership of seventeen states and six urban school districts was created to develop a set of standards that specified what children should know and be able to do at benchmark grades (initially 4, 8, and 10) in English language arts (ELA), mathematics, and science, and also provided meaningful examples of student work that met the standards, along with explanations of why they did so. The latter qualities—examples and explanations—are what distinguished these performance standards from their more basic brethren, content standards. The New Standards Project also advocated the idea of "effort-based learning," whereby teachers, and by extension students, must believe that all students can learn, because it is with that belief that teachers will provide challenging content and instructional attention to all students (Resnick & Hall, 1998). The New Standards Performance Standards, which are considered exemplary materials, are widely used in states, districts, and schools across the nation.

The New Standards Performance Standards became the springboard for the New Standards Reference Examinations, which were designed to align with the new standards. New Standards Reference Examinations were developed in ELA and mathematics, and later in science, for grades 4, 8, and 10. They were intended to embody a more robust method of assessment, including both short-answer and open-ended student writing prompts. Portfolios were also envisioned as part of the Reference Examination, although they were later curtailed because of psychometric concerns.

Both the New Standards Performance Standards and the New Standards Reference Examinations became backbones of NCEE's comprehensive school reform model, America's Choice. America's Choice sought to combine the crucial elements of standards, assessments, curriculum materials, school leadership, school organizational restructuring, and intensive teacher professional development into one coherent and unifying program for school improvement.

With federal support, the NAS's Comprehensive School Reform (CSR) models, including America's Choice, became increasingly widely used options for low-performing schools under intense pressure to improve. In 1998, Congress began the CSR program. The current CSR program, authorized as part of the 2001 No Child Left Behind Act, allocated over $300 million for its efforts. States were authorized to provide $50,000 per year for three years to eligible schools to adopt a design of their choice. By 2003, thousands of schools across the country were implementing a CSR model (Datnow et al., 2003).

THE DEVELOPMENT OF AN INSTRUCTIONAL FRAMEWORK
IN DUVAL COUNTY, 1998–2004

In the summer of 1998, preparing to take over the Duval County superintendency, Fryer was in Southern California, finishing cancer treatment and devouring the literature on education management and reform. He was compelled by the arguments of economic imperative that underlay the standards movement. Coming across Tucker and Codding's (1998) *Standards for Our Schools*, he called Codding and began to explore the possibilities of bringing NCEE into Duval County to help with their reform efforts.

So, in August 1998, when Fryer officially became school superintendent of Duval County, the district began contracting with NCEE. Initially NCEE consultants conducted leadership training with a cadre of the district's central office leaders. Over time, the reform philosophy of NCEE, embodied in the America's Choice school reform design, became the cornerstone of standards-based reform in Duval County. County leaders used their unique and close relationship with NCEE, federal backing of CSR, best practice findings from international research, and National Science Foundation support in mathematics and science as catalysts for their own development of a district-wide comprehensive reform strategy. What follows is a brief description of the evolution of reforms in the major content areas of English language arts, mathematics, and science in Duval County.

America's Choice: A Model for School Reform

The America's Choice school reform is organized around five "design tasks": standards and assessment, aligned instructional systems, high-performance management, professional learning communities, and parent/guardian and community involvement. As a central part of America's Choice, NCEE provides professional development for principals and for coaches employed by the school. Principals are charged with leading the reform in their schools, while changing literacy instruction across the schools is the primary responsibility of the coaches. Coaches receive intensive training triennially from

TABLE 2.1

Duval County Major Capacity-Building Activities 1998–2004

	1998–1999	1999–2000	2000–2001	2001–2002	2002–2003	2003–2004
Schoolwide/Literacy	America's Choice Cohort I (14 schools) ————————————●					
		America's Choice Cohort II (48 schools) ——————————————————●				
		NCEE Literacy Workshops		Schultz Center Literacy Workshops ——————————→		
					School Standards Coaches ————————→	
						District Standards Coaches ——→
Mathematics						
Curriculum	Connected Math chosen as middle school curriculum	Investigations chosen as elementary school curriculum		College Preparatory Math (CPM) chosen as high school curriculum for algebra and geometry.	Introduce two safety net mathematics programs. Knowing Math, an afterschool program for grades 3–7 and CPM's Foundations for Algebra.	
Professional Development	Training of 2 teachers (grades 6 and 7) from each middle school on standards as a way of introducing math reforms.	Training of one 8th grade teacher in each middle school to introduce math reforms. Training of 3 teachers (grades 3–5) from each elementary school as a way of introducing math reforms. Training of all 6th & 7th grade teachers in Connected Math begins.	Training of all middle school teachers in Connected Math continues. Training of all elementary school teachers in Investigations begins.	Started CPM algebra in 3 lowest performing high schools.	Training of high school teachers across district in CPM algebra.	Training of high school teachers across district in CPM geometry.

Math & Science

NSF funds Urban Systemic Initiative (USI) in math and science in Duval County.

USI supports development of leader teachers in both mathematics and science, assists with curriculum selection process and training of both teachers and principals.

USI gets new director, adjusts to become more aligned with America's Choice.

USI grant renewed.

Science

Curriculum

Middle school science comprehensive science curriculum developed around standards.

Elementary comprehensive science curriculum developed.

HS curriculum revision & adoption of NSF approved science materials.

9th grade integrated science curriculum implemented, driven by greater alignment with FCAT.

Professional Development

6th grade science professional development begins.

7th grade science professional development begins.

8th grade science professional development begins.

Science professional development in all grades ongoing.

Leadership Development

USI sponsors summer leadership institute ongoing thru 2003.

District leaders begin to develop standards-based leadership training.

National Institute for School Leadership (NISL) training for middle and high school principals begins.

NCEE and then return to their schools to train teachers. There are two kinds of training for teachers. ELA teachers receive intensive training in NCEE's form of literacy instruction, called writers and readers workshop. These workshops present intensive hands-on techniques for students to develop their skills as authentic readers and writers. Other subject-area teachers initially receive more general instruction on standards and on the development of classroom rituals and routines that facilitate more individualized instruction. Training for mathematics coaches follows the initial literacy rollout. The America's Choice design advocates the reorganization of the school day for longer blocks of uninterrupted time for reading, writing, and mathematics. Coaches lead teacher meetings and study groups in which teachers examine the standards, student work, and instructional approaches and the relationships among them.

In 1999, fourteen schools in Duval County adopted America's Choice, joining the second national cohort of America's Choice schools. Fryer intended these schools to be the vanguard in the system. In 2000, forty-eight more schools adopted America's Choice, and Duval County, with sixty-two schools in the design, about 40 percent of the schools in the district, became the largest single consumer of America's Choice.[1] While these schools intensively implemented America's Choice, the district also contracted with NCEE to introduce its literacy model into other county schools.

Thus the key components of America's Choice became the backbone of the instructional vision in Duval County. This included an emphasis on standards, considerable attention to assessment issues in general and student work in particular, a focus on extensive reading and writing practice and authentic literacy experiences, and the prominence of intensive professional development, largely based within each school.

Yet NCEE was not the sole source for the county leadership's emerging vision for instructional improvement. While America's Choice provided the overarching framework for the district's vision and its central views on literacy instruction, parallel developments in mathematics and science were also shaping reform policy in the district. Table 2.1 is intended to guide the reader to follow the trajectory of reforms across the content areas within the

1. Duval is still the largest single district to adopt America's Choice, although some states, including Georgia and Mississippi, have facilitated larger numbers of their schools to implement America's Choice.

district. The table gives a year-by-year encapsulation of the major developments in the district from 1998 to 2004.

Mathematics: Addition by Subtraction

Even before Fryer arrived in Duval County, the city's New Century Commission had clearly identified the district's middle school curriculum as a focus for reform. At the same time, the district's mathematics supervisor, Marita Eng, was trying to digest the implications of the Third International Mathematics and Science Study (TIMSS) for the district. The TIMSS study, conducted in fifty nations in 1995, was the largest multinational comparative study of educational achievement to date. After analyzing the results, researchers found that American elementary school students fared well compared to their overseas counterparts, but middle schoolers were performing in the middle of the pack. By high school, America's average student performance was near the bottom. Only three countries—Lithuania, Cyprus, and South Africa—did worse. After examining the curriculum and textbooks of each country participating in TIMSS, researchers concluded that the reason for America's increasingly poor performance was that our curriculum was "a mile wide and an inch deep." That is, we covered every possible topic almost every year, but engaged deeply in virtually no topics.

Duval County's mathematics and science leaders set out to rectify the curricular flaws identified by TIMSS. "We really examined the TIMSS report and decided that what it said was that we can't do everything every year," said Eng. "So we decided to narrow down the curriculum in middle school. We chose only eight topics per year." Following the advice of the New Century Commission, mathematics reforms in the district initially focused on grades 6–8.

In 1998, working closely with Fryer as he came on board, Eng chose Connected Mathematics as the district's middle school curriculum, based upon its parsimonious approach, which aligned with the "less is more" approach recommended in the follow-ups to the TIMSS studies. Rather than immediately training teachers in Connected Math, Eng chose to emphasize the need for a new curriculum that was aligned with standards. Eng asked each of the district's two dozen middle school principals to select two teachers from each grade level to come to a series of weekly sessions. The sessions were focused on discussing standards and the need for standards. "We did this very methodically and did our background work first," said Eng. "We talked about standards first, so they would have some idea why were moving toward standards, why we need standards, what the standards were, and then why our current textbook and instructional materials were very difficult to use with a standards-based approach," Eng explained. Eng used a similar strategy the following year in the elementary schools before beginning training on Investigations, the chosen elementary school curriculum. In January 2004, Eng estimated that 90 percent of her elementary teachers had gone through mathematics training in Investigations. "We are down to the reluctant and new teachers," she said. Eng found middle school numbers harder to estimate, because of the constant flux of middle school teachers. High school training had just started in 2004, so few teachers had been trained at that point.

Science: Collaborative Investigations

Science reform in Duval County in the late 1990s followed a path similar to mathematics in concept but took a more grassroots form. Like mathematics, science reform in the county was catalyzed by the New Century Commission's emphasis on middle school reform and the TIMSS findings that emphasized curriculum depth and measured progress rather than broad coverage. As in mathematics, district science leaders restructured the curriculum sequence to create a spiraling curriculum that exposed students to the major disciplines of science while minimizing repetitive coverage. According to Ruth Sentflebber, the district's science supervisor who spearheaded the process, "We really wanted a seamless curriculum for kindergarten through high school. So we left out some standards on purpose in various grade levels because they can't teach it all. But by the end of the key junctures all of the standards will be covered. We tried to make it less redundant." Philosophically, science instruction in the county emphasizes the inquiry concepts that scientists use and the constructivist approach to learning that contends that students who are led to construct their own understanding of a phenomenon achieve deeper understanding. As Sentflebber explained, "We are trying to encourage teachers to move towards more student-centered, rather than teacher-centered, instruction."

Unlike mathematics, district science leaders developed the science curriculum more locally, relying less on external materials. Spurred by the New

Century Commission's emphasis on middle schools, they transformed the middle school curriculum from the more traditional general science, life science, and physical science toward more comprehensive science, with new content built toward the standards. The elementary school curriculum followed a similar integrated approach to science instruction.

One particularly notable thing about the troika of the literacy, mathematics, and science reforms that were proceeding in the district was the philosophical similarity among all three reform efforts. Reforms in all three content areas were heavily centered on standards and inquiry-oriented instructional activities and emphasized active student-centered approaches. As mathematics supervisor Eng told me in 2002 about the alignment of mathematics reforms and America's Choice:

> What we are doing in mathematics matches perfectly well with . . . the literacy program that America's Choice is using, because everything we do is standards-based, so everything meshes in exactly. In fact, when we're doing the writing in mathematics, our steps in helping the students develop their writing is exactly the same as what they use in language arts and science. . . . And when we do the rituals and routines in mathematics, it's exactly like the rituals and routines that they're doing in language arts. . . . So it's not that the students have to go to math class and learn a different routine and different structure, and then go to the language arts and do a whole different thing. It matches perfectly well.

A third major reform initiative in Duval County added additional epoxy to the emerging curricular alignment. A National Science Foundation Urban Systemic Initiative (USI), funded in 1999, became an additional support for curricular coherence in Duval County. The USI provided funding for curriculum development in science, professional development in both mathematics and science, and the training of a cadre of school-based leader teachers in both mathematics and science who provided training and support in their subject areas, much as the America's Choice literacy coaches did in reading, writing, and English language arts. The USI also funded an annual week-long summer principal leadership institute, which built principals' capacity to support improvement in their schools in all content areas. "When we talk about our successes," said Carolyn Girardieu, the USI director, "we talk about how the alignment has made a significant impact in this district.

And when I say alignment, I don't mean just within mathematics or science. I mean the alignment of all initiatives."

A FRAMEWORK TO ARTICULATE THE INSTRUCTIONAL VISION

When Fryer first came to Duval County, he introduced "Fryer's High Five" as a way of communicating his early focus. The original High Five were (1) standards and assessment, (2) instructional systems, (3) high-performance management, (4) public engagement, and (5) community support. As standards-based reform began to take shape in the county, the High Five and the America's Choice design tasks were melded together into what district leaders called the Framework for Implementation of Standards (shown in figure 2.1). This framework, which defines the standards-based expectations for principals, teachers, and district support staff, emphasizes five things for school and district leaders: (1) academic performance, (2) safe schools, (3) high-performance management, (4) learning communities, and (5) accountability. Each of these categories includes a series of key elements for district-wide focus.

The frameworks are the embodiment of district leaders' efforts to specify and articulate exactly what they want principals to foster in their schools and teachers to enact in their classrooms. While the frameworks have matured immensely over time, they contain the central elements and latest thinking on the district's instructional vision. As Charles Cline, the district's long-standing, just retired, associate superintendent for curriculum and instruction, told me at the end of 2002, "We've begun to articulate . . . our expectations. The frameworks are our standards-based expectations for all our schools."

Ed Pratt-Dannals, a former teacher, principal, and regional superintendent who has now taken Cline's place as the associate superintendent for curriculum and instruction, saw the framework as kind of roadmap of the district's vision for school personnel. "Everything goes back to the framework," he said. "It has all our expectations for schools. . . . You can see that they're supposed to have model classrooms set up in each subject, and what it means to develop professional learning communities. . . . What do we expect to see when we go into schools? That is where the whole framework came from." As I visited schools across the district from 2001 to 2004, I saw

FIGURE 2.1
Framework for Implementation of Standards in Duval County Public Schools

Purpose: To define standards-based expectations for all Duval County Public Schools
Target Audience: Principals and district support staff

The framework aligns with the Superintendent Fryer's "High Five" in the district strategic plan.

Target 1: Academic Performance

♦ Understand and use the New Performance Standards and Sunshine State Standards.
♦ Align standards, curriculum, instruction, and assessment.
♦ Connect student work to standards.
♦ Develop common expectations by course and grade.
♦ Adopt common assessments.
♦ Integrate technology with course content.
♦ Literacy: Establish model classrooms at each grade level that exemplify standards-based literacy instruction, including:
     a. Writing Workshops
     b. Reading Workshops
     c. Skills Block/Phonics
♦ Mathematics: Establish model classrooms at each grade level that exemplify standards-based mathematics instruction using the following materials:
     a. Elementary—Investigations
     b. Middle School—Connected Math
     c. High School—Algebra I–College Preparatory Mathematics
♦ Science: Establish model classrooms at each grade level that exemplify standards-based science instruction
♦ Implement safety nets (both internal and external) that give every student the fullest support and opportunity to meet standards.
     a. Intervention: support tutoring/mentoring; establish before school, after school, and/or Saturday school remediation
     b. Double blocking and or flexible time (secondary)
     c. Performance-based course/GPA recovery (secondary)
     d. Grade recovery

Target 2: Safe Schools

♦ Implement a schoolwide discipline plan.
♦ Implement Foundations/Sprick Training (MS/HS).

Target 3: High-Performance Management

♦ Regularly use data to inform your decisionmaking.
♦ Utilize Distributed Leadership Teams to guide refinements in schools' efforts to reach standards.
♦ Align School Improvement Plan with school and district priorities.
♦ Use operational and tactical strategies for school improvement
♦ Provide materials and reallocate resources to support instructional improvement.

Target 4: Learning Communities

♦ Create comprehensive professional development plan aligned with the School Improvement Plan.
♦ Develop and maintain a cohesive, positive, professional, and constructive school culture.
♦ Establish smaller learning communities for teachers and students.
♦ Facilitate parent and community involvement and education.

Target 5: Accountability

♦ Establish annual school performance goals and explicit intermediary indicators as evidence of progress toward school performance goals.
♦ Use data to plan for improvement and monitor progress toward performance goals.
♦ Analyze and document student work.
♦ Implement formative, ongoing and summative assessments.
♦ Conduct performance reviews using implementation rubrics and snapshots.
♦ Compile school portfolios (school, grade/course, class, and student progress and results).

many copies of the frameworks thumbtacked behind principals' desks, laminated in school leadership team meeting rooms, and even taped to the walls near teachers' desks.

It is no secret that much of the frameworks are derived from the five design tasks of America's Choice.[2] "A lot of what has formed our framework so far has been what we learned through America's Choice and other reading," Pratt-Dannals told me in February 2003. "You compare it with the implementation rubric of America's Choice and see what you find," observed Barbara Vandervort, a longtime Duval County principal who went to work for NCEE in 2002 and later returned to the county. "There is a very large overlap."

GOING DEEPER: THE IMPLEMENTATION RUBRICS

In its attempts to forge a deeper, more detailed vision, Duval County leaders have entered into a licensing agreement with NCEE that includes both the licensing of NCEE materials for training and the rights to use and modify ("Duvalize") the America's Choice implementation rubrics. Based on the America's Choice version, Duval County has developed its own rendition of school implementation rubrics.

Introduced across the district in 2004, Duval County's standards-based education implementation rubrics are detailed specifications of expectations for elementary and secondary school faculties to follow when implementing standards. The implementation rubrics are organized around the five targets in the district's framework and provide detailed guidance for schools. Each of the five global targets (academic performance, safe schools, high-performance management, professional learning communities, and accountability) has a series of subcategories in which implementation at different levels (getting started, initial implementation, formative implementation, and full implementation) is described in some detail. The implementation rubrics include statements of what principals, leadership teams, teachers, and students will do at different levels of implementation. According to Ed Pratt-Dannals, the associate superintendent for curriculum and instruction, the implementation rubrics are a way for district leaders to provide guidance to

2. The America's Choice design tasks are standards and assessment, aligned instructional systems, high performance management, professional learning communities, and parent/guardian and community involvement.

schools on district expectations for organizational and instructional emphasis and practice.

In the spring of 2004, the regional superintendents and directors began conducting three intensive, day-long annual visits to each school in their region. Given that there are roughly thirty schools in each region, this was a major commitment of time and resources from district leaders. "It has created a common conversation and a new sense of direction. . . . It takes almost a whole day to go in and talk about where they are on the rubric, to come up with a 5-3-1 which becomes their action plan," said regional superintendent Theresa Stahlman. "Then we go back in the middle of the year and see how much progress they have made, visiting classrooms and walking the schools to see where they are going. The conversations are pretty honest about where people think they are." Thus the implementation rubrics became a way to guide school faculties in their implementation of the district's reform efforts.

In 2005, the regional superintendents and directors began scoring school-level implementation on each component of the implementation rubric and analyzing the results for patterns both within and across schools, levels, and regions. Because these developments are relatively recent, they were not a factor when most of the analyses of this study were conducted.

THE DISTRICT'S INSTRUCTIONAL VISION
FROM THE SCHOOL PERSPECTIVE

In some ways, district reform efforts are like playing a gigantic game of telephone. District leaders trigger the chain with voluble and repeated pronouncements. From their perspective, what they are asking teachers and school leaders to do is clear and well communicated. Yet the message that reverberates within schools is far from crystalline. What principals and teachers hear is often a scratchy echo of the original signal. This is perhaps not surprising, for two reasons. First, there is a cacophony of events, activities, and dramas that permeate schools each day that compete for teachers' and principals' attention. These events often demand an immediate response, and the urgent often drowns out all else. For example, I once asked a middle school principal to make a list of the things that had demanded her attention over the previous few days. Her list read like a soap opera lineup: student pranks, last-minute teacher absences, an angry parent upset about how her child was treated by others in her sixth-grade class, a fight in the cafeteria, a teacher announcing her engagement, students being released early for the big football game, other students breaking the school dress code, and so on. It is easy to see how the larger picture of reform strategy could get lost in the daily details of school operation.

The second reason, perhaps even more powerful, is the strong tradition of autonomy that schools and teachers enjoy. Principals tend to view their schools as their domains, the territory for which they are responsible. Teachers see their classrooms similarly. Once the bell rings, they close their doors and teach as they see fit. District efforts to influence what happens in schools and classrooms push against both the insular culture of schools and the long-standing custom of school and teacher independence.

As their vision became more precise, Duval County's leaders repeatedly stated their vision and the strategies for achieving it in public venues, and reproduced their message in countless handouts and memos. While the district's communication and capacity-building strategies are an important part of this story, I will save a close examination of them for the next chapter. What is important here is the extent to which the vision was heard and understood in the corridors and classrooms of the Duval County schools.

In the 2002–03 school year, I set out to understand the extent to which the instructional vision of Duval County's leaders had penetrated the district's schools five years into reform efforts. Over the school year I visited ten schools, each for a full-day visit. Four of the schools were elementary (K–5) schools, three were middle (6–8) schools, and three were high schools (9–12). Three of the schools (one at each level) were America's Choice schools, one school was implementing the direct instruction program, one was an academic magnet school, and the other five were regular neighborhood schools. In each school I interviewed the principal, the school standards coach, a literacy teacher, and a mathematics teacher. I also observed a literacy class. Time permitting, I also interviewed a science teacher. Appendix A describes the design of my research and the data collection and analysis plans in greater detail.

In interviews with the principal, school standards coach, and teachers in each school, I asked whether the respondent felt that the district had a clear vision of what good instruction looked like, and in what ways it was clear or not. You might think this would be a no-brainer. After all, how could school

FIGURE 2.2

Percentage of People in Different Positions Who Believe That the District Has a Clear Vision of What Instruction Should Look Like

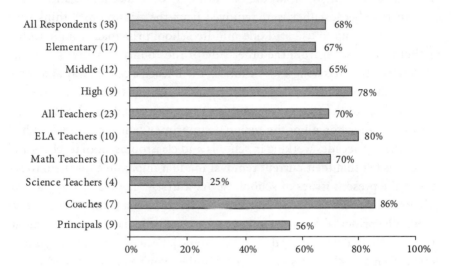

people not be aware of the central district reform effort five years into the effort? But the variety and complexity of the responses was surprising.

On the whole, it appears that the district was fairly effective at communicating its instructional vision to school faculties, with important exceptions. Overall, about 70 percent of the school personnel I interviewed felt that the district had articulated a clear vision of instructional quality. More specifically, as represented in figure 2.2, twenty-six of the thirty-eight teachers, coaches, and principals (or 68%) that I asked believed that the district had communicated to them a clear vision of what effective instruction should look like. Faculty tended to focus on the standards as the cornerstone of that vision. As one elementary school English teacher explained, "Their philosophy is . . . that our instruction is to be based on the standards and drawn from the standards. So we're to start with the standard, and instruction comes from that." Another typical response was: "I think the district has a great idea about what makes better instruction, because right now they are requiring all schools to be standards based. I think that they are now seeing what will help student performance, student scores, and also classroom instruction." Overall responses were roughly similar among respondents in elementary, middle, and high schools.

Those who did not think the district had articulated a clear instructional vision tended to cite the tradition of autonomy or to discount district leaders' expertise because they were removed from the classroom. "I think they kind of leave it up to us," said one middle school principal. A high school mathematics teacher from the other side of the county concurred: "I don't think the district has done a whole lot. . . . I will teach a certain way and some other teachers will teach a different way. And both of us can be effective."

Regardless of the fact that, except for the superintendent who was not a traditional educator, all of the regional superintendents and directors had spent literally decades working in schools and classrooms, both teachers and principals felt that their current removal made it impossible for them to relate to the present issues of schooling. As a first-grade teacher explained, "They haven't been in the teachers' shoes. They think a form will fix everything." The principal of an elementary school expressed a similar sentiment: "I'm not sure that everybody does [understand], because I don't think, unless you've been a teacher for so many years, unless you've been here and you've walked the walk in their shoes, I'm not sure they do understand completely. I think they understand somewhat, but I'm not sure they do completely."

Among teachers, a similar number to that overall, 70 percent, said the district had articulated a clear vision of what effective instruction should look like. Among the teachers interviewed, a high percentage of English language arts and mathematics teachers felt that the district communicated a clear instructional vision. Interestingly, while English teachers often cited the district's emphasis on standards as the core of the its vision, mathematics teachers overwhelmingly referred to the district mathematics supervisor, Marita Eng, as the personification of the district's mathematics vision. One elementary mathematics teacher said, "[Marita] has brought this district a long way in mathematics." A high school mathematics teacher echoed this: "Because of our district supervisor, Marita, we have somebody there who knows what she is doing." This suggests that there is more than one way to communicate an instructional vision to schools, and that individual personalities can have a powerful influence.

Although the sample of science teachers was small, it does not appear that the district was as effective at articulating a vision of science instruction to this group. Only one of the four science teachers interviewed felt that the district had a clear vision of effective science instruction, and she was at best ambivalent: "I would say yes and no. I say yes to the people . . . who are science teachers. But if you're not a science teacher you just don't know." The perceived lack of a clear vision for science instruction may have been due to the slower, more evolutionary nature of science reform in the district.

It is important to recognize that although teachers generally concurred that they had received a clear message from the district, they did not necessarily agree with the district's vision of instructional quality. Some frankly stated that they felt their subject area was heading in the wrong direction. Others felt the district was out of touch with their student populations. As one middle school mathematics teacher explained,

> They do [have a clear vision of quality mathematics instruction]. But unfortunately they don't tailor it to the populations that we teach. I think everybody knows what good-quality instruction is. I think it's spelled out beautifully as far as how fast we should go, what we should test, what we shouldn't test. . . . But I think a lot of people don't take the students' needs into consideration. And that becomes a snowball of a question.

In chapter 4, I will examine the extent to which teachers actually adopted the instructional practices advocated by the district and their reasons for doing so or not.

Not surprisingly, school coaches, who received specialized training on the district's reform efforts, overwhelmingly responded that the district had communicated a clear vision of instructional quality. "The district has a great idea about better instruction, because right now they are requiring all schools to be standards-based," said one elementary school coach. Coaches also tended to have the most fine-grained explanations of the district's instructional vision and strategies.

Principals were split in their responses, with only five of the nine principals that I interviewed responding that they felt the district had communicated a clear vision of instructional quality. Most of their hesitation seemed to come from their uncertainty as to how deeply the district's vision had penetrated the insular culture of their schools. One high school principal with over twenty years' experience in the district felt that the district had projected a larger vision "in a general sense," but that it lacked specificity. He noted that the reform efforts had only been in effect "within the past five years or so that Fryer's been here. So it is basically new to everybody." This comment reveals a perspective on the time it takes to deeply infuse a vision into an organization. While five years is an eon in the life of educational reform, it is a minute in the cultural life of a school.

But an elementary school principal who was new to Duval County noticed a distinct contrast between her old district and the coordination in Duval County. "I am impressed here because of what I've seen in the last two years," she said. "My regional superintendent has come into classrooms . . . and asked students questions. I was really impressed with that. I've never had a superintendent who has done anything like that. So I think that most people do have some understanding of the district's vision of standards." Despite these impressions, however, she also wondered how deeply the vision had penetrated the culture of her school.

The results of a survey of Duval County principals conducted in the spring of 2003 also provides insights into the extent to which the district's standards-based instructional vision was understood and accepted by school leaders after five years of implementation. (See Appendix B for a description of the survey instrument, method of data collection, and response rates.) Figures 2.3 and 2.4 show the degree to which principals agreed that the district clearly articulated its instructional vision of standards-based reform.

The responses in figure 2.3 show that principals overwhelmingly believed that district leadership supported their efforts to introduce standards-based reform into their schools, that they believed standards-based reform was more promising than previous reform efforts in the district, and that they felt standards-based reform was improving the quality of the education children in the district were receiving. Furthermore, over 85 percent of the principals reported that they believed the implementation of standards-based reform in their schools would improve their state test scores. In each case, the percentage of principals who strongly agreed with each statement was greater than the percentage that somewhat agreed, indicating that their accord was substantial.

Like the responses of school faculty members, there was also variability in principals' views on the clarity of the district's instructional vision across subject areas. Figure 2.4 shows principals' responses to a series of questions about the clarity of the district's vision in English language arts, mathemat-

FIGURE 2.3

Principal Understanding and Support of District Instructional Vision of Standards-Based Reform

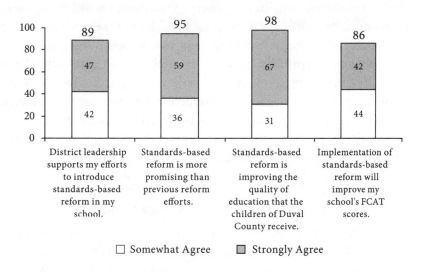

☐ Somewhat Agree   ▨ Strongly Agree

FIGURE 2.4

Principal Understanding of District Instructional Vision across Content Areas

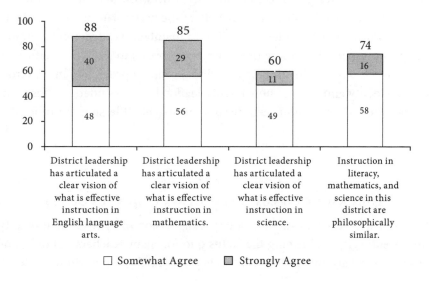

☐ Somewhat Agree   ▨ Strongly Agree

ics, and science. More than 85 percent of the principals felt that the district had articulated a clear vision of effective instruction in both English language arts and mathematics, although the response was somewhat stronger in English than in mathematics. In science, the subject for which the district had developed its own curriculum, principals did not feel strongly that the district had developed a clear instructional vision. Interestingly, the pattern about science among principals was similar to that found in the school fieldwork. On the survey, three-quarters of the principals also agreed that there was a philosophical similarity to the instructional approaches across literacy, mathematics, and science, although this agreement tended to be lukewarm. This was perhaps driven by their views that the district had failed to articulate a clear vision of effective science instruction.

IMPLICATIONS OF A DISTINCT VISION

Should a district's leadership press for a particular set of instructional practices in schools, there will be several almost inevitable implications. First, the constraints will give rise to all manner of opposition, both passive and active. This will range from individual teachers and schools who just want to "do their own thing" (more on that in chapter 4) to advocates of alternative instructional approaches who will confront leadership about their favoritism and seek district resources to continue their own work. Second, there will be constant threats and distractions that affect the particular instructional emphasis, which will test leadership ability to maintain its istructional emphasis. In this section I examine these common threats to a district's efforts to promote and sustain a distinct instructional vision. I provide examples from Duval County and discuss how county leadership responded to these particular circumstances, and then discuss more general lessons for other district leaders.

COMPETING VISIONS:
THE CASE OF DIRECT INSTRUCTION IN DUVAL COUNTY

When district leaders articulate a particular vision of instructional quality, they are directly challenging the status quo for many teachers, schools, and other interest groups. Individual teachers or small groups will have developed expertise in, and commitment to, instructional approaches that differ from those advocated by district leadership. In some cases, entire school faculties or teachers in certain content areas or grade levels may have adopted particular instructional approaches that are not consonant with district leaders' vision. In other cases, community advocacy groups may support competing instructional visions. Whatever the case, district leaders who advocate a particular instructional vision must recognize that there will certainly be many sets of educators with entrenched interests that have invested their efforts in, have funding for, or otherwise gain their legitimacy from a different instructional approach.

The strategies that district leaders employ with those who advocate alternative instructional visions will help determine the extent to which the leaders are able to spread their ideas among schools and teachers. One example in Duval County, the case of Direct Instruction, dramatically illustrates the implications of advocating a particular instructional vision and the turbulence this can cause for schools, district leaders, and the community. The response of Duval County leaders in this case is also noteworthy because it exemplifies a strategy for addressing the ensuing friction.

In 2000, just as Duval County's leaders sought to expand America's Choice from fourteen to sixty-two schools, a religious-based community advocacy group began agitating for the adoption of Direct Instruction in Jacksonville's lowest-performing, poorest schools. Direct Instruction represented a dramatically different instructional approach than America's Choice. Direct Instruction is a highly structured, regimented, teacher-directed, phonics-based reading program in which teachers use scripted lesson plans and repetition to teach students the foundations of reading. Developed in the 1960s, Direct Instruction has a long track record and substantial research evidence that it builds basic reading skills in students from high-poverty backgrounds. America's Choice, by contrast, is based on a more contemporary instructional philosophy that contends that children learn better when they are encouraged to engage in their own learning through immersion in authentic literature and extensive writing practice. Direct Instruction and America's Choice represent two radically different philosophies of how children, and particularly children from high-poverty backgrounds, learn best.

In Duval County, Direct Instruction was championed by a local nonprofit community group cleverly called the Interchurch Coalition for Action, Reconciliation, and Empowerment, or ICARE. ICARE, representing thirty-eight congregations from twelve denominations, was formed in 1995 to advocate for the disempowered on a range of neighborhood issues, like crime, city support services, and education. ICARE began pushing the school system to expand direct instruction across its low-performing schools. According to the *Florida Times-Union*, "ICARE has noticed Fryer's allegiance to America's Choice and demanded that equal attention be placed on Direct Instruction" (Diamond, 2000a).

ICARE was known for persevering in its causes. As ICARE member Montgomery Harlow said about the community organization, "ICARE was there yesterday and it will be there tomorrow, next week, next month, and next year. . . . I've been in a host of religious organizations, but ICARE is the only one I've seen that is so specific and has objectives. You can count on us to be here for a long time" (Richardson, 1998). Through meetings and the media, ICARE doggedly pushed Fryer to provide the same resources for Direct Instruction as he was investing in America's Choice. The alignment of the religion-based social advocacy group with some of the poorest and highest-minority schools in the district against the mostly white district leadership added a racial tinge to the dynamic of the situation.

Fryer resisted the expansion of Direct Instruction in Duval County, as he perceived it as a threat to his reform agenda. He was particularly worried about the effect Direct Instruction would have on teacher engagement. "How do you even make a better teacher [with this model], because all the questions they ask are in the script?" he wondered during an interview in June 2001. "I mean, what is a good teacher under that kind of model? I don't know."

ICARE's resolute advocacy of Direct Instruction eventually led to a heated meeting with Fryer in the spring of 2000, where Fryer held a flexible but firm line.

> They started in with me and said, "We want forty-three schools with the Direct Instruction model." I said, "I'm sorry, that's not my vision of where we're going." And I saw this guy get tight-jawed about it. They asked me to be just as passionate about direct instruction as I was about America's Choice. I said, "I'm sorry, I can't." I just had to be honest. I just can't be. But I'm not trying to undercut Direct Instruction. They're all our children and we want whatever we do to succeed.

The Duval County school board also became involved in the reading program controversy. In an attempt to mediate the situation, the board requested that both programs present their approaches. In June 2000, representatives of America's Choice and Direct Instruction formally presented their instructional model to the board. Seeking a compromise but revealing a lack of understanding of the philosophical incompatibilities between the two models, one school board member questioned why the two reading programs couldn't be combined within schools, rather than running simultaneously in different schools. Board members were split in their support of the two programs, which increased the pressure on Fryer and his team to resolve the situation.

Fryer, however, resisted pressure to impose either America's Choice or Direct Instruction on schools and the community, even though he openly preferred the former. Fryer's tactics during this time when his instructional vision was under siege are particularly instructive. He was always open and steadfast about his belief that America's Choice represented his vision of effective instruction, yet he never mandated that all schools adopt America's Choice or not implement Direct Instruction. His message to schools was clear; he had a preference, but schools had to make their own choice and take ownership for that choice. As Fryer explained, "The school and principal must be passionate about [their choice] or else it won't work. Have I persuaded schools? Yes. But tell them or order them to participate? I never did that. I said that I personally believe America's Choice is the easiest way to implement standards, but they must make their own decisions" (Diamond, 2000b).

This approach was persuasive to many school leaders. The story of Dinsmore elementary is a telling example. At the beginning of the 2000–01 academic year, the school considered using both America's Choice and Direct Instruction. But after examining both programs, they decided to adopt America's Choice. As the school's principal explained in a newspaper interview, "We visited schools using America's Choice and their students were stronger than ours. We would have liked to do both programs, but we couldn't. We had to pick one, and this was just the right thing for us to do" (Diamond, 2000b). Others perceived more camouflaged coercion in Fryer's approach. According to a school board member critical of Fryer, "People will do what the hierarchy is doing. This is a voluntary program, kind of, sort of.

But we know how the system works. If you are upwardly mobile, you better be for this" (Diamond, 2000b).

As these comments suggest, Fryer walked a fine line between advocacy and authority. He made his preferences clear without mandating a particular approach because, he argued, this removed the school's responsibility, and hence its commitment, to make its own choice. This illustrates the leadership dilemma between a top-down mandate, which forces coherence but weakens commitment, and a bottom-up choice, which creates ownership but results in a programmatic hodgepodge. By voicing preference without a mandate, Fryer was attempting to sidestep this dilemma. He held firm to his instructional vision in the face of alternate visions, without removing a demand for commitment on the part of school leaders and faculties. In chapter 3 I focus in greater detail on Fryer's particular techniques and strategies for implementing his instructional vision, but the takeaway point here is the steadfast commitment to an instructional vision.

Over time, the controversy surrounding Direct Instruction settled down. The school board continued to support both programs. Direct Instruction expanded in the district from eleven schools in 2000 to sixteen schools in 2001. America's Choice and its standards-based philosophy continued to dominate the district's overall attention and resources. The school board commissioned an external evaluation of Direct Instruction to inform its consideration. The evaluators found that the program was generally implemented as it had been designed, and that principals and teachers in schools using Direct Instruction were overwhelmingly in favor of the program because they believed it helped their children improve their reading (Hamann, 2001). An internal district evaluation of Direct Instruction found that the program significantly improved student performance in first and second grade but that students in Direct Instruction schools performed in some cases no differently and in other cases significantly lower than students in schools not using Direct Instruction in grades 3–5 (Ballentine, 2002). Direct Instruction continues to operate, primarily as a reading program, in a small number of Duval County elementary schools. In 2005, 15 of the 104 elementary schools in the district used Direct Instruction, largely in grades K–2. All of these schools remain part of, and accountable for, implementing the district's standards-based instructional approach.

ICARE's passionate advocacy of Direct Instruction, Fryer's firm but non-authoritarian response, and the school board's involvement are instructive for educational leaders who seek to implement a distinct instructional vision. First, they must recognize that school districts have a long history of decentralization and attempts to cohere traditional instructional diversity around a particular approach are bound to meet with mistrust, passive resistance, and, quite possibly, open opposition. Second, as the involvement of ICARE and the school board demonstrate, these issues rarely play out solely in the programmatic realm and are likely to become entangled with sensitive social and political issues. In the face of a potentially explosive situation, school leaders must find a balance between holding their ground and addressing legitimate complaints. As I examine in great depth in chapter 3, Fryer's distinct strategy of compelling principals and teachers to adopt his conception of standards-based instruction without mandating that they do so had profound implications for the progress of reform in the district, as well as the response in the schools.

EXTERNAL DISTRACTIONS: BUS CONTRACT DIVERTS ATTENTION FROM THE INSTRUCTIONAL MESSAGE

While alternative instructional visions are one threat to reformers' attempts to cohere an educational system around a distinct instructional vision, another threat comes from distraction. In his book on school leadership, Larry Cuban (1988) frames this as an epic battle between three sets of demands on educational leaders—administrative, political, and instructional. Administrative demands make up the managerial tasks—procedural requirements, budgeting, and plant management—that can chew up the time and energy of education leaders. Political tasks, including negotiations and relations with the school board, mayor, and state government, require another set of skills. The instructional role, in Cuban's view, represents the responsibilities of activities like developing and monitoring the curriculum; helping teachers improve their pedagogy, content, and classroom management; and establishing a climate focused on learning. Given the immediacy of the managerial problems (Bus 68 never gets kids to school on time! School 58 has a leaky roof!) and political tasks (The school board wants to change district policies for textbook adoptions! The mayor wants to use education reform in his reelection platform and wants to know if you will support him!), it is small wonder that instructional efforts often get crowded out. In a summary of fifteen studies that were conducted between 1911 and 1981 of how school principals spent their time, Cuban found that principals spent only about a quarter of their time on instructionally related activities (p. 62). This conforms with many of the studies described in chapter 1. Similarly, Duval County's leaders continually faced the same unremitting tug of war between managerial, political, and instructional demands.

Instructional leadership is the buzzword of today's educational improvement gurus. Their diagnosis, much like Cuban's, is that educational leaders tend to give short shrift to instructional improvement. Their prescription is "all instruction, all of the time." This is greatly overstated, as a major function of school district leaders is to attend to managerial and political issues. What education leaders can do is preserve time, space, and resources for instructional improvement. Additionally, managerial and political issues can be used to reinforce attention to instructional issues.

A major transportation imbroglio in Duval County in 2000 demonstrated how distractions can innocently arise, balloon into a crisis, distract from the emphasis on instruction, and corrode relationships in their wake. The story illustrates the intricately intertwined relationships among instructional, managerial, and political issues within education and how an instructional vision can suffer from external distractions.

One challenge in maintaining an instructional focus is dealing with the sheer size of many urban school districts. The Duval County public school system is a vast organization with an annual budget, as of 2002, of over $1.41 billion, according to George Latimer, the district's associate superintendent of administration and business services. The district employs a workforce of more than 13,000 full- and part-time employees. This includes over 7,300 full-time teachers and approximately 400 school-level administrators housed in 149 schools that educate over 126,000 students. To support its schools, district employees perform a variety of functions ranging from payroll to purchasing to accounting to transportation to facilities management. Each of these areas requires attention to a variety of matters that are in some ways precursors to teaching and learning and in other ways peripheral to them. In such an immense and complicated system, with each department demanding attention, it is easy for instructional issues to get crowded out.

For any district, transporting students to and from school is a major undertaking—the bigger the district, the more complex the scheduling. In Duval County, about sixty thousand students are bused to and from school each day. The county spends about $37 million on transportation each year, splitting the cost 40/60 with the state. Thus, $15 million to cover the cost of transporting students each year comes out of local wallets.

For the last half of the twentieth century, local contractors had provided transportation for the county's students. Over that time, as the county's population increased and the school system expanded, the busing system grew increasingly convoluted. By 2000, there were 119 contractors covering 913 bus routes. Jacksonville's antiquated system was also unique in the state. By 2000, sixty-four of Florida's sixty-seven counties ran their own bus systems. Two of the other three had long instituted open-bidding processes for service providers. Only Duval County had never had contractors bid on their transportation contracts.

At the end of 1999, the district formed a committee to suggest ways to improve the transportation system. The committee issued a report that recommended that the school board bid out the county's bus services. Calculating that a competitive bid could save the county $3 million a year, Superintendent Fryer called for bids for the 2001–02 school year. Fryer's motive was to reallocate the savings into professional development for teachers. In early 2000, Fryer told me in an interview how he was trying to generate additional resources for his instructional reforms. "We need to work on our resource base," he said. "For example, we spend $35 million on transportation and we can save some of that. This money will be going into professional development for teachers." At first the decision seemed to be what an editorial in the *Florida Times-Union* described as "an easy call" ("Education: An Easy Call," 2001). The suggestion was supported by the city's general counsel, who issued a "binding opinion" that the school board bid out its transportation contract.

But the managerial motives for the decision resulted in an intense political backlash. The local bus companies, to protect their livelihoods, decried the loss of local jobs. They put enormous pressure on school board members, flooding their offices with emails and faxes, demonstrating at school board meetings and enlisting political allies to lobby on their behalf. The pressure on board members became so intense, the *Times-Union* reported, that school security officers had to escort them to their cars and follow them home after meetings. "It's been the most intense ever, I'd have to say, by far," remarked then school board chair Susan Wilkinson, who felt the pressure was more impassioned than during the contentious debates over school desegregation and sex education (Pinzer, 2001). Even the mayor got involved, chastising the contractors for their "inappropriate" public pressure.

Eventually, the board settled on two national companies, a local company, and a consortium of local companies to cover the routes of the county's five regions. But this came about only after several board votes, the rescinding of a vote, threatened legal action, and a great deal of acrimony. To make matters worse, due to political compromises by the school board, the promised savings never materialized. After the contracts were finally filled, the estimated savings were projected to be only about $370,000, just a fraction of what Fryer had hoped for. The dust stirred by the debacle was slow to settle, as the selected bus companies had trouble finding enough qualified drivers to cover their routes when students headed back to school the following August. The service delays were highly publicized by the media.

The controversy also had a corrosive effect on the relationship between Fryer and the seven-member school board, at least in the short term. The hard feelings engendered by the bus contract contributed to stormy relations between Fryer and the board that lingered for many months. In retrospect, however, Fryer believed that the bus situation became a catalyst for realigning district governance relations.

The bus contract situation demonstrated the interconnectedness among instructional, managerial, and political issues in education. While Fryer's initial motivation was simply to increase the amount of money available for his instructional initiatives by improving the efficiency of the bus system, he underestimated the political hornets' nest he was walking into. The situation also demonstrates the differing incentives and unique dynamic in education between publicly elected school board members and appointed superintendents. While the decision was relatively straightforward for Fryer, different and powerful constituencies were pressuring the publicly elected school board members. While Fryer's unswerving commitment to instructional improvement and fiscal responsibility undoubtedly earned him respect within both the educational and business communities, he paid a heavy price. The situation eroded his relationship with the school board and cost him political capital in the community. But perhaps more damaging was the dissipation of energy and attention to implementing the district's instructional vision caused by the volatile and distracting situation. Ironically, in attempting to increase the focus on instruction, Fryer actually did exactly the opposite.

THE CLAIRVOYANCE AND FRAGILITY
OF AN INSTRUCTIONAL VISION

In this chapter I have sought to establish the central importance of a well-articulated vision of powerful instruction as the core element of district improvement. Using the experiences of Duval County leaders as an example, I have described and contextualized the key components of their vision for instructional improvement, which centered around clear standards for student performance; curricular specification in the major content areas; pedagogical alignment across literacy, mathematics, and science; structural reorganization of the school for a better use of instructional time and resources; school-based professional development; and the development of collaborative learning communities. By examining the extent to which the vision was understood and interpreted by school leaders and teachers, I have tried to illuminate the ways in which school faculties are likely to interpret district leaders' efforts and to point out possible reasons for those interpretations.

While there are many similarities and important points of coherence across the major content areas, there are also critical distinctions among them. Most obviously, there are important differences in the content and developmental processes across literacy, mathematics, and science. This requires that each subject be treated distinctly and limits the extent to which approaches in one content area may be appropriate in others. Second, and perhaps connectedly, each subject-matter curriculum in the district was developed differently. While literacy came largely through America's Choice, mathematics was a melding of district curriculum choices (Investigations, Connected Mathematics, and College Preparatory Math for High School) and America's Choice processes. Science, by contrast, was much more of a grassroots development in the district. The way the curricula of these subjects came to be, and the way the district rolled them out and supported them, may be connected to the reactions from school-level respondents. Third, there are important differences in the extent to which external pressure for performance was being asserted by the state. Literacy and mathematics were much more high-stakes subject areas than science, which may have allowed science to develop more organically in the district and also may account for the view that the instructional vision in science was less clear than in literacy or mathematics.

Developing a robust instructional vision requires district leaders to probe the commonalities and distinctions across subject areas and to continually refine the meaning of a coherent instructional vision that accounts for the particularities of subject matter and developmental level. Developing a powerful instructional vision is like chiseling a fine marble statue out of a rough-hewn block of stone. Leaders must start with the coarse block of an idea and shape it to their need. After much chipping and polishing, a coherent vision begins to take shape that accounts for the different parts of the form and the different grains of the material. Only after much time and effort is a vision specific enough to provide guidance yet general enough to allow professional latitude. This continuous refinement process is a theme that I return to many times in this book.

In this chapter I have also identified several central issues that are likely to arise in any attempt to unite a school system around a particular instructional approach. One crucial challenge that district leaders face is the degree of prescription associated with their instructional vision. The balance between specificity of instructional reform and teacher autonomy is delicate. An instructional vision must be specific enough to provide guidance for teachers and school leaders while at the same time allowing them to exercise professional judgment and ownership. This is a particularly tricky issue because of the heritage of instructional autonomy in American education, which is organized within a fairly regimented organizational apparatus. Thus, while the lives of school faculty are constrained in many ways, teachers have traditionally had wide latitude over what they teach and how they teach it. The design of America's Choice, perhaps its genius, places this reform adroitly between designed prescription and user sovereignty. Standards, and to some extent curriculum, are fixed in such a model. Yet, in order to diagnose student work in relation to those standards and employ instruction methods that shepherd students toward those standards requires a high level of teacher skill and professionalism. Similarly, the structure of readers and writers workshops that are employed by America's Choice provides a regimented framework for instruction. But within this framework, teachers must have wide latitude to make sophisticated decisions about what learning strategies to use with which students and how to effectively deliver them. This is a balance I will explore further in subsequent chapters.

A second key issue that seems all but inevitable when district leaders enact an instructional vision is that it will threaten other existing approaches and therefore attract opposition. Teachers no doubt are using some existing approach, so that a broad instructional vision is almost certainly going to replace some existing approaches. Leaders' instructional vision may be philosophically close to or far from what teachers are using. In some cases these are approaches developed by teachers and in other cases they are more formal programs. Since most school systems, and most schools within them, are extremely decentralized, any efforts to align classroom instruction around a particular set of ideas is likely to be met with at least healthy skepticism and at most open opposition. The situation in Duval County surrounding ICARE's advocacy of Direct Instruction is a vivid example of what can happen when visions clash. Superintendent Fryer's delicate approach of advocating clearly without mandating that all faculty adopt his preferred methods represents one possible strategy for navigating the pitfalls of ceding instructional authority or removing the responsibility for ownership that is essential for quality implementation.

External distractions are a third threat to attention to, and the ultimate effectiveness of, an instructional vision. School districts are large, complicated systems, and instructional reform efforts are only part of the complex processes that need to be managed within them. District leaders hold a host of responsibilities and face myriad challenges. As Cuban's historical investigations have shown, it is relatively easy to allow managerial and political concerns to crowd out instructional ones. The bus contract story in Duval County is a poignant reminder of how even the best of intentions to garner resources for instruction can turn into political or managerial distractions. Leaders cannot realistically hope to focus only on instruction, but they can make their instructional initiatives the emphasis of their efforts. Only by preserving substantial space for instructional attention amid managerial and political demands can leaders attend to enhancing the central mission of their organizations.

3

Gardening and Engineering:
A Dual Approach
to Educational Change

I think it is dangerous to try to create great changes in human nature in any short space and time. If you're going to change a civilization, it can be done only as the gardener does it, not as the engineer does it. That is, it's got to be done in harmony with the rules of nature and can't all be done overnight. That's why I'm against practically all revolutions—because they usually end badly by trying to do too much at once.

—*George Kennan*

Attempts to make broadscale instructional changes across education organizations, in their own humble way, are potentially as dramatic and radical as the geopolitical changes that foreign policy expert George Kennan wrote about following World War II. Meaningful, large-scale instructional reforms—reforms that seek to reach deeply into classrooms and change the way teachers engage students with ambitious content—imply fundamental changes in the ways that teachers think about their work with students, how district leaders introduce teachers to the often uncomfortable notions of change, and how leaders provide training for teachers so they can develop new skills. Leadership of meaningful educational change requires *both* the nurturing skills of the gardener *and* the constructing skills of the engineer. Education leaders must attend to the sometimes seismic shifts in peoples' psyches brought about by the introduction of change and, at the same time, build learning opportunities to provide people with the needed skills to enact the proposed changes. Kennan's analogy reminds us of the very real risks associated with ambitious reforms that do not lay sufficient groundwork. The graveyard of American educational history is scattered with the bones of once promising, yet failed, reform efforts.

Gardening and engineering are apt metaphors for the work required to lead educational change because they embody the two major challenges education leaders face. First, and most fundamentally, district leaders must cultivate the need and rationale for change and address peoples' natural aversion to the disruption it entails. Whether they acknowledge it or not, district leaders' efforts to meaningfully change teachers' practices challenge many aspects of their deeply rooted professional identities. In order to successfully foster change, district leaders must shepherd school faculties through the psychological transformation that accompanies retraining. This requires an understanding of the psychological implications of change and a set of strategies that will convince teachers and school leaders that proposed changes are worthwhile and merit their commitment.

Second, district leaders must construct learning opportunities for school faculties and district staff that develop their competence with the new skills required by the reform. In doing this they must retool the way professional development systems are organized and learning opportunities are delivered to employees at all levels of the organization, including teachers, school leaders, and district administrators. Training, in order to be effective, must be based on what we know about the ways adults most effectively learn and grow. The scaffolding of learning opportunities within the organization provides employees with the skills to successfully apply the ideas of reform.

Strategies to introduce change and to build individuals' proficiency to enact change are the yin and yang of the capacity-building process. Education researchers and policymakers talk about these twin concepts as the will and capacity for reform (Fuhrman & O'Day, 1996; McLaughlin, 1987). The first builds the rationale and commitment for change, while the second develops the competence to enact change. Each without the other is unlikely to produce meaningful differences in the way things are done.

In this chapter I describe how Duval County leaders sought to build both the commitment and the capacity of school faculties and district administra tors to enact their instructional vision, and how they used a range of motivations, incentives, and evidence to coax, cajole, convince, and even compel school faculty members to adopt new instructional approaches. First I use the literature on change theory to describe several frameworks for thinking about how organizational leaders foster an understanding of the reasons for, and value of, change. I then point out some of the key strategies used by Duval County leaders to encourage, inspire, persuade, and even pressure people to change. Within this conversation I will point out several of the debates and challenges that district leaders faced along the way. I then present an emerging framework for thinking about organizational capacity-building and what constitutes effective adult professional learning experiences. Using this framework for reference, I describe Duval County's learning opportunities for teachers, coaches, principals, and district leaders, and how the district is in the process of articulating a career progression continuum.

LEADING AS GARDENING:
THE CULTIVATING ASPECTS OF CHANGE LEADERSHIP

Perhaps the most fundamental challenge faced by education leaders who embark upon major change efforts is to develop ways to introduce people to new ideas about their work. Introduction to change must honor peoples' experience and professionalism and take into account the implications of this dislocating process on people's psyches. Leading change requires an understanding the process of change and how to constructively lead people through that process.

One way to go about this is simply to damn the torpedoes and demand that people do what is required. This approach has never proved very fruitful in education, with its tradition of local control, teacher autonomy, and loose coupling between administrative policy and local practice (Weick, 1976). There is a long line of research on the implications and limitations of mandated reforms, in both education and other public policy fields. Required change may bring about compliance, but it is usually superficial (Fullan, 1991). Overt mandates also may produce substantial resistance because they do little to convince people that the required act is worthy of their commitment (Evans, 1996). The education system seems particularly immune to mandates because of several distinct characteristics. First, teaching is not an easily reproducible process but stems, rather, from a series of fine-grained decisions and adjustments that teachers must continually make and thus is impervious to general rules and requirements (Elmore, 1993). Second, and related, education has a strong tradition of teacher autonomy; what goes on behind the classroom door is the purview of the teacher, regardless of the rules and requirements of more powerful administrators (Berman, 1978; Firestone, 1989; McLaughlin, 1987). Policy research in education has repeatedly shown that policies are reinterpreted, often selectively, to suit the needs of local actors (Cohen, 1988; Weatherly & Lipsky, 1977).

So, if educational leaders reject pure directives as weak levers to bring about deep and meaningful change, then the question remains: How do they win over the hearts and minds of school faculties to adopt a desired instructional reform? An important prerequisite to answering this question is to understand the process that individuals go through as they experience change. Only through understanding this process can education leaders support people to make productive changes.

Several different frameworks can help education leaders understand the implications of change for individuals. Hall and Hord (1987) developed a model for understanding and managing change, called the concerns-based adoption model (CBAM) (for a short description, see also Horsley & Loucks-Horsley, 1998). CBAM frames change through two parallel dimensions: stages of concern and levels of use. The stages of concern are affective, how people feel about doing something new and different. The levels of use are behavioral, how people act as they move from doing something one way to doing it another way. The affective stages of concern propose that people go through four general levels of concern with change. Initially, people are either unaware of or uninterested in a proposed change. Second, people begin to ask questions and wonder how it might affect them. Third, a range of concerns emerge as people engage in new skills. Fourth, people describe their thoughts about how to make a reform work better, collaborate with colleagues to do so, and seek ways to build on the reform.

The levels of use identify three levels of typical behaviors that individuals going through during the process of change. First is nonuse, in which a person takes no action with regard to the program or practice. Second is orientation, where individuals seek information about the program or practice. Third is the preparation level, where an individual makes a decision to adopt a new practice and actively prepares to implement it. The CBAM framework is helpful in thinking about the stages individuals go through as they grapple with change.

Evans (1996) takes a much more psychological view of the change process in individuals. In his insightful book "The Human Side of School Change," Evans lays bare the psychological implications of school reform efforts. He argues that change implicitly challenges the competence of the individuals who are the targets of change efforts and introduces a sense of loss as they abandon familiar practices. He stresses how important it is for leaders of change to develop strategies to "unfreeze" people from this initial state of confusion and conflict, and to build new commitment and competence in the desired practices. He argues that change efforts, first and foremost, must attend to people, culture, meaning, and motivation rather than structure, roles, and rules. This requires going beyond technical training to change the deeper culture of schools.

Spillane, Reiser, and Reimer (2002) view the level of individual transformation in response to a reform as a product of those individuals' ability to make sense of the new ideas. They contend that individuals' cognitive responses to reform have a major influence on the depth of reform implementation and, ultimately, the impact of reform. They develop a framework of sense-making in which individuals' existing cognitive structures (attitudes, beliefs, and knowledge) interact with policy signals and the specifics of the situation to shape their responses. For Spillane et al., low levels of reform implementation are less the product of overt resistance than misunderstanding and misinterpretation of the intent of reform. They argue that the implementing agent as sense-maker is heavily influenced by biases favoring prior beliefs and values, the need to protect their self-image, and social context and interactions. Like Evans, Spillane et al. believe that the organizational context and structure have a huge bearing on individuals' sense-making and reaction to reform ideas.

Yet another way to gain insight into how reform resonates with individuals is through motivation theory. Motivation theorists also stress the psychological aspect of spurring people to change. Researchers on motivation across disciplines (Mohrman, 1989; Mohrman & Lawler, 1996) explain that peoples' actions are driven by their desire to perform in ways that lead to fulfillment of their needs. Approaches to motivation are based upon peoples' deep need for self-efficacy, a sense of competence, effectiveness, and achievement. Two key expectancies shape the power of a particular idea for change—that the effort will lead to success and that the success is consistent with important personal outcomes. Incentives for change can be both intrinsic (internally motivated) or extrinsic (externally motivated).

Although they emphasize different things, all of these frameworks attempt to shed light on the internal reactions that people go through during the introduction of change. Change confronts people's conceptions of their expertise, value, and pride in their work. Change can spark confusion, fear, and resentment in stressful and transitional times. Even if conceived of neutrally, reform efforts are personal in that they ask people to do their work in ways that are different from how it is presently conceived. Technical solutions often fail because they do not adequately take into account the personal and psychological shifts that accompany new ways of working. A deeper understanding of people's psychological reactions to change can help leaders craft responses in ways that are more sensitive to the internal unease and transition that accompany requests for change.

NURTURING CHANGE IN DUVAL COUNTY

We can learn a tremendous amount about both the process of change and efforts to lead it by taking a critical look at how Duval County leaders chose to frame and introduce their instructional vision. The blend of strategies employed by county leaders to inform, encourage, convince, cajole, and even compel teachers and school leaders to adopt a preferred set of instructional strategies created a powerful set of dynamics within the district. The approaches of Duval County leaders are quite revealing in terms of both the thoughtfulness of their approaches and how they speak directly to the various theories of human change, (e.g., Hall & Hord, 1987; Evans, 2001; Spillane et al., 2002; Mohrman, 1989) including the limitations of these approaches.

Advocacy without Mandate

Foremost in their efforts to introduce change in Duval County was the decision to openly advocate for the essential tenets of the America's Choice design without mandating that schools adopt them. Fryer himself was a passionate advocate of America's Choice, and he sought to encourage schools to adopt the design but did not require them to do so. As he said in an August 2000 interview with the *Florida Times-Union*, "In any system there is a tendency to follow what I like, but the school and the principal must be passionate about [America's Choice] or else it won't work. Have I persuaded schools? Yes. But tell them or order them to participate? I never did that. I said I personally believe America's Choice to be the easiest way to implement standards, but they must make their own decision" (Diamond, 2000).

The delicate balance of offering strong encouragement without issuing a mandate can be seen in the way district leaders responded to the call for more resources from advocates of Direct Instruction (see chapter 2). In that case, Fryer refused to provide equal support to the Direct Instruction program and clearly did not favor it, but he also did not force schools to abandon it. It is worth repeating Fryer's response to ICARE leaders' requests that he provide the same support and resources to Direct Instruction as he did to America's Choice: As he said in 2001, "They asked me to be just as passionate about Direct Instruction as I was about America's Choice. I said 'I'm sorry, I can't.' I just had to be honest. I just can't be. But I'm not trying to undercut Direct Instruction. They're all our children and we want whatever we do to have to succeed." By taking this stance, Fryer was walking the fine line between encouraging schools to adopt his preferred approach and mandating that they do so.

On the face of it, it may seem strange for a leader trained in the command-and-control culture of the military to stop short of ordering people to adopt a particular approach. But this tactic was consistent with the leadership philosophy Fryer had developed during his military career. Drawing from his leadership experience, Fryer used the language of intrinsic motivation to describe the difference between following someone else's order and making one's own choice:

> That has been my whole philosophy all my life as a leader. There are some people who lead with the power of the gun, . . . but when you take the gun away it is gone. I want to build this deep. I want people to say, "the boss is pretty good. He lets me run with a lot of rope, he gives me guidance, he gets out of my way, and I own it now and I feel responsible for it."

Implicit in the strategy to advocate an approach without requiring it is a belief in the power of people taking ownership of a reform. When a leader mandates a reform it is owned by the leader, but not necessarily by those who are under orders to enact it. This allows those actually implementing the reform to maintain a certain distance from responsibility for its success, yet when somebody makes their own decision to adopt a reform, they are committing themselves to the effort involved in adoption. They have moved from a passive to an active position. With choice comes ownership.

Yet some felt it was unseemly for Duval County's leadership to advocate for a particular instructional approach. Perhaps this was because people were not used to district leaders being involved in instructional issues that were usually left to the schools. Perhaps it was just the grumbling of those who preferred other approaches. Whatever the case, some did not appreciate Duval County leaders using their positional authority to advocate their preferred approach. As one of the Duval County School Board members interpreted it, "People will do what the hierarchy is doing. This is a voluntary program, kind of, sort of. But we know how the system works. If you are upwardly mobile, you better be for this" (Diamond, 2000). Taking a strong stance was not without political cost.

Fostering Urgency for Change

To further motivate change in the district, Duval County leaders regularly pointed out external threats to public education in order to foster a sense of urgency. From the get-go, Fryer and his leadership team stressed the urgent need to improve performance in the district. At monthly principal meetings and countless talks to teachers and the community, district leaders repeatedly pointed to external calls for improvement of the schools. The Duval County leadership team pointed to competition for students from private schools in the county as one reason for a sense of urgency within the district. District leaders also used economic arguments to urge change. NCEE and America's Choice had long used the economic imperative—the argument that in order to remain globally competitive, the American economy needs a highly educated workforce—as the primary rationale for instructional change, and Duval County leaders adopted this position.

Duval County leaders also used state and federal accountability requirements to reinforce their message of the urgent need for improvement. Florida law states that students in schools that are graded F on the Florida Comprehensive Achievement Test (FCAT) for two years in three are eligible for vouchers to attend any school in the district, public or private. County leaders capitalized on the pressure created by the state's high-stakes testing and accountability system to further legitimize their call for teachers and school leaders to adopt their instructional vision.

A clarion call by Superintendent Fryer at a May 2003 gathering of the district's principals is a perfect example of leaders' efforts to convey the urgent need for principals to improve their schools' performance. In his speech, Fryer pinpointed the array of forces, both within Florida and across the nation, that advocated competition in education. Fryer began by pointing out the increases in McKay scholarships; Florida offers these state tax breaks for companies that give scholarships for private schools. "There are a lot of folks out there trying to help kids leave the public school system," Fryer told the principals. He continued with a litany of arguments as to why education was already a competitive market and naming those advocating for furthering this trend:

> "We must keep reminding our teachers [that] this is a global economy and our kids are competing in . . . an internationally competitive marketplace. I had lunch with Secretary of Education Paige a few months ago in California and he made the same point. He listed all the Democrats and Republicans in both the Senate and the House who were for everything from vouchers to charter schools and who were certainly supportive of high standards and accountability that are buried in No Child Left Behind. . . . Like every business, we have to compete for our customers. So let's get that word out.

These efforts to stress the necessity for change represent a strategy that Evans (1996) refers to as "unfreezing." According to Evans, "Unfreezing is a matter of lessening one kind of anxiety, the fear of trying, but first mobilizing another kind of anxiety, the fear of *not* trying" (p. 56, italics original). By fostering a sense of besiegement, district leaders were making the status quo untenable.

Building Existence Proofs

It is not enough to make people unsatisfied with where they are; leaders must also show them where to go. A third strategy adopted by Duval County's leaders to encourage schools to adopt their preferred instructional approach was to use the first cohort of fourteen America's Choice schools to demonstrate the potential of this approach to improve teaching and enhance learning. When Fryer and other district leaders chose America's Choice as their instructional reform engine, they wanted not only to transform the schools that adopted the design, but also to use the America's Choice schools as "existence proofs"—as examples of the kind of school all the schools in the district could become.

At \$60,000–\$85,000 a pop (the annual cost per school of America's Choice), district leaders soon realized (if they even initially intended so) that it would not be feasible for all 149 schools in the district to purchase America's Choice. But this did not deter them from folding the key concepts of America's Choice into the district's standards-based reform efforts and spreading the core techniques of the model to other schools in the district. They called these the standards-based schools, as distinct from the America's Choice schools. In this way, district leaders sought to initiate a kind of domino effect of adoption. Fryer explained in 2000:

> I had a strategy. The strategy [for] the first year [was] to build a consensus on the need for this kind of reform. The next year was to build the zealots. Fourteen schools were picked. I personally convinced those schools to do it. I spent more than two hours with each faculty. I wanted an 80 percent buy-in. Even though a couple [of the schools] have had real struggles, most of them have done pretty well. The next year I knew that I wanted to create the critical mass that would begin to sustain this [model] in the district, so that no one could erase it, assuming it kept producing results. And forty-nine more schools signed up. Now . . . the job is to implement that . . . and then to begin to take the elements of that design and spread them to other schools [in the district].

Duval County leaders carefully selected the zealots to represent a broad cross-section of district schools, with particular emphasis on the low-performing schools, so they could demonstrate the effectiveness of the design for schools in different contexts. For this reason, the first fourteen America's Choice schools looked much like a microcosm of schools from across the district.

The first America's Choice cohort had ten elementary schools and four middle schools, which mirrored the district in many ways. They ranged from

TABLE 3. 1

Comparison of District Characteristics and America's Choice First Cohort

Characteristic	District	America's Choice First Cohort
Number of Elementary and Middle Schools	105	14
Avg. percent Free/reduced Lunch	57%	68%
Percent Minority	51%	66%
Number/percent A/B	14 (13%)	1 (7%)
Number/percent C	52 (50%)	5 (36%)
Number/percent D/F	39 (37%)	8 (57%)

schools like North Shore Elementary, a school in danger of receiving an F from the state, to Thomas Jefferson Elementary, a solid C school that was interested in using brain research to encourage multiple intelligences, to Chets Creek, one of the highest-performing elementary schools in the district. Table 3.1 compares the characteristics of the first cohort of America's Choice schools to the rest of the district's schools. The first cohort covered the spectrum of schools in the district, although they were slightly above average in terms of minority student populations and poverty. While they had schools at every performance level, they performed slightly more poorly than the district average.

While the America's Choice schools were getting underway, Fryer and his leadership team also introduced the America's Choice literacy model to a wider set of district schools, the standards-based schools, and in doing so, introduced teachers across the district to the potential of the standards-based literacy instruction.

So in 1999, as the first fourteen schools were beginning their journey with America's Choice, the district simultaneously contracted with NCEE to provide literacy institutes at all levels (elementary, middle, and high school). Those trained at those first literacy institutes were asked to implement the literacy model in their own classrooms. According to Superintendent Fryer, creating the opportunity for teachers in all the district schools to see the America's Choice literacy model in action was a way to show them what the model looked like within their own schools. He did not unrealistically expect that a few teachers trained in the literacy model would be able to train others in their schools. Rather, he believed that this would let other teachers see what the model looked like in their own schools and whet their appetites to try it themselves. As Fryer explained, "What we did is try to provide as much opportunity as we could for all the nondesign schools to get a literacy trained person. That was the thing . . . let other teachers see what was happening."

A perhaps unintended benefit of these initial adopters was that they formed the talent pool for coaches and the testing ground for schools in the district's next cohort of America's Choice. As Barbara Vandervort, one of the initial district leaders engaged with America's Choice (and later an NCEE employee), explained, "A lot of those people that attended those literacy institutes became the coaches in cohort 2 because they had the knowledge and were sought after. And it is interesting to see that many of those schools that had people attend the literacy institutes that first year became America's Choice schools in cohort 2 because they saw the success of the design in their own schools."

Creating Cross-Visitations

A system of visitations by school faculty to the America's Choice schools provided a fourth key ingredient to district leaders' efforts to encourage schools to adopt the America's Choice design and its standards-based instructional practices. Even as America's Choice was getting underway in those first fourteen Duval County schools and the literacy model was being introduced to a wide range of teachers across the district, Fryer and his leadership team were facilitating visitations of principals and teachers from across the district to the America's Choice schools. These cross-school visitations were an important component of the strategy of leaders' strategy to spread understanding of the model and its potential to teachers across the district, and a way to capitalize on the legitimacy of peer advocacy.

In order to create critical mass for standards-based instruction, Fryer believed he had to "have teachers convince teachers, and principals convince principals." In his view, this was a far more powerful way of encouraging people to consider the design because of the legitimacy of peer recommendation. He was convinced that people who visited their peers and saw the power of the design for themselves would be swayed by what they saw. "I believe in creating an example that works, and then having visitations," Fryer told me in 2003. "Having people who are the leaders of other schools and who are the key teachers in other schools go look at it because the work proves itself. The output, the student work, and the data show things they can't argue with. It's far better than just having some expert say, 'if you'll do this, I guarantee it will work." Evans (1996) also stresses the importance of what he calls personal contact, noting that "those who are being asked to adapt respond better when they have regular attention from, and access to, those who are responsible for it" (p. 61).

These cross-school visitations became a common practice in the district. In my fieldwork in schools I came across a number of teachers who described visits to other schools for the purpose of being introduced to and gaining a deeper understanding of the district's reform approaches. For example, a teacher in an elementary school that I visited in March 2003 described a recent visit to another school and the influence it had on her:

> Yesterday, we had the opportunity to go to another school, and I was so glad that I had that opportunity. It's different, but it's a real school with real kids, with real problems, and you get to see it being done. . . . That gave me a fresh perspective. It gave me a feeling [that], "OK, I can do this," and it gave me ideas.

This teacher's experience encapsulated many of the intentions behind the cross-visitations. They allowed teachers to view standards-based practices in schools similar to theirs with children similar to theirs, and gave them a sense of the pragmatic possibilities of adopting the district's reform practices.

District leaders later expanded the concept of visitations to include visitations across grade levels. As Fryer explained in 2001:

> The visitation has been really pretty enormous. We decided recently that now it was time for a vertical kind of visitation program. We've done enough of this 'Let's go see how the elementary school works.' Now I wanted high school teachers and principals to see what the elementary school students were doing. And when high school principals and teachers went to [the elementary school]—they just couldn't believe it. There were reactions, I am told, by the teachers: "Oh my God, our children cannot do as well as these children do and we're teaching high school. How can we do that?" And then they got enthusiastic about [standards-based practices]

because they realized that they really need to understand how these standards work.

The expansion of visitations beyond similar grade-level schools suggests that district leaders were using cross-visitations not only as a way to show teachers how their schools could look under the district's standards-based reform approach, but also as a tool to communicate the district's expectations for implementing the reforms. By having high school teachers and principals visit some of the highest-performing elementary schools that were implementing the reforms, Fryer sought to ratchet up expectations for all schools.

Building Islands of Evidence in Each School

A fifth strategy district leaders used effectively to spread their preferred model of instruction was the concept of the model classroom. The idea of a model classroom—a place in every school (and ideally in every grade and subject area) where teachers can see, touch, and smell for themselves what a reform looks like with kids like theirs—was brought to Duval County by NCEE and America's Choice.

In the America's Choice design, the main focus of a school coach's energy is to set up model classrooms at key grade junctures within each school. The model classroom is a place where teachers can go to see the America's Choice instructional model in action, observe its key tenets, and then return to their own classrooms to try it out for themselves, all with the encouragement and under the watchful eye of the coach. The model classroom is vital because it provides an accessible place for teachers to see the instructional techniques in action. The model gives teachers a concrete picture of what instruction looks like with their population of students in their own environment. When teachers see their colleagues having success with kids like their own, they cannot easily dismiss a reform idea by saying, "It may work there but it won't work in my school with my kids." Creating these oases of evidence within schools is part of the genius of the America's Choice design. The model classroom is a way to demonstrate to teacher that a reform is attainable and that it can improve the learning of their students.

Duval County's leaders capitalized on this idea and incorporated it into their own strategy for spreading reform in the district. The model classroom became one of the central components of implementation in the district's framework and a focus of the district's early implementation strategies. The teachers who went to NCEE's initial literacy workshops became de facto model classroom teachers, although the model was made weaker by the fact that at that time there were no coaches in their schools to support their efforts, nor a schoolwide design within which to implement the model. John Thompson, one of Duval County's five regional superintendents at the time, described the America's Choice model in January 2000: "The [goal] is to set up model classes within a school. You are trying to get people to buy in. You expect different rates of implementation, but if you have models within a school, you have a powerful force for others to emulate."

Mary Brown, the director of another region in the district at that stage of the rollout, described the model classroom as a catalyst for discussion of effective instruction among teachers: "We start with the model classroom and encourage all teachers to visit classrooms within their school . . . and it has spurred a discussion of best practices amongst teachers." Another district administrator concurred, "It's pretty amazing. I think this is what is allowing us to move ahead. It is because they have a place to *see it.*"

The concept of the model classroom as a locus for change was well understood by a broad spectrum of district administrators in a set of interviews conducted in January 2000, early in the district's reform cycle. For example, the district's supervisor of alternative education and English as a second language, an office that operates in isolation from trends in the core the subject areas in the typical district, explained the model classroom technique. "It's like osmosis with the model classroom. This kind of change is hard to bring about, but America's Choice gets at this by starting with a small group and spreading. Teachers seeing the model classroom helps them help other teachers buy in, and then they are beginning to buy in without being told to do it."

Teachers and principals in schools across Duval County quickly noted the influence of this particular approach. When I asked one elementary principal of an America's Choice school how she convinced teachers to adopt the reform, she responded as if the results of the reform itself did the convincing: "I really didn't need to convince them. The proof was in the pudding. They went into the model classroom and saw what was going on there, and began to dig in and do the work. And then they started seeing results. So it's the results that convinced them, not me."

A model classroom teacher in a low-performing high school that was not part of America's Choice recounted the moment when the school's faculty began to look at her instruction with interest:

> I think there was a turning point when we had an in-service day and I was asked to give a presentation. And after that presentation it was like a whole new light was shed. It was a lesson where I actually [posted] the standard and I took student work and attached it to my lesson plan and highlighted it, showing them what I was expecting and where the child actually did it. And they [said], "You got this child to do all of this in one work period? How did you do it?" I could almost see them thinking, "Okay. Well, maybe she does know what she's doing. Let's just listen a little." So that made it easy for me and they started to come by and see what I was up to.

In each of these cases, changes began to occur only after faculty members noticed the influence the techniques were having on students and their performance. The model classrooms provided places for them to see the new instruction in action, but it was the results that provided the push to adopt the practices.

THE COLLECTIVE EFFECT OF GARDENING

The collective effect of the Duval County leaders' push for change quickly developed a powerful momentum in the district. The district leaders' methods of encouraging adoption of their preferred instructional approaches—fostering a sense of urgency and external competition, demonstrating that America's Choice worked in similar district schools, facilitating inter-school visitations—all helped create unprecedented awareness, anticipation, enthusiasm, and expectation for the reform model.

Fryer and his leadership team's advocacy of America's Choice created a sense of desirability around the reform model that gave it its own momentum. Many principals felt they had to have America's Choice in their schools because it had proved successful in the model schools, and would be good for their schools too. As one principal described:

> I think my children deserve anything that any other group of children in this district deserves. So if it's good, then let me in on it. . . . I saw what was

happening in the other schools and was able to appreciate the success that those children were having . . . and I just thought, this is for me!

In effect, district leaders had created a demand for the skills and strategies of America's Choice across the district. School leaders who were not part of the design even began trying to implement pieces of it on their own. America's Choice became so desirable that forty-eight schools signed up to adopt the design in the second cohort.

On the flip side, the phenomenon engendered a sense of jealousy among schools, creating a sense of haves and have nots. As Regional Superintendent Thompson noted, "It took until after Christmas in the first year before I saw any change, and it's been a gradual recognition . . . the ripples spread out to more teachers in each school, and then more schools . . . once there [was] recognition that things were going on in these [America's Choice] design schools, then the other schools felt, 'I'm slipping behind.'"

In a district used to having lots of different home-grown approaches and emphases, where teachers and school leaders were used to having lots of latitude and control over their instructional approaches, squeezing everybody into a particular instructional approach, regardless of the latitude within that instructional approach, created several interesting dynamics. First, there was the predictable dynamic of resistance, of people saying, "We don't want to do that thing" or "It's not for us."

Reforms that are successful enough to create a sense of intrigue and possibility around them create a different dynamic, a dynamic of demand. But along with that demand also comes a sense of inequity—why are those schools and teachers getting access to that desirable thing while we are not? In this case, it was obvious that the America's Choice schools were getting more resources than the other schools in the district. ICARE's crusade for Direct Instruction was about getting the district to allocate resources equitably across schools with different philosophical approaches to instruction.

At least some Duval County leaders were surprised by the dynamic resulting from their own success at creating a demand for America's Choice and the instructional approaches advocated by NCEE. As Thompson told me, "Early on, nobody in the district was concerned, or was alert to, the fact that we were getting a division among schools between the haves and have-nots, and . . . it really was a struggle to do something for the other schools."

Having created a demand, district leaders were now faced with the challenge of building capacity to meet that demand. In the next section I turn to the organizational systems and structures Duval County leaders created to build the capacity of people across the system to deliver and support standards-based instruction.

LEADING AS ENGINEERING: BUILDING CAPACITY FOR CHANGE

I think it's training at all levels, a massive amount of investment in professional development, that makes a difference. What did we do in the armed forces to bring ourselves to where we are? First of all, we did a lot of self reflection. What was wrong with our profession? We learned to work jointly in the military, instead of in silence. Then we invested in a whole lot in professional development. . . . For example, when I commanded a fighter wing we trained against either real enemy airplanes we had acquired, with pilots trained in their tactics, or we had airplanes that simulated all that. . . . Plus, we built things like red flag and green flag, which were these massive gigantic exercises that came as close to real war as possible. Our training [concept] was "train as you will fight." Professional development has been a large part of why [the armed forces are] so much better.

—Superintendent Fryer

Attending to the process of change—and how individuals are introduced to, understand, and experience change—is only one part of the puzzle for systematically improving instructional quality within educational organizations. The second crucial piece is developing a capacity-building system that provides teachers, school leaders, and district administrators with the knowledge and skills to enact more ambitious instruction. For teachers, this means training that is in part generic and in part highly specific to their grade level and content area. It includes such matters as how to organize their classrooms, how to provide more targeted instruction to students, how to diagnose students' skill levels, and how to develop a wide range of instructional strategies to move students toward standards. School leaders need to develop the skills to support teachers in their efforts by restructuring school schedules and monitoring the work of teachers. District leaders need to be prepared to support, monitor, and motivate the efforts of school faculties. Creating an effective professional development system that builds the capacity of people at all levels of the system is the second great challenge for district leaders.

Over the past twenty years, approaches to professional development in education have changed substantially, as their form and structure have been stretched to fit a growing understanding of how adults learn most effectively. A once dominant approach, the "one-shot" workshop, has been increasingly disparaged as generally insufficient and ineffective (Smylie, Bilcer, Greenberg, & Harris, 1998). In its stead, researchers and educators are beginning to forge a remarkable level of consensus about what constitutes effective professional development, which is defined as structured learning experiences for teachers that produce changes in their instructional practices and enhance the learning of their students. Effective professional development contains at least seven critical components.

First, professional development must show teachers how to connect their instruction to specific and ambitious criteria for student performance (Hawley & Valli, 1999; NRC, 1996). Work in cognitive development suggests that more complex knowledge and problem-solving skills require more sophisticated teaching strategies (Borko & Putnam, 1995) and that this kind of teaching can be achieved through setting higher learning goals (Resnick & Klopfer, 1989). One major finding from the Third International Mathematics and Science Study (TIMSS) was that high common standards for student performance are strongly related to national achievement (Schmidt, 1999).

Second, effective professional development must immerse participants in techniques of active learning (Arons, 1989; Bybee, 1993; McDermott, 1990). Little (1993) argues that ambitious reforms "constitute a departure from canonical views of curriculum and from textbook-centered or recitation-style teaching" (p. 130), requiring teachers to model more student-centered forms of learning. Marek and Methaven (1991) found that the programs that employed questioning and experimentation had a greater influence on student achievement than programs that taught teachers to follow specific curricula.

Third, reformers argue that professional development must be both intensive and sustained (Hawley & Valli, 1999; Smylie, Bilcer, Greenberg, & Harris, 1998). In order for teachers to incorporate new practices, they must be able to try new techniques in their classrooms and then have time to reflect on their experiences. Supovitz and Turner (2000) found that more intensive professional development experiences were related to changes in teachers' instructional practices. Consequently, professional organizations call for more long-term, coherent professional development plans (National Council for Teachers of Mathematics, 1989; NRC, 1996).

Fourth, staff development must engage teachers in concrete teaching tasks that they can employ with their students (Darling-Hammond & McLaughlin, 1995). Research on situated learning suggests that knowledge transfer increases in tightly contextualized situations (Anderson, Reder, & Simon, 1996). Studies have shown that staff development undertaken in isolation from teachers' classroom duties seldom have much impact on teaching practices or student achievement (Zigarmi, Betz, & Jennings, 1977).

Fifth, professional development must focus on subject-matter knowledge and deepen teachers' mastery of their content area (Cohen & Hill, 1998). The National Science Education Standards, for example, call for professional development to emphasize essential science content (NRC, 1996). The teaching of reading requires that teachers understand the building blocks of phonics, phonemic awareness, fluency, vocabulary, and comprehension (National Reading Panel, 2000). Kennedy (1998) examined the evidence of effective professional development and concluded that "programs that focus on subject matter knowledge and on student learning of particular subject matter are likely to have larger positive effects on student learning than are programs that focus on teaching behaviors" (p. 11).

Sixth, adult professional development must capitalize on the experiences and expertise of peers. Joyce and Showers (1996) found that teachers who worked regularly with adult peers practiced new skills and strategies more frequently and applied them more appropriately than teachers who worked alone. Wenger (1998) has studied both formal and informal learning across organizations and contends that learning comes from "communities of practice that sustain enough mutual engagement in an enterprise together to share some significant learning" (p. 86). Lieberman (1995) argues that the definition of professional development must be expanded to include "authentic opportunities to learn from and with colleagues *inside* the school" (p. 591).

Finally, reform strategies must be connected to other aspects of school change (Corcoran & Goertz, 1995; Fullan, 1991; O'Day & Smith, 1993). One of the most persistent findings from the research is the intimate relationship between staff development and school improvement. As Fullan (1991) states, "Staff development cannot be separated from school development" (p. 331). According to Lieberman (1995), reform plans that have a chance to succeed must create a "culture of inquiry," which is an "ongoing part of teaching and school life." Marsh and LeFever (1997) find that school leadership is critical to school reform.

This emerging framework offers a skeletal outline of the form and content of effective professional development and provides guidance for the engineering challenges (to use Kennan's term) facing school district leaders who seek to build a cutting-edge professional development system on a large scale.

Building Capacity in Duval County

In Duval County, the district leadership's ambitious instructional vision implied nothing less than a massive rethinking of the ways that teachers and school and district leaders approached their jobs. Fryer and his leadership team took a macro approach to capacity-building. Drawing on his military background, Fryer viewed his role as the strategic coordinator of resources in the battle for the advancement of learning. He used the analogy of how a general sees a battlefield to distinguish between the strategic work of district leadership and the more tactical front-line work of principals and teachers in schools. According to Fryer, schools were where the "close-in battle" was taking place, where teachers and principals were fighting ignorance and advancing knowledge. His job, by contrast, was to marshal and provide resources in support of the work in schools. These could include the allocation of fiscal resources; community resources; and the district's levers of command and control; as well as flexible resources that could be allocated to areas of high need; and the reserve resources of the local community, government, and businesses.

Fryer's analogy of the district's work as a battle against the social and historical forces that impeded education underlined the magnitude of the challenge the district faced. As Fryer recalled, "That's where we've had the biggest problem. How do we continue to do what we are doing on such a massive scale and still develop a capacity to do more? It's stretching our resources to the limit."

To meet this challenge, Duval County leaders developed an increasingly sophisticated multilevel system to build the capacity of educators at different levels to provide standards-based instruction and support the delivery of standards-based instruction. This includes direct training of teachers; institutionalizing school standards coaches to model instruction and provide ongoing support to teachers; training district standards coaches to facilitate school improvement; providing leadership training for principals to support standards-based instruction in their schools; and creating professional growth opportunities for district leaders.

It would not do justice to this system to solely describe its present state, as if it sprang fully formed from the heads of district leaders. In fact, Duval County leaders' thinking about providing learning opportunities to people at different levels across the system has been evolving and changing in important ways. In the following section I first describe the key components of the system, including the direct training of teachers, the development of a coaching system that embeds ongoing professional development within schools, and district leadership development. I then discuss a key dilemma the district grappled with over time. In the case of materials development, the district was torn between self-sufficiency and reliance on external expertise.

Direct Training of Teachers

Duval County funds ongoing professional development for teachers through the Schultz Center for Teaching and Leadership, an independently operated, nonprofit training facility that serves five surrounding counties, including Duval. Working closely with the district, the Schultz Center staff (many of whom are district employees) provides a scaffolded sequence of teacher training, particularly in the content areas. Standards-based literacy training, for example, has three levels of increasingly advanced courses. Teachers take each course for a particular grade level, so materials are customized to meet the particular needs of teachers at that level of literacy instruction. Mathematics courses are also customized for each specific grade and closely track the district's math-pacing guides so that teachers receive "just in time" development. Most courses are targeted to specific grade and skill levels and are delivered intermittently, with time in between for teachers to return to their classrooms to apply the techniques they have learned. All courses are offered for state in-service points (and in some cases, university credits) as extrinsic motivators for participation.

One challenge facing independent professional development centers that serve large school districts is to provide training that is tightly connected to districts' reform ambitions. Often hampered by having small staffs, these training facilities have traditionally provided generic fare or brought in external professional developers for short-term workshops that are not tightly connected to district goals. There is a large body of research indicating that such workshops have little or no impact on instructional practices. But Schultz Center staff members have apparently learned from the shortcomings of other independent professional development providers. Working closely with district leaders, the Schultz Center offers training that is tightly aligned with the needs of Duval County educators. Many of the trainings are offered by district employees, including school and district standards coaches and regional superintendents and directors.

Several features of teacher training are common across content areas. First, training is ongoing and connected to teachers' current work. In almost all cases, participants come together multiple times over the course of the school year and leave with practical information and strategies to apply to the units they are teaching or about to teach. Second, training is specific to either particular grade levels or small grade ranges, so that teachers get information targeted to their needs. Third, trainers are often expert teachers from the district who have "walked in participants' shoes."

School Standards Coaches

One of the district's central capacity-building strategies was the placement of a full-time standards coach in each school, beginning in 2002. The coach's job is to work with the school principal to implement the elements of the district's framework. This includes analyzing student performance data and helping to develop and train teachers on instructional responses, to facilitate the implementation of safety-net programs for students who need additional time and/or assistance, and to train and work with the school faculty to deepen their understanding and application of standards-based instructional practices.

Duval County leaders absorbed the idea of school-embedded professional development from the America's Choice design. In the America's Choice model, the full-time literacy coach is the core mechanism by which the ideas of standards-based instruction are introduced throughout the school. According Regional Superintendent Thompson, "One of the things that we saw from America's Choice . . . was the importance of in-school professional development." Duval County leaders became convinced that school-embedded professional development, conducted by coaches, was the ideal means to bring about deep change within its schools. Yet Duval County's model differed from the America's Choice model in several ways. In the America's Choice model, the coach essentially becomes a literacy expert who provides all training to teachers, while the principal takes the role of organizing school structures to support the model. In Duval County, the coach is more of a generalist and shares school reform leadership with the principal, while content-based training is provided at the Schultz Center. These distinctions between Duval County's standards-based reform approach and America's Choice have sparked considerable debate among district leaders as to which is the better model.

In their evolving efforts, Duval County leaders have come to distinguish between the purpose of coaches at the elementary and the secondary level. Elementary school coaches are intended to provide a level of support that has never been available to them before. In secondary schools, coaches' aims are to re-energize and focus the work of departmental structures around instructional engagement. As Superintendent Fryer explained, "What I think we really need in middle and high school is functional coaches. . . . You need someone with the expertise to sustain and deepen knowledge in a given area. Now, that traditionally should have been a department head. It hasn't worked that way, it really hasn't."

District Standards Coaches

In the summer of 2003, Duval County and NCEE contractually extended their relationship through what they called a "design license agreement." The agreement called for the certification of district standards coaches to support the implementation of standards-based reform in Duval County schools and gave Duval County the right to use NCEE's copyrighted training, curriculum materials, and the NCEE's detailed school implementation rubrics. The certification process was designed to ensure that district coaches were qualified to support the implementation of the design in schools. The district coaches were provided training similar to that of America's Choice cluster leaders, who are employed by NCEE to provide support to geographic clusters of between eight and fifteen schools. The agreement also allowed Duval County to "Duvalize" NCEE's implementation rubrics to account for distinctions between the America's Choice design and Duval County's standards-based reform.

Most of the district standards coaches have had experience with America's Choice. They are largely former America's Choice cluster leaders and school coaches. Like America's Choice cluster leaders, district standards coaches are assigned to work with between six and ten schools to support their implementation of the district framework. The coaches are asked to spend approximately 80 percent of their time working with schools and 20 percent developing curriculum materials and providing training to teachers at the Schultz Center. The coaches are under the supervision of the six district regional superintendents. The coaches' work is wide-ranging, depending on the level of implementation in the schools they are working with and the level of autonomy they have within their region. Like most early reforms, the work of the district standards coaches is undergoing substantial refinement as the district adjusts to this new layer of support.

Principal Leadership Development

Early on, district leaders realized that principals were integral to the support and spread of their instructional reform efforts. As Superintendent Fryer explained in 2003, "Leadership is now my focus, because once we get the principals understanding this stuff and confident they can lead it, we will keep it going." The evolution of district-sponsored professional development for principals, including monthly principal meetings and the development of a principal-training curriculum, reflects the district's bumpy evolution toward more targeted, more instructionally oriented professional development.

For many years, the district has brought all its principals together for monthly meetings, which have been used to communicate the district's programs. The meetings often are broken into two parts. The first part is a whole-group meeting or presentation by either district leaders or an external speaker. In the afternoons, the principals usually break out by geographic region (about thirty schools each) for a session of several hours that is led by the regional superintendent and director. Fryer focused these meetings more on instructional leadership and brought in many leading national figures—Lucy Calkins, Jim Stigler, Bill Schmidt, Ruby Payne, and Roland Barth to name a few—to explore the many dimensions of instructional leadership with principals.

During the 2002–03 school year I had the opportunity to attend most of the district's monthly principal meetings. Examining an overall picture of this aspect of leadership development is noteworthy because it demonstrates the district's movement toward a more disciplined emphasis on their instructional vision (see table 3.2). Taken as a whole, the district's leadership meetings reinforced their emphasis on instructional leadership and were organized around the key elements of the district's vision.

The first two monthly principal meetings of the school year were largely devoted to the district's new principal evaluation system. The initiative was developed in response to a 2002 Florida state law that required school boards to adopt a performance pay policy for principals. Rather than adopt a generic evaluation system, district leaders snatched the opportunity to establish a system that fit the desire both to have accountability and to build principal capacity through action research. The September principals' meeting was therefore devoted to an overview of the new principal evaluation system. In October the district brought in a specialist in action research to work with principals on developing investigations to facilitate their work with their faculties and to develop demonstrable evidence that their schools were moving toward their teaching and learning goals.

The January principal meeting was devoted to a thorough examination of the district's reading program. Janice Hunter, the district's elementary school coordinator, provided a comprehensive overview and description of the key components of reading (phonemic and phonological awareness, fluency, vocabulary, and comprehension); a description of what the reading process should look like inside both literacy classes and in other content areas; a discussion of a range of strategies that teachers could use with challenged readers; the professional development available to teachers for training to teach reading; and an outline of how principals should describe the district's comprehensive reading program to parents and the community. The superintendent then led a whole-group think-aloud on ways schools could strengthen their reading programs and instruction, after which principals broke up into their regional subgroups to continue to discuss reading strategies and the ways they could improve reading instruction in their schools.

TABLE 3.2

Principal Leadership Development for 2002–03 School Year

Month	Featured Activity
September 2002	Presentation on Appraisal Plus
October 2002	Presentation on how to use Action Research to deepen knowledge of standards-based reform and satisfy Appraisal Plus requirement
November 2002	Half day—Regional breakouts only
December 2002	No meeting
January 2003	Overview of District Reading Program
February 2003	No meeting
March 2003	Overview of district Science and Mathematics Curriculum reforms; Presentation on TIMSS by William Schmidt of Michigan State University.
April 2003	Half day—Regional breakouts only
May 2003	Ruben Gonzalez—Motivational Speaker

The March principals' meeting was focused on the district's curricular revisions in science and mathematics. William Schmidt, an internationally renowned curricular expert and one of the principal investigators of the TIMSS, which examined the mathematics and science performance of elementary, middle, and high school students in forty-one countries, presented the findings of the TIMSS study and their implications for curricular design. One of Schmidt's central points was the importance of a spiraling curriculum that may overlap from year to year, but did not try to repeatedly cover most topics every year. Schmidt had a long-running relationship with Duval County, having been hired as a consultant by the district beginning in 2000 to help to revise the district's curriculum to reflect the knowledge from his work. The principals' meeting was a way to share the curricular revision work with leaders from across the district.

After Schmidt spoke, the district's science and mathematics supervisors described how they had streamlined and focused the science and mathematics curricula on the big ideas within their subject and how it reflected Schmidt's findings. To illustrate the point in mathematics, the supervisor displayed three charts, which reflected the mathematics topics by grade level in the countries that had performed high on TIMSS, the mathematics topics by grade level in the state of Florida, and Duval County's mathematics topics by grade level. By resequencing and carefully scaffolding their curriculum, Duval County's looked more like that of the high performing TIMSS countries than it did the Florida state curriculum.

The last principal meeting of the 2002–03 school year, however, reflected district leaders still in transition from old traditions of disconnected professional development experiences to the newer, more connected and thoughtful ways of fostering growth in leaders in support of change. By that spring, district leaders clearly felt that principals needed motivation and support after the long and exhausting school year and responded to this need with a motivational speaker. Yet they failed to connect this need to the goals and purposes of the district's reform movement. The result was an experience right out of a *Saturday Night Live* comedy sketch.

For the May 2003 principal's meeting, the district hired motivational speaker Ruben Gonzalez to talk about persistence in meeting life's goals. Gonzalez, born in Houston but the child of Argentineans, had decided in the 1980s, "I just wanted to be in the Olympics, I didn't care at what sport" (Gonzalez, 2004a). Looking around for a sport at which he could achieve his goal through sheer persistence rather than any particular skill, and recognizing that he could represent Argentina because of his heritage, Gonzalez chose the luge. Luge was the perfect sport for Gonzalez because "there are going to be so many quitters that I can rise to the top just on the attrition rate" (Gonzalez, 2004b). So Gonzalez became a three-time Winter Olympian for the temperate-climed Argentina. Despite the fact that he finished at the bottom of the competition each time, Gonzalez was the self-proclaimed "luge man." He spun his story of earnest doggedness into a career as a motivational speaker and "peak performance expert." Gonzalez's self-deprecating humor and engaging story of perseverance against the odds in a bone-crunching sport were carefully constructed to motivate people to persist in their work and meet their personal goals. As Gonzalez's website boasts, "Your attendees will leave the program with a new, ironclad, commitment to their goals. . . . They will walk out with the exact knowledge they need to construct their own bold, daring, and imaginative vision of accomplishment. They will stop making excuses, and start getting better results" (Gonzalez, 2004c).

The Duval County principals left their session with Gonzalez both amused and bemused. They enjoyed the story but wondered what this had to do with their work. The principals I talked to after the session thought the talk was entertaining but ultimately unfulfilling, because it gave them no firm guidance for their work in schools. How did this help them improve education in their schools? As one principal said after the meeting, "We didn't need that. What we need are stories about schools that have made a difference to the lives and performance of children. Those would be motivational for us." The session with Gonzalez represented an anomaly in the district's leadership development sessions for the year, which were generally focused on their instructional leadership goals. Perhaps because the district's leadership development sessions were becoming more focused on instructional leadership issues, the Gonzalez session awkwardly stood out.

But most of the district's leadership development plans were on target and tightly aligned with the district's goals. In 2002, Ed Pratt-Dannals, at that time one of the district's regional superintendents, who later became the associate superintendent for curriculum and instruction, and Terri Stahlman, then the principal of one of the district's outstanding elementary schools who was later promoted to regional superintendent, began developing a curriculum to prepare principals in the district's schools to lead change and support the implementation of standards-based instruction in their schools. The leadership training program, developed by these two knowledgeable leaders of the district's change efforts, was tightly aligned with the district's frameworks. The curriculum was designed to steep principals in experiences that developed their knowledge of the district's instructional reform vision and what constituted strong instructional practice so that the principals could lead and monitor instructional improvement in their schools.

As they worked to flesh out their principal leadership program, however, Duval County again found that NCEE offered a more fully developed alternative. In 2003, Duval County became one of the pilot districts for NCEE's principal leadership program, called the National Institute for School Leadership (NISL). During their experience working with schools around the country to implement America's Choice, NCEE's leaders Tucker and Codding became acutely aware of the critical role that the school's principal played in the success of the design. After first bulking up the role of the principal in America's Choice, NCEE leadership embarked on the development of a training program focused on school leadership, with a heavy emphasis on instructional leadership. The culmination of that effort was NISL, a two-year principal training program. NISL is designed to increase principals' facility with the ideas and skills needed to lead, support, and monitor on-going instructional improvement in schools. NISL was informed by a multi-year examination of leadership practices in both a range of fields, including the military, business, and other public service industries, as well as cross-national comparisons.

As their work deepens, Duval County's leaders are starting to develop a vision of a continuum of leadership development from the classroom to the principal's office. While schools are traditionally very flat organizations, Duval County leaders have begun a leadership development program that brings promising and successful candidates through a long-range professional career ladder from teacher to teacher instructional support to assistant principal or standards coach to vice principal to principal. The development program, which includes both university coursework and district training, "combines workshops, readings, and performance-based applications with on-site experiences that are specifically designed to prepare the candidate for the Principalship" (Duval County Schools, 2003, p.3).

District Leadership Training

From early in their journey, Superintendent Fryer was careful to provide training to the district's top level of leaders, including his cabinet, associate superintendents, regional superintendents, and directors. In 1999, even before the schools were starting to implement the America's Choice model, a group of senior district leaders participated in a training session with NCEE on the rationale for change, the need to prepare students for a globally competitive world, the logic for having standards, and the emphasis on student performance. As the NCEE training became more detailed and focused on school faculties, district leaders tried to maintain their deep engagement.

Nevertheless, the flow of expertise from the external provider directly into schools created a kind of inverted dynamic in the district for a time. The top layers of leaders, who traditionally had held both the authority of knowledge and the authority of position in the district, lost the first of these two bases of their power. While they were still the supervisors of the schools, which required that they monitor and evaluate schools' performance, they did not have the detailed expertise in the new instructional approaches and the level of understanding necessary to support schools' ability to implement them. As one principal recalled, "They have been threatened since this reform started. The regional superintendents and directors for the most part know that the principals know more than they do about the reform, and therefore they felt inadequate in some regards to monitoring us. . . . And that caused a problem because we worked under them." This has been redressed to some extent over time, as the district's leadership layers have absorbed the reform more deeply and the superintendent has strategically replaced retired members with the strongest and most knowledgeable principals.

An Engineering Dilemma: To Build or Buy

One of the truly extraordinary stories of the efforts to reform instructional practice in Duval County was the relationship between Duval County leaders and NCEE. The relationship began when Fryer first learned about NCEE's vision of standards-based reform. Fryer called NCEE's Tucker and Codding as he convalesced from cancer treatment in California even before he started his Duval County superintendency. The relationship thrived as 62 of Duval County's 149 schools went through the three years of America's Choice training. It flourished as the district became a pilot site for NCEE's leadership training program. It deepened further as NCEE certified a group of district standards coaches to oversee the schools' continued implementation of standards-based reform.

It was, however, in many ways an uneasy relationship, as both parties sought to define their appropriate roles in supporting the school improvement process. Although Duval County leaders recognized the need for and value of NCEE's abundant expertise, they also perennially tried to bring these qualities in-house and gain independence from external help. When it came to NCEE's expertise, Duval County leaders were always asking themselves "Should we buy it or should we make it?" Throughout the evolution of their partnership, Duval County leaders repeatedly sought to bring the expertise provided by NCEE into the district's functions in order to become self-sufficient, only to find that they were better off, for a variety of reasons, to continue to utilize the external expertise.

Whether to purchase or develop instructional training materials for teacher professional development is a perfect example to illustrate the pendulum of Duval County's leaders' thinking about what the role of external providers ought to be, relative to the district's function. In the space of four years, from 2000 to 2003, Duval County went from purchasing NCEE training and development materials to developing them internally, then back to purchasing them. They were constantly concerned about how well the purchased materials were suited for their context and sought to customize them.

The buy-make-buy story is worth telling in more detail. When Duval County leaders initially adopted America's Choice, they had every intention of using the program as a way to build the district's internal capacity. As Pratt-Dannals said in 2002, From the beginning there was an agreement between the Superintendent and Judy Codding [of NCEE] that the ideal would be that over a three- to five-year period we'd be creating internal capacity." Superintendent Fryer, in his typically vivid way, expressed the same idea in a December 2002, interview: "I told them [NCEE] from the beginning that I am not interested in a model where I have to stay connected by an umbilical cord forever. I wanted their capabilities for a fast takeoff, rather than a slow climb. I saw what other districts had done. I saw what was going on in New York's District 2 and I saw that it took them ten years to build and understand standards and I didn't have ten years. I wanted to get going."

So, as NCEE was training teachers and school principals in Duval County, they were also training the people that Fryer hoped would build the county's capacity to take over NCEE's role as the developer of high-quality instruction in the district. By the fall of 2002, although Fryer was disappointed at the slow pace of internal development, he still believed that the district was on track to build its own capacity. As he explained in an interview:

> My plan was that . . . by the end of three years we would have our own capacity to continue this work in the rest of the schools. It didn't work out that way. . . . I saw by the end of the second year that we weren't going to have a capacity if I didn't create one. . . . So I created a team of the very best people we had in our reform and made them trainers, and asked them to develop parallel materials that were not proprietary.

Throughout 2002 and the first half of 2003, a cadre of Duval County's top-notch people developed a set of materials that were in many ways similar to, yet did not infringe upon, NCEE's materials. By many accounts, the quality of the materials and training developed by Duval County curriculum developers was fantastic. But the price was high.

As Fryer concluded in the spring of 2003, "I didn't want to pay the internal price of having our people develop materials. We costed out what we did last year. It probably cost a couple of hundred thousand dollars to develop the materials. And if you figure it from staff time—it's not worth it when for $700,000 I have eternal right to [NCEE's]. So you know, I'd rather do it with them." So Duval County leaders grudgingly relinquished their efforts to make professional development materials. The county continued to license the rights to NCEE's materials, but demanded the right to "Duvalize" them.

The complexity of the district's relationship with NCEE was exacerbated by political problems associated with the visibility of America's Choice. The more Fryer advocated that schools adopt America's Choice and the more he increased funding to support the program, the more politically charged the presence of the external assistance provider became. The controversy was fueled by local radio talk shows, which wildly mischaracterized the instructional methods used by America's Choice.

Slowly, Fryer came to the conclusion that maintaining a high-profile relationship with NCEE was "just politically not sustainable." He became more strategic and began to reduce the visibility of his reliance on and relationship with NCEE, even as he continued to mine their expertise for ideas and techniques he could adopt or adapt. He reflected in the fall of 2002, "When you attach a name to something it makes it a lightning rod. It's just amazing how people have attacked America's Choice. Most of them having no idea what it means, but it's a very convenient target . . . and it's amazing [that] once you call it standards-based training in your own district, even though it's the same thing, all that fire goes away."

Education is strongly perceived as a local good, paid for, constructed, and directed by the local community, and communities do not like to feel that their education system is being controlled by outsiders. Both within and outside the school district, the relationship with NCEE made people uneasy and ambivalent. Even as district leaders marveled at the expertise infused in their district by America's Choice, they felt a pressing need to be self-sufficient, to control the provision of educational services to their schools. For this reason they felt a strong desire to tinker with NCEE's materials, at times unnecessarily. As the visibility of America's Choice became too high, it became a source of division in the community. All of these factors raise questions about the appropriate relationships between local school districts and external providers, an issue I will return to in chapter 7.

THE NEW "GARDINEERS"

The gardening and engineering metaphors that frame this chapter are useful ways to think about the complex work of district leaders as they attempt to gain buy-in while they build capacity to enact instructional reform. A central lesson is that both the gardening and the engineering aspects of change are necessary to introduce deep and lasting reforms in education and that the psychological aspects of change are not addressed simply through training and professional development. The tools of the gardener are intended to prepare the soil for planting. While the growing season takes time, it prepares people to take advantage of new techniques of practice. Conversely, capacity-building strategies that are delivered before people are ready for change will rarely take root. By effectively fusing the forces of gardening and engineering together, district leaders become "gardineers" and reap the synergetic advantages of both (see box).

The gardening side of the equation involves the softer tasks of nurturing change: Understanding people's psychological reactions to the introduction of new ideas, building a case for change, increasing comfort with taking risks associated with change, and fostering an environment conducive to trying new ideas are all necessary for reforms to take root in people's hearts and minds. Duval County leaders chose several "gardening" strategies to nurture these necessary components of the change process.

This set of strategies addressed many of the central components of the conceptual frameworks for understanding and responding to how humans react to change. Duval County leaders' strategies made people uncomfortable with the current state of things, created pressure for change, demanded ownership from those who adopted new practices, developed a clear alternative for people to move forward, provided opportunities for people to learn about and become comfortable with the desired practices, and offered local access to promising alternative ideas.

"Gardening" and "Engineering" Strategies
Employed in Duval County

"Gardening" Strategies for Nurturing Change

1. Fostering a sense of urgency.
2. Advocating a particular approach to instruction and school organization without mandating it.
3. Building existence proofs by implementing reforms in selected schools.
4. Creating cross-visitation opportunities for teachers and other school faculty members.
5. Establishing model classrooms as "islands of evidence" in each school.

"Engineering" Strategies for Building Capacity to Support Change

1. Enhancing the quality and coordination of professional development provided to teachers.
2. Developing nested levels of support in the form of school and district standards coaches.
3. Expanding principal leadership training.

County leaders were simultaneously scaffolding a system to provide employees across the district with the knowledge and skills to adopt new practices. These capacity-building "engineering" strategies were consistent with the emerging criteria of what makes effective professional development, in that they were tightly linked to external standards for student performance, practically connected to the daily instructional tasks of teaching, provided both intensive and sustained experiences for participants, were subject-matter specific, capitalized on the benefits of social learning opportunities, and were embedded in a larger framework of school change.

What made the work of Duval County leaders so distinctive was the coherence across the gardening and engineering strategies. While many of these components were evolving over time, they refined and adjusted their efforts based upon experience, feedback, and new considerations and were able to bring them together into a coherent set. The techniques to build commitment fed into the array of professional development opportunities, just as the capacity-building methods capitalized on the demand created by the commitment strategies. Together, gardening and engineering can be powerful and symbiotic forces for encouraging change and building competence.

Duval County's experiences also raise a particular set of predicaments for district leaders who seek to develop similar commitment and capacity-building strategies for instructional change. District leaders face a dilemma when they advocate a particular approach yet must rely on suasion to convince school faculties to adopt their methods of choice. Such a voluntary approach is problematic in that people are able to opt in or out based on their preferences. On the flip side, maintaining this choice is crucial if people are going to adopt a set of practices with the passion and commitment necessary to produce meaningful improvements. In theory, leaders who use persuasion over mandate can argue that a critical mass for change will eventually sweep up those who are reluctant to participate. But those who are reluctant have an equally strong historical force on their side: the common tendency for change to quickly cycle through educational systems. Thus the voluntary approach, no matter how skillfully leaders prevail upon people to choose a particular approach, will eventually produce diminishing returns. At some point down the line, district leaders will have to change their tactics toward conversion. This issue is developed further in chapter 6, when I consider the issues surrounding the sustainability of reform.

A second implication of the sequenced approach used by Duval County leaders, in which successive cohorts of schools adopt a particular reform, is the creation of a sense of haves and have-nots across the district. In Duval County there was a lingering belief that some schools were receiving preferential treatment. From a leadership perspective, this creates a positive demand to adopt the reform model as schools interpret the signal of what is organizationally desirable, but it also creates resentment among those who, for whatever reason, are not interested in or able to adopt the new reforms. In Duval County this created some lingering bad feelings at schools that could have been won over earlier. One lesson that leaders can draw from this is that even as they create a sequenced adoption plan, they must have a strategy to make the transition to systemwide implementation and support. Much of the consternation in the district could have been minimized by spreading the reform ideas across the district sooner.

A third issue that arises from Duval County's experiences is how to develop increasingly advanced learning opportunities to deepen implementation for early adopters. Several of the first cohort of America's Choice schools in Duval County felt that they were left without support after their three years of work with NCEE, because district leaders were, quite naturally, focused on spreading support throughout the district's standards-based schools. Duval County leaders addressed this in two ways. First, they developed a sequence of course offerings for teachers that included both introductory and advanced courses. Second, the coaching model was used to provide more differentiated support as, presumably, both school standards coaches and district standards coaches were able to provide more sophisticated and advanced assistance and support as warranted.

A fourth and perennial challenge faced by district leaders is maintaining local leadership's focus on the core mission of promoting and supporting instructional improvement. This means that district leaders must be thoughtful when constructing meaningful learning opportunities for district leaders and school principals. It is relatively easy to turn to generic professional development activities, rather than staying focused on the tenets of effective professional development. Duval County leaders did a fairly good job of connecting their leadership development activities to deepening principals' knowledge of instructional interventions and leaders' personal skills to support instructional improvement in their schools.

Fifth, the dilemma to build or buy curricular materials raises a distinct challenge for district leaders. On the one hand, districts are rarely as well-positioned as outside providers to invest the time, resources, and expertise into curriculum development. At the same time, districts want materials that are well-suited to their distinct context. Even if they use external materials, particular needs will always create the temptation to tweak the materials to conform to the district's unique conditions and circumstances. Duval's County's vacillations demonstrate the powerful and contradictory motivations on both sides of this issue. I contend, as I argue in chapter 7, that it is better to partner with external providers around curricular materials, as most districts are just not equipped to develop curriculum materials in-house as efficiently and of as high quality as external providers. If we accept this premise, the question becomes how districts can take ownership of externally developed materials and apply them to their needs and circumstances.

These and other issues show how concerted efforts to till the soil of schools in order to plant new instructional ideas and enhance teachers' skills in applying the new instructional ideas to their teaching will considerably change the context and environment of schooling and introduce new pressures and considerations into the school environment. District leaders who skillfully foster commitment and simultaneously build capacity are "gardineers" of the first order and are more likely to make headway in their efforts to bring about the quality instruction that enhances educational outcomes. But the responses in schools and classrooms are diverse. In the next chapter I examine how both school faculties and individual teachers respond to district leaders' efforts to encourage, promote, and push for change, and show comments from Duval County teachers about their reactions to change and the motivations and beliefs that underlie their responses.

4

Schools' and Teachers' Implementation of Reform

The gardening and engineering strategies introduced in chapter 3 were intended to describe how leaders might build commitment and capacity for systemwide enactment of an instructional vision. The goal of these strategies is to encourage teachers to commit to a preferred set of practices and to build their proficiency to implement those practices skillfully. But is it possible to spread a set of distinct instructional practices across a wide range of classrooms and schools? Is it realistic to expect a diverse set of teachers in a spectrum of settings to adopt a particular set of instructional approaches? Is the uniform implementation of an instructional philosophy even consistent with teachers' views of their work? What challenges do leaders face in trying to conform practice around a particular vision of instructional quality? In this chapter I explore these questions by examining the levels of implementation inside of schools and classrooms and teachers' rationales for adopting or rebuffing change.

Before doing so, I want to point out that, from a perspective outside education, these questions might seem strange. Most industries put a premium on predictable and replicable activity. Organizational theory is dominated by the precept of essentially rational (albeit bounded) functioning (Cyert & March, 1963). Many industries and professions rely heavily on the replication of task to produce predictable results. Xiao and Moss (2001), for example, provide the case for high reliability in the work of medical trauma teams who depend on highly structured routines in time-dependent situations. Weick and Roberts (1996) describe the need for replicable, error-free actions on aircraft-carrier flight decks to guarantee effective functioning. Macduffie (1995) shows how human resource stability acts as a performance indicator in the auto industry. Production reliability is also cited as a major factor in high-technology competitiveness (Kim & Kuo, 1999). Thus, while employees may have considerable input into what their routines look like, efficiency and competitiveness generally require a high degree of consistency across production units. In education, however, whenever such arguments for high reliability are raised, the retort is that educating students is not at all like landing airplanes, producing automobiles, triaging patients, or manufacturing semiconductors.

Indeed, education has several characteristics that make it distinctly different from many other professions. Most notable is the complexity of teaching that defies the routinization found in other professions. Furthermore, the act of teaching involves skills that are highly contextualized in application. For example, teaching effectively requires making a series of fine-grained decisions. In order to target instruction to students' existing knowledge and cognitive ability, teachers must be able to identify students' skill levels and introduce appropriately challenging information and tasks that push their understanding to a higher level. Thus, effective teaching requires teachers to have the ability to assess students, manage the classroom, and incorporate content and pedagogical expertise into appropriately focused learning experiences. Because of the complex contextual nature of instruction, there is no dominant, unified system of best practice in education.

Moreover, producing results in students involves more than simple expert application of the craft of teaching. It also involves developing relationships that motivate children to learn. Teachers must establish an emotional link with their students in order to motivate them to participate in the learning process (Labaree, 2004). For this reason, Cohen (1988) likens teachers to social workers or therapists whose influences are the results of coproduction. He sums up the complexity of teaching nicely, observing that "teaching is a practice of human improvement. It promises students intellectual growth, social learning, better jobs, and civilized sensibilities. . . . Practitioners try to produce states of mind and feeling in other people or groups by direct work on and with those they seek to improve" (p. 55). No matter how hard and skillfully teachers work, their success is dependent on their students.

The fine-grained, contextual nature of instructional decisionmaking would imply that teaching requires a high degree of autonomy, and the profession is marked as such. Teachers normally work behind closed doors and are often the only adult in the room (Labaree, 2004). Shulman (1983) argues that the very complexity of teaching demands a certain level of professional autonomy. Lortie (1977) maintains that teaching is "least controlled by specific and literally enforced rules and regulations [and] provides considerable occasion for the exercise of personal discretion by classroom teachers" (p. 30). Weick (1976) calls education a loosely coupled system because of the low level of organizational production coordination, weak managerial authority, high employee autonomy, and the ambiguous relationship between organizational goals and means.

The extent to which teachers have control over their professional lives, however, depends on where you look. Many observers of teaching have also noted the abundant constraints within which teachers function. Teachers must work with a curriculum they did not formulate, accept crowded and inflexible schedules, and have little time within the workday to prepare new lessons or reflect on past ones (Labaree, 2004). Furthermore, teachers often have added responsibilities like hallway or lunchroom monitoring, coaching, or other tasks when they are not teaching (Sedlak, Wheeler, Pullin, & Cusick, 1986). Ingersoll (2003) argues that teachers have relatively little control over most of the organizational aspects of their school environments. His research demonstrates that teachers generally perceive that they have low levels of control over such areas as hiring, school policies, and resource allocation. Because teachers feel relatively disempowered to influence many aspects of their workplace, job satisfaction is low and turnover high (Ingersoll, 2003). Thus, teaching could be characterized as having high instructional autonomy and low organizational influence.

These constrained organizational conditions of schools, combined with the individually autonomous profession of teaching, create a particular ethos into which district reforms enter. In this chapter I attempt to give the reader a picture of how Duval County's instructional reforms were received and applied, on both the school and individual teacher levels. My purpose here is twofold. First, I seek to approximate how deeply reform had penetrated five years into the district's reform efforts. In doing so, I hope to shed light on what constitutes a reasonable timeline for instructional reform efforts

to substantively change practice across large systems. Second, I seek to describe what the journey of instructional change might look like for individual teachers and take a closer look at teachers' rationales for their level of adoption. Therefore, the chapter is divided into two parts. First, I use
a holistic technique to assess the range of school-level implementation of
the district's reforms five years after they were introduced and to describe
school-level progress. Second, I introduce a model to describe the array of
teacher responses to the introduction of Duval County's instructional vision
five years after its inception, and explore how teachers explained these responses. It concludes with a discussion of both school and individual level
progress and their implications for reform leaders.

The sample this chapter is based on consists of ten schools that I visited
during the 2002–03 school year. These schools were purposefully sampled
as representative of the district as a whole on a number of dimensions. Each
visit consisted of an interview with the principal of the school, an observation of an English language arts class, an interview with the teacher of that
class, interviews with at least two other teachers in the school (one mathematics), and an interview with the school's standards coach. At each school,
the principal chose the teacher to be observed and those to be interviewed,
which I took to represent that principal's conception of some of the strongest
faculty members in the school. During the ten visits, I interviewed twenty-
nine teachers, all ten principals, and coaches in eight of the ten schools. Appendix A provides more details on data collection, including the sampling
strategy for schools and teachers.

HOW SCHOOLS HAVE IMPLEMENTED DUVAL COUNTY'S
INSTRUCTIONAL VISION

> I worked on disseminating the vision among the senior district level [ad-
> ministrators and principals], and I think the vision is well understood. But
> I would guess that seven thousand teachers are probably not totally into
> the vision. —*Superintendent Fryer*

Assessing the level of implementation of the ten schools in the sample provides a sense of how deeply Duval County leaders' reform efforts have penetrated schools across the district. This can also provide insight into expec-

tations for reform leaders who seek to implement large-scale instructional changes. I did not set out to systematically assess the level of implementation of each school in the study but, as I began to analyze the data for this book, I became interested in the extent to which the ten schools were implementing the district's vision of instructional reform. These schools represent a nice cross-section of the district in terms of performance, grade levels, and experience with different reform approaches, and the extent of their adoption of reforms is a marker of the penetration of the district's efforts across the system.

I constructed a framework to guide my judgment of the level of school implementation. I considered the following criteria in making my assessments:

1. The principal's advocacy and understanding of the district's reform efforts, both in terms of my interview with them and their faculty's perceptions
2. The school standards coach's knowledge and understanding of the district's reform efforts and the extent to which they adopted them in their job was deepening implementation at their school
3. The existence of model classrooms in literacy/English in which teachers were implementing the workshop model
4. The extent to which the principal, coach, and other school leaders were putting pressure on teachers to move their practice in the direction of the district's reforms
5. The proportion of interviewed/observed teachers who reported or demonstrated that they were implementing the reform model; this criteria was adjusted to take into account the maturity of the reform at each school (i.e., the number of years that the school had been implementing the reform)

To assess each school's level of implementation, I reread each of my interviews with faculty members and reviewed the field notes I took during my visit. Then, using the criteria above, I made a judgment of the level of implementation of each of the ten schools. After applying these criteria, I arrived at the following conclusions. Two of the schools, one elementary and one middle school, were approaching full implementation. Both of these schools had been involved in America's Choice, so it was not surprising that they were implementing standards-based reform more deeply than their counterparts. Four other schools, two elementaries and two high schools, were moderate adopters. One middle school was a low to moderate implementer. Finally, one elementary, one middle, and one high school were low implementers. At lease some district reforms were visible at all ten schools. My assessment of each school is shown in figure 4.1.

What follows is a brief description of each school, their level of implementation, and the unique challenges each school faced. These short vignettes highlight the diverse situations within the district and contribute to understanding of their levels of implementation. Pseudonyms are used for each school, and their demographic statistics are approximated to protect their identities.

Johnson Elementary School, 750 students
70 percent minority students, 65 percent free/reduced-price lunch
Moderate Implementation
2002 State Grade: C

Johnson was a school that combined a neighborhood and magnet school into a single building. The principal was a strong advocate of standards after seeing America's Choice operating in other district schools. She eagerly sought to adopt components of the design even before training was offered to non–America's Choice schools in the district. The principal saw standards as a mechanism for integrating the neighborhood and magnet components of the school. Teachers' reactions to the district's reform efforts were mixed: One of the three teachers interviewed was a strong supporter of the district reforms; a second bought into the district's science reforms, but less so mathematics; and the third had reservations about the instructional direction of the district.

Fillmore Elementary, 650 students
95 percent minority students, 90 percent free/reduced-price lunch
Approaching Moderate Implementation
2002 State Grade: D

Fillmore was implementing Direct Instruction for reading in grades K–3, and readers and writers workshops in the upper grades. The principal and Direct Instruction coach believed that Direct Instruction was working for foundational reading skills, but that the standards-based approach was bet-

FIGURE 4.1

Range of School Implementation across a Sample of
Ten Duval County Schools

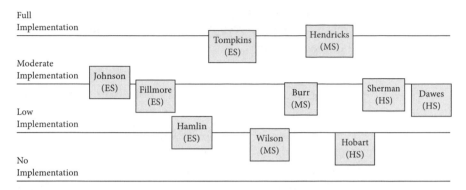

ter for comprehension and writing. The Direct Instruction coach seemed uncertain about her role in supporting standards. Lower elementary teachers recognized and expressed worry about the inconsistent experience for students going from a Direct Instruction approach to a standards-based approach. Upper elementary teachers were mixed in their support of the district's instructional approaches.

Hamlin Elementary, 570 students

10 percent minority students, 50 percent free/reduced-price lunch
Low Implementation
2002 State Grade: B

Hamlin was a solidly performing elementary school struggling to implement the district's reforms. The school's principal was a recent transplant from another district who seemed strongly committed to the district's reform agenda but did not appear to be pressing her faculty to adopt it. Hamlin's standards coach was a fifteen-year veteran of the school who complained of the lack of time to work with and train teachers. Adoption of the district's reforms reported by teachers were generally minimal. One mathematics teacher spurned the district-advocated curriculum for her own test-prep approach. A veteran second-grade teacher who acknowledged that "the old fashioned way [of teaching] is just not working" was converted by the "practical, usable, workable" information provided in literacy training workshops but was incorporating new practices into her teaching methods at a slow pace.

Tompkins Elementary, 275 students
90 percent minority students, 90 percent free/reduced-price lunch
Approaching Full Implementation
2002 State Grade: C

Tompkins, one of the second cohort of America's Choice schools in the district, had been implementing the reforms since 2000. Everyone interviewed at the school seemed convinced that standards-based instruction was improving teaching and learning. "We believe it because we see it in our kids" was a major theme in interviews. The standards coach had a tight relationship with the principal and was playing a major role in deepening reform practices. The school had been through three literacy coaches; the previous two had been reassigned by the district in an effort to spread reform. The school was in flux because the principal was about to retire after six years on the job.

Wilson Middle School, 1,250 students
25 percent minority students, 20 percent free/reduced-price lunch
Low Implementation
2002 State Grade: A

Wilson was an academically gifted and talented magnet school, one of the highest-performing middle schools in the state. The principal was a strong advocate of standards-based reform as a means to improve learning for all children in the school. Wilson teachers, on the other hand, resisted the imposition of external standards. They believed that common standards were actually *limiting* instructional quality at the school because they operated as a standardized expectation that was lower than the school's expectations. In fact, Wilson teachers viewed low student performance as a validation of their rigor rather than a failure of their instruction. They argued that giving students repeated opportunities to achieve certain results reduced student responsibility and effort. While instruction at the school was engaging and of a higher order, it did not follow the reform formats.

Burr Middle School, 750 students
50 percent minority students, 50 percent free/reduced-price lunch
Approaching Moderate Implementation
2002 State Grade: B

Burr's principal appeared to have only a superficial understanding of the district's reforms. She said she was hesitant to describe standards to the faculty and was not utilizing the school standards coach to deepen teacher implementation. The standards coach was new to the school and the position and was unsure of her task and purpose. The teachers who were interviewed, however, could articulate the district's reform efforts and appeared supportive of standards. Two of these were from other district schools with America's Choice experience, and they described their Burr colleagues as divided in support of the district's reforms.

Hendricks Middle School, 1,000 students
99 percent minority students, 80 percent free/reduced-price lunch
Approaching Full Implementation
2002 State Grade: D

Hendricks was one of the first cohort of America's Choice schools in the district. Both the principal and standards coach were strong advocates of standards-based reform. The principal was very charismatic and eloquent in describing support for the reform: "We're a good school on the way to becoming a great standards-based school." She described her recent emphasis on teachers' common lesson plan development, on fostering professional learning communities, and on using data to plan for results.[1] The school's standards coach was leading faculty study groups that examined student performance data and state test results. The English class I observed was solid and followed the literacy workshop structures. The teachers I interviewed expressed strong support for America's Choice.

---

1. Planning for Results was the America's Choice student performance data analysis strategy to examine test results in order to determine instructional strategies and emphases.

Hobart High School, 2,200 students
50 percent minority students, no lunch assistance information available
Low Implementation
2002 State Grade: C

The principal of Hobart High was in her second year as principal; she was the school's third principal in ten years. In contrast, the faculty was very stable and many were nearing retirement. The teachers who were interviewed did not see much influence of standards in the school and did not feel much push for standards from the district. The standards coach had district experience and was in her first year at Hobart but was already considering moving back to a district position. She was focusing on tailoring training to each content area. The principal viewed faculty retirements as an opportunity to increase support for standards; current pressure for change was low.

Sherman High School, 1,200 students
30 percent minority students, no lunch assistance information available
Moderate Implementation
2002 State Grade: D

Sherman High was a career preparation school that was divided into an academically oriented lower division (grades 9–10) and a series of upper division (11–12) vocational academies. The school was led by a longstanding district veteran and was implementing the America's Choice high school design in its lower division. The upper division, which was geographically separate on campus, was relatively untouched by either America's Choice or the district's standards-based reform initiative. The standards coach described the upper/lower division divide as a "rift between the academic and vocational teachers." Only one of the school's mathematics teachers was using the college preparatory mathematics curriculum that the district had introduced in high schools the year before.

Dawes High School, 1,600 students
99 percent minority students, no lunch assistance information available
Approaching Moderate Implementation
2002 State Grade: F

The principal of Dawes was an ambitious former America's Choice middle school principal who was placed at Dawes to get the school off the state's low-performing school list. The principal's strategy was one of triage—focusing reform efforts on literacy and mathematics at the high-stakes grade levels, while leaving other subjects and grades more or less alone as long as they did not confront her authority. To implement instructional change, the principal brought in strong literacy and mathematics teachers from her previous school. These classes had a distinctly America's Choice feel, while others in the school did not. The pressure to improve performance permeated the atmosphere of the school.

SUMMARIZING SCHOOL-LEVEL IMPLEMENTATION

Even these brief pictures of implementation in a cross-section of Duval County schools suggest the diverse range of struggles that school leaders and faculties faced as the district's ideas for reform filtered through the system. Perhaps not surprisingly, the schools with America's Choice experience seemed to have the deepest reform implementation, but this may also say something about how the spread and replication of reform inevitably produces fainter versions of the original ideas. It is also noteworthy that while there was extensive variability in the extent to which schools were implementing the district's reforms, standards-based reform practices and rhetoric were visible to at least some extent in all schools. There was also no particular correlation between reform adoption and school performance; some low-performing schools exhibited fidelity and willingness to adopt the district's practices, while some high-performing schools were low implementers.

This sample of schools also reveals interesting within-school variations in adoption, which seems to reflect local emphases. In some schools, implementation varied by grade level, with some grades more assiduously adopting the district reforms than others. In other cases adoption varied by subject area, with penetration deeper in literacy than math, or vice versa. Impediments to reform also differed across the sample; at some schools progress was constrained by weak pressure for change from the principal; in other schools resistance came from entrenched faculty; in other schools there were philosophical disagreements with the reform by individuals or groups of faculty members.

Also noteworthy were the common challenges that transcended the contextual and demographic particularities of the schools. The struggle with standards was not just a challenge for the low-performing schools. In fact, schools at different places across the performance spectrum shared surprising similarities in their efforts to adopt the standards-based framework. In the high-performing magnet school, for example, the faculty struggled to incorporate the philosophy of all children performing at high levels with their own conception of rigor, which implied that some children could succeed while others would fail. At the low-performing Direct Instruction school, teachers similarly struggled to integrate two distinct philosophies about the strategies by which children learn.

HOW TEACHERS HAVE IMPLEMENTED THE DISTRICT'S INSTRUCTIONAL VISION

While leaders' efforts to introduce change have their own logic and coordination, things look very different on the ground. Looking down into the microscope, one finds a teeming variety of instructional responses to any concerted effort to influence instructional practice. These responses reflect teachers' deeply held individual and collective beliefs about their capacity, responsibilities, latitude, and effectiveness. Sometimes teachers welcome new ideas, but reform more often engenders at least some degree of skepticism. While reformers may interpret teacher wariness toward change as resistance, it actually comes from a very pragmatic place. Change often does not bring about improvement, and there is a natural human disinclination toward the risks associated with change.[2]

The culture of schooling within which educational changes occur has a bearing on teachers' responses. In education, a constant barrage of ideas are introduced into schools every year, whether they be new programs; new textbooks, curriculum materials, or pacing guides; new ways of organizing classrooms; or the seemingly perennial adjustments to the external high-stakes testing system. In such a context it is natural that teachers would develop a protective layer of skepticism against this cavalcade of reforms, which are often sold with unreasonably optimistic rhetoric. The reforms often amount

---

2. See the "gardening" section of chapter 3 for more information on psychological reactions to change.

to little and peter out without so much as a whisper, replaced by the next fervent legion of ideas. Change is seemingly the only constant in the lives of educators.

In this section I try to capture and make meaning of the teachers' responses to district policies from the perspective of the classroom. To help both myself and the reader make sense of the range of practices that teachers described in response to the district's reform efforts, I offer the heuristic depicted in figure 4.1. The figure represents the interplay between the introduction and continuation of an instructional reform and teachers' current practice. In figure 4.2, teachers' current practice is represented by the box labeled X. Current practices (X) are really made up of an amalgam of practices that teachers have acquired over time from a variety of sources. Influences on current practice, represented at T, U, V, and W, include preservice training, professional development experiences, discussions with colleagues, and their own experiments that shape their practices and form their prevailing knowledge of their craft. This stew of past practices is represented by box TUVW. These experiences are fused together to produce current practice (X). The relative influences of T, U, V, and W may provide hints about what may be harder or easier to change about teachers' current practice. By generally representing teachers' current practice as X, I do not mean to imply that these practices are the same for each teacher. In fact, the X for each teacher may look quite different, as the influences of T, U, V, and W are disparate and distinct for every teacher. While X may look similar among some teachers, there will be a considerable range.

When district leaders persist in their advocacy of a chosen instructional reform, they are asking teachers to move their practice from X to Y. Reform practice, the form of instruction that leaders seek teachers to adopt, is represented by Y, on the far right of figure 4.2. In some cases the distance between X and Y will be very great, while in others, teachers' current practice will look very similar to the practice advocated by leaders, and therefore X and Y will look similar to each other from the outset.

The influence of reform efforts on current practice can produce results along a broad continuum. This continuum is represented by the three boxes between X and Y. Box Y|X represents one form of reform influence on teacher practice. In this case, practice still consists largely of X, with a layer of Y papered over it. XY represents cases where teachers are amalgamating their current practices with the new practices, which I call instructional patch-working. Y_x represents teachers whose instruction consists largely of reform practices, with a residue of preexisting ones. Although I have represented the move from X to Y as a continuum, there are far more gradations than the few way stations I have represented in figure 4.2.

Relatively few teachers may ever get to a pure form of Y, and moving more teachers to Y_x may be the best district leaders can hope for. Thus, the goal of reformers' efforts is to increase the proportion of teachers that are approaching Y, and supporting and motivating teachers to move across this continuum.

One of the trickiest things about layering and patchworking is that the resulting effect may produce higher- or lower-quality instruction. In art-less cases, layering or patchworking may send inconsistent messages to students, produce bizarre combinations of instructional techniques, and result in thoughtless mishmashing of different practices. The addition of reform practices to a teacher's standard repertoire may, for all intents and purposes, produce instructional practice that is no closer to Y than where the teacher started. In other cases, teachers may be using their prior practices to supplement the reform ideas, such that students' learning opportunities are enhanced. One of the challenges facing advocates of reform is to distinguish between these two kinds of cases and encourage the latter while discouraging the former. There are a multitude of implications for district leaders and their change strategies, which were discussed in chapter 3. Here I am simply interested in describing how teachers in the ten schools where I conducted fieldwork fell upon the continuum.

Teachers in the ten Duval County schools I visited represented the various stages described in the continuum of figure 4.2. In discussions about the district's reform efforts and their responses, teachers candidly described their own instructional practices and the reasons they did or did not adopt the district's preferred methods. In my school visits, I did not encounter one teacher who was unaware of the district's efforts to introduce standards-based reform, although their understanding of what that meant, as we shall see, varied widely. I interpret this as evidence that the district's reforms had penetrated deeply into schools and the consciousness of teachers, although my sampling approach (whereby principals nominated teachers to be observed and interviewed), hinders my ability to be definitive about this.

FIGURE 4.2

Model of Influences of Reform on Teaching Practice

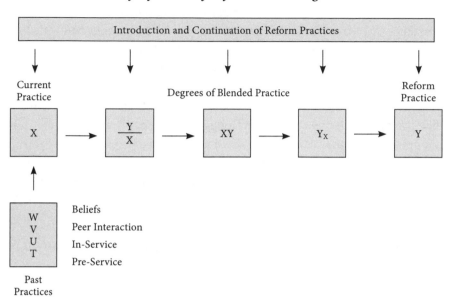

In the following section I describe four types of instructional responses teachers made to the district's efforts to cohere teaching around its instructional vision. These include teachers who essentially refused to change their practices, those who layered the district-advocated practices on top of their own practices, those who integrated their own practices with those advocated by the district, and those who adopted the district's preferred practices virtually wholesale. In each case I explore teachers' rationales for their actions. While I do not attempt to array these teachers systematically according to the extent they implemented the district's initiatives, their responses do provide particular insights into the variety of reactions, and the rationales behind those reactions, that leaders who seek to institute a distinctive instructional vision will encounter.

Staying at X

Several teachers reported that their instructional approaches had not been influenced by the district's efforts. Despite these teachers' general familiarity with the preferences and goals of the district's instructional vision, they chose not to implement the district's preferred instructional strategies and did not appear to feel much pressure to do so.

They offered several rationales for not adopting the district's preferred approaches. Three reasons stand out. First, teachers felt that they had wide latitude to teach as they desired, which was tied into their motivation to become teachers in the first place. Second, several teachers noted inconsistencies in the district's message and used these as a rationale to reject the preferred instructional approaches. Third, teachers felt that their effectiveness justified their instructional methods. As long as they were producing results, this group reasoned, they should be allowed to use methods of their choosing.

Of the teachers who did not adopt the district's approaches, instructional autonomy was the most frequently cited rationale. Several teachers explained that they became teachers because of the autonomy it promised. As one middle school English teacher explained:

> I think the reason people become teachers—because it couldn't be for the money—is to have their own effect on a group of kids, you know, on a certain population. And in a sense, it's a way of living forever, you know, because something that I've done, something that I've said really affected these kids. And these kids are liable to tell . . . their kids, and so on and so forth. So, I think one of the reasons why people become teachers is to affect a group of kids, to teach their own thing. They want to teach what they want to teach.

For teachers who stayed at X, externally introduced change efforts were generally perceived as constraints on the instructional autonomy they so highly valued. State and federal high-stakes assessments and accountability laws, state standards, and district reform efforts were generally lumped together as unwelcome impingements on preferred methods of practice. As one elementary school mathematics teacher lamented, "It almost makes you lose the love of teaching, when you feel like you have to do this, [the district's standards-based reform program] . . . where it used to be that you could just teach." An eighth-grade mathematics teacher expressed a similar sentiment: "You know, wow, I became a teacher because I have individuality. I wanted to do my own thing and teach it my own way, and now someone says, wham, you've got to do it like this." The tradition and expectation of high instructional autonomy conflicted with external expectations and demands.

Several teachers, across the different levels of adoption, pointed out weaknesses and inconsistencies in the district's reform efforts and leaders' lack of understanding of the challenges of their particular schools and their work with students. In a few cases teachers used these critiques as rationales for not adopting the district's instructional approaches. One middle school mathematics teacher, for example, felt that the district standards were too low, and therefore did not apply to her. This, she felt, provided her with license to ignore the district's standards-based approach. "As they [the district] move towards standards," she said, "I feel they are trying to make a cookie-cutter approach where they try to tell us all kids are different and learn at a different rate, but yet they want to script everything we do now, because we feel that for what we do it goes too slow for the bulk of our students." According to this teacher's logic, the standardization associated with standards was constraining her latitude to teach challenging concepts, which justified her decision to eschew the district math curriculum in favor of her own materials.

Other teachers felt no reason to adopt the district's approaches because they believed that their own methods were producing results. One story that stands out in this regard was that of a fifth-grade mathematics teacher who rejected the district's mathematics curriculum in favor of an elaborate test-preparation curriculum of her own devising. Although she had participated in the district's training on Investigations, she opted not to use it. "I have never felt real comfortable with the Math Investigations," she explained in the spring of 2003. She continued:

> Mr. —— [her coteacher] and I developed more math in which the children are actually learning how to subtract, multiply, divide. Math Investigation seems to be a little bit more of the analytical thinking part of it, and we noticed that's not what these children are being tested on . . . computational skills. That's what they're having to have for this test, and so Mr. —— and I a couple of years ago developed an FCAT [Florida Comprehensive Assessment Test] review curriculum in which we were able to put together different packets of things that had come from different sources, of how to best prepare children for testing. And we were never so high in our math scores, so we really felt like that was a successful program.

Several things stand out in this teacher's alternative approach to that advocated by the district. First is what she perceived as a misalignment between the district curriculum and the high-stakes test. As we shall see, many teachers observed this mismatch, although not all used it as a rationale to shun implementation. Second is her argument that her method has evidence of effectiveness. The importance of some form of evidence as a rationale to adopt a certain instructional approach was a technique also employed by the district (see chapter 3), and this raises the interesting question of whether the district's use of this rationale for adoption of its preferred approaches opened up the way for advocates of alternative views to adopt the same argument. Another striking component of this story is the latitude that this teacher enjoys within her (moderately implementing) school. There seemed to be no external pressure on her to adopt the district's mathematics curriculum. In fact, I later learned that this teacher was named the school's Teacher of the Year. Thus her autonomous instructional approach was, in fact, sanctioned and rewarded by the leaders of her school.

Layering

A more common response than overt rejection of the district's instructional approach was a layering of the new on top of the tried and true. In these cases, the practice looked largely like traditional practice with some elements of reform laid on top. Unlike the teachers who stayed at X, the teachers who layered their practice did not appear to have any philosophical disagreement with the district's reform strategies, but seemed to choose and use elements of the reform that to suited their notions of effective instruction. The demand to change practice in the midst of everyday pressures seemed to provoke a layered response. Test alignment and deeply rooted beliefs about student learning capacities were also cited as rationales for layering.

Layering took many forms. Some teachers simply interwove the district's advocated instruction with their own approaches. This was most startlingly expressed by a fifth-grade elementary teacher who described how mathematics teachers at her grade level "do Monday, Wednesday, Friday computation skills. They don't vary away from the textbook. And then on Tuesdays and Thursdays they develop their Math Investigations that go along with it. We'd like to integrate them more but haven't found the time to fit them together."

Another common form of layering was to adopt the outer form of the district's instructional approaches without appearing to understand or internalize the purpose behind the reforms. For example, several teachers talked about how they were putting up standards-based bulletin boards, as the district advocated, without being able to explain that the purpose of bulletin boards was to provide students with concrete examples of how their work demonstrated elements of the standards. The bulletin boards were quite literally external to any actual changes in the instructional practices of teachers. For these teachers, the additional task of putting up bulletin boards was layered onto their existing work.

The demands associated with the high-stakes assessment also seemed to play a contributing role in teachers' decisions to layer new ideas on top of old practices. One fourth-grade English teacher, for example, described how she used a "sort of modified readers workshop format" in which she incorporated test-preparation skills with the readers workshop structure. "The reason that I'm not doing a pure readers workshop is I feel like they need to do more preparation for the FCAT," she told me. "So a few times a week we do an FCAT practice page or we do comprehension questions" out of the FCAT preparation book.

Another elementary mathematics teacher provided a similar rationale for layering test preparation with the district's curriculum. "We cannot do it [use Investigations] every day, because the children have to have the computational skills," she said. "So again, it's just a matter of working it out, to see how we can best integrate it and get the children the computation skills that they need as well. So, now that FCAT is over we're going to focus more on the Math Investigations, more so than we've done so far this year. And then next year we plan to really develop it a whole lot more, because I know the county wants this to be done, so we're going to work it in the best we can," she said. This teacher's response shows a layering of Investigations and test preparation but suggests that she will continue to integrate the two over time. This illustrates that teacher practice is not always static, and there are many teachers who will continue to move along the continuum represented in figure 4.2.

Beliefs about student capabilities also cropped up as a rationale for layering. One first-grade teacher with a background in Direct Instruction (who was not in a Direct Instruction school in the sample) explained that she used Direct Instruction techniques heavily at the beginning of the school year, and then made the transition into workshop approaches later on. She explained that she did this because she was trying to build and assess student abilities to handle what she believed were the higher comprehension levels necessary for the workshop literacy model. "I think the first step is to focus on basic skills and do some diagnostic testing to see where the children are, and then let's see if the standards movement is feasible," she said.

Beliefs about students' learning abilities also motivated a fourth-grade mathematics teacher to go back and forth between the Investigations curriculum and the more traditional textbook. Although trained in Investigations, she said that she was still basing many of her lessons and assignments on the materials of the district's old textbook. "I think with the Investigations you are teaching them [the students] to be critical thinkers, and not all children can think that way," she explained. In both of these cases the teachers were quite open about their beliefs as to the limitations of their students' learning capabilities, which influenced the extent of their use of the district's reform approaches.

Instructional Patchworking

A more sophisticated teacher response to the district's instructional change efforts was instructional patchworking, which involves the integration of traditional and reform approaches so that they exist in practice in complex combinations. Given the pressure to adopt the district's standards-based approaches, combined with teachers' own hard-earned experiences as to what works (through the T, U, V, and W in figure 4.2), instructional patchworking represents a reasonable response to the introduction of a new reform, particularly in the eyes of experienced teachers who have already developed a range of practices. In the best cases, patchworking represents the incorporation of new ideas into the repertoire of practices that teachers can draw on to develop appropriate instructional responses to assessments of student need. Less skilled teachers may jumble practices together, creating an instructional hodgepodge that may actually confuse students and constrain their progress.

Instructional patchworking often involved incorporating techniques into the larger set of routines of experienced teachers. In one middle school, I observed an eighth-grade English lesson in the school's model classroom. The lesson had two components. The teacher first asked students to write a response to a provocative phrase from a Pink Floyd song comparing education and mind control, and to contrast the two in their sourcebook. Sourcebooks are a writers workshop technique to encourage students to record ideas, strategies, and general writing tips that they may use in the future. A lively discussion ensued on the similarities and differences between education and mind control. In the second component of the class, students reviewed attributes of folktales and described a folktale they were planning to write. The class did not follow the workshop structure of a minilesson, independent work period, and closing, but jumped from one to the other of these activities in no particular order. The teacher began the class by outlining the agenda for the day and asked students to describe what standards each part of the class was focused on. Student responses were substantive and demonstrated that they knew what skills they were developing. While the lesson was authentic, engaged students, and focused on higher-level thinking skills, its format did not resemble the workshop model advocated by the district. This was a good example of high-quality instruction that did not conform to the district's model.

In my ensuing interview with this teacher, she described many of the components and techniques of the district's advocated approaches that she had incorporated into her instructional repertoire, including sourcebooks, student-developed rubrics, and the connection of standards to lessons. "I've taken some neat ideas that I have put into practice in my classroom," she told me. "One of them is the sourcebook. I enjoy using it. I think the kids like it and it becomes an outlet for them. It's sort of a part journal and part vent for their feelings. . . . I can't imagine me not using a sourcebook now," she said. She also explained how she used rubrics, a key reform component, differently than before. "I used rubrics before we took the standards thing," she said. "I use them more now. I think it opened my eyes; I would never have used a rubric for sustained silent reading, for example. It would never have occurred to me. Just either you do it or you don't do it. And that's not fair for a twenty-minute period of time. And to be honest with you, the rubrics the kids come up with are great. . . . Sometimes they are not to the level you would want, but I think they have more buy-in and you have a little more influence," she said. These are two examples of how an experienced and skillful teacher patchworked powerful reform strategies into her set of practices to make her practice deeper and stronger.

Other teachers patchworked similar new ideas into their repertoire of practices without abandoning old ideas that they deemed effective, even if they were inconsistent with the new reforms. One kindergarten teacher in an America's Choice school, who considered herself an "eclectic" teacher, explained how she was incorporating Direct Instruction phonics techniques, which she learned during a previous stint at a Direct Instruction school, with America's Choice comprehension strategies. "I use a lot of phonics instruction," she told me. "Direct Instruction taught me, as a teacher, how children learn to read, and I have the confidence that I can teach a child how to read. And that is a wonderful thing to have." I have a lot of children who come to school with a very limited literacy set," she continued. "And so the Direct Instruction is a very structured, fixed way to get the basic letters and sounds in the kids and teaching them how to blend. But in Direct Instruction, as a teacher, I wasn't aware of some of the other parts of reading until I came to an America's Choice school,"

This teacher felt unconstrained by programmatic ideologies. She found that patchworking was a way to explore and incorporate different instructional techniques into her repertoire of effective practices. Her response to both her Direct Instruction and America's Choice experiences was not to abandon one for the other, but rather to incorporate elements of both. From her perspective, this created a more powerful learning experience for her students.

Moving to Y

Finally, there was a subgroup of teachers that seemed to jump straight from X to Y. Some of these were teachers who likely were not teaching very differently from Y before the district's reforms were introduced, and the district's instructional approach merely sanctioned their preferred methods of practice. For these teachers, the distance between X and Y was very small.

Other teachers seemed to gravitate directly from X to Y because they did not hold any deep convictions about the subject in question, nor did they feel comfortable with their instructional approach in that subject. Therefore, they were less attached to their current methods of instruction. One fifth-grade mathematics teacher explained this sentiment:

> One reason I think I jumped on the bandwagon with Investigations is because I have always been departmentalized and never taught math. So I was hungry for someone to tell me how to teach math when I took the courses two summers ago. So I had no preconceived notions about how you should

teach math, and it's not like I've been doing it for 100 years. So I, you know, bought in hook, line, and sinker, whereas some of the other teachers who had taught in a different way were more unwilling to change.

In a few cases, teachers reported adopting the district's standards-based reform techniques because they believed they maintained professional judgment, even as they implemented the district's curriculum. An eighth-grade mathematics teacher, for example, found that he could use Connected Math and still maintain his professional judgment. "People forget, you can still do your own thing, but you just got to do it like this." This teacher seemed to conclude that he could satisfy his need for professional autonomy within the standards-based instructional framework, and therefore did not consider the district's reforms a curb on his professional judgment.

Bounding Autonomy

A frequent question of those leading reform is, How long will it take for a reform to penetrate deeply enough within a system to produce changes in practice and have a positive impact on student learning? Of course, this question depends on the complexity and ambition of the reform, the size of the system, and the cultural context within which it functions. Even so, in this chapter I have attempted to shed some light on this question by showing how schools and classrooms looked five years into Duval County leaders' efforts to influence practice across schools in the district. As a global assessment, seven of the ten schools that were examined were implementing the district's reforms at least moderately. In these schools, multiple efforts were made to adopt the district's preferred organizational and instructional strategies. However, only three or four of the schools could be considered to be deeply implementing them. In general, elementary schools were implementing them more strongly than middle and high schools. While there was apparent variability in implementation, the district's reforms had succeeded in touching all schools in the sample at least to some extent. The low implementing schools were just more likely to be implementing the district's reforms in pockets.

Another thing that comes through in taking a deeper look at implementation is that the intended recipients of school reform are rapidly moving targets. Even as a district seeks to introduce new ideas into schools and classrooms, teachers and school leaders are constantly entering and exiting and moving around within the system. These factors, coupled with the uneven receptiveness to any new educational ideas, raise questions about how deeply reforms can reasonably be expected to penetrate into a system at any given time. Efforts to deepen reform often are slowed by the need for backfilling because there is a constant supply of new teachers who need to be introduced to reform ideas. Duval County's mathematics coordinator noted this when she commented that a perennially low proportion of middle school mathematics teachers had been trained in Connected Math because of the high rate of teacher turnover. Over time, programs can even find that the number of teachers they have trained well exceeds the number of teachers in the system (Supovitz & Goerlich-Zief, 2000) In sum, there is no tidy answer to the question of how long it takes, but three to five years of solid and consistent effort are a good estimate for at least widespread introduction of instructional reforms.

The picture of implementation gets even more complex when one peers more deeply into classrooms. Fieldwork from this study indicates that teachers were stretched along the continuum of reform implementation, ranging from outright rejection to full adoption of the district's reform efforts. Most likely, however, are the two combinations of layering and patchworking. In these cases, teachers were integrating district reforms with their own pre-reform practices. This represents an important accomplishment for reform advocates in that their practices have become part of the repertoire that teachers are using. One weakness of this study is that there is no way to estimate the proportion of teachers that reside at each place along the implementation continuum.

Although we tend to look at reforms as the introduction of fresh ideas that are more powerful than those that have come before, this is rarely the case. From a teacher's perspective, the current reform is likely to be just one of several change efforts that have promised better and more effective methods of practice. The underlying message to teachers is that change is not always an improvement and that caution is warranted. In fact, one reasonable interpretation of the reason reforms do not stick is that the practices they advocate are no more effective than those they seek to supplant. From this perspective, the patchworking and, to a lesser extent, the layering that teachers use to incorporate new ideas into their practices is entirely reasonable. If reforms are not entirely better wholesale, at least parts of them are likely to make sense. Furthermore, the constraints imposed by the way teaching is organized in American schools make it necessary for teachers to slowly absorb instructional changes and incorporate them into of everyday instruction. But from a district's perspective, patchworking is a problem because there is no way to help teachers determine if their decisions are impeding or facilitating student learning, or for observers to judge whether variations on a model are ineffective or effective.

It is one thing for teachers to incorporate elements of reform into their practices based on their best judgment of effectiveness or on their ability to absorb different practices within the constraints of their work. It is quite a different thing for teachers to receive training on a reform and to reject it wholesale. To some extent, the variation in teacher implementation reveals the autonomy they enjoy to adopt instruction in their classrooms as they see fit. The variation in teacher adoption also represents the variation in school leaders' response to the district's standards-based reform strategy, because it is school leadership that allows teachers to exercise their autonomy.

One thing that is quite astounding in teachers' responses to Duval County's instructional reforms is the sense of autonomy that teachers feel, not just in terms of how to implement the district's instructional reforms and which elements to implement, but whether or not they should adopt the new practices at all. The terrain on which teachers act autonomously is as wide open as the Mohave Desert. There are currently no boundaries that allow leaders to distinguish between legitimate and illegitimate forms of teacher autonomy. In such an environment, it seems that all expressions of autonomy are legitimate because no clear distinctions can be made.

Drawing boundaries around teachers' expression of autonomy is the first step toward narrowing the range within which teachers can legitimately express their professional expertise. Two areas of research suggest that the field could make progress with reform implementation by distinguishing between the realm in which teachers should more readily accept guidance (areas of illegitimate autonomy) and that in which they should retain substantial latitude to apply their professional judgment (areas of legitimate autonomy).

First, we are learning that teachers in fact desire different levels of autonomy in various classroom areas. In other research we have been asking teachers how much autonomy they want in certain areas within their classrooms (Supovitz & LaCoe, 2006). It turns out that they want different amounts of autonomy in such areas as classroom environment, pedagogy, assessment, curriculum, professional development, and student discipline. My point is that teachers want significantly more autonomy over the classroom environment and pedagogy (how to teach) than they do over student discipline and curriculum (what to teach). This suggests that teachers are more willing to accept curricular guidance, even though they seek to maintain substantial influence over how to teach a specified curriculum.

Second, there are some aspects of instructional practice that are more effective than others. For example, it is becoming increasingly accepted that students who are just starting to write are better off being allowed to use invented spelling rather than being forced to spell correctly. While there is an intuitive desire for teachers to want students to spell correctly, the research shows that allowing students to write words as they hear them will allow them to attend to the relationships between letters and sounds and how these work together to form words. If we expect students to write in ways they are not hearing, they will not make connections between what they hear and what they write. This will distract from central idea development, which is more important than orthographic accuracy (Garan, 2002; National Reading Panel, 2000). Therefore, teachers who insist on correct spelling as students are just learning to read may actually be limiting students' phonemic awareness and phonics development.

This example shows that some expressions of teacher autonomy clearly go against the evidence. Now, I grant you, the terrain gets much more contested the more nuanced the conversation becomes. This is, to continue the example, because there is less definitive evidence as to what grade or developmental level students no longer benefit from invented spelling. There comes a point when teachers need to hold students accountable for standard spelling. This is when professional judgment comes into play.

One central argument teachers make repeatedly, and often voiced in this chapter, is that autonomous actions are a prime motivation for teachers in an otherwise underpaid and organizationally constraining environment. But I contend that the level of latitude currently enjoyed by teachers is a byproduct of the lack of progress in developing evidence-based practice in the field of education. Doctors, who enjoy considerable latitude in the decisions they make about many types of patient treatment, do not resist the boundaries around their decisionmaking that are represented by accrued knowledge in their field. It is similarly incumbent upon professional associations and educational researchers to begin to build accepted knowledge of good practice. Such knowledge can act as a foundation upon which teachers employ professional judgment that is bounded by consensus on instructional effectiveness. By joining autonomy with knowledge of effective practice while still retaining ample room for professional judgment, the debate about reform implementation can be channeled into more productive questions about the level and mix of implementation, not whether reform is to be attempted at all. To assess the level of reform implementation, and to provide actors at all levels of the system with information to inform their actions, people need various forms of data. In the next chapter, I turn to systems that provide data to teachers and leaders.

5

Districtwide Data Use

If educational leaders develop an instructional vision and build a system with the organizational capacity to enact the vision, will people follow their lead? How will the leadership know if teachers and principals are implementing their vision? How will they provide teachers, principals, and themselves with the information they need to guide their decisionmaking and monitor the influences of those decisions? How will they know if their efforts are making a difference for students? Educators at all levels of the system—from teachers to principals to district administrators—need data to inform their decisionmaking and help them understand the implications of their choices. District leaders need to define which data are regularly needed, build systems to deliver those data in meaningful and useable forms, and provide people at all levels of the organization with the training to ask the right questions of the data and make sense of what they find. This requires a *system of districtwide data use.*

Using data is all the rage in school reform today. You can hardly read a study of school or district reform without seeing data use as one of the core elements of the reform (data-driven decisionmaking, for example, figured prominently in the district analyses of Snipes, Doolittle, & Herlihy, 2002; Togneri & Anderson, 2003). And why not? The onslaught of technological capability brought on by the computer revolution makes it possible for us to compile more data more quickly than ever before. Over the last twenty years, education, like many other industries, has gone from a struggle to get any data in relatively quick and useable forms to an environment in which too much data are readily available. But the availability of data is a far cry from useable information that can inform decisionmaking. The challenge for education leaders of the twenty-first century is to go from data to information to knowledge to policy.

Why are data and their effective use considered so central to successful organizational functioning? The theory underlying the importance of using data is relatively straightforward. At whatever job we hold, we need information to guide our decisions. Teachers need data about students and their current skill levels in order to guide their instructional decisionmaking. Leaders need information about the utility of programs in order to inform their decisions to support, modify, or end them. Administrators need data to measure progress in order to hold people accountable for their performance. People use data informally all the time to guide their decisionmaking. But the more accurate the information on which a decision is based, the better the decision is likely to be (Mehrens & Lehmann, 1973). Data are the essence of any learning activity, whether individual or organizational.

In the business world, systems to acquire and manage knowledge are associated with organizational competitiveness (Chakravarthy, McEvily, Doz, & Rau, 2003) and innovation (Almeida, Phene, & Grant, 2003). The systematic accumulation of knowledge is a way to understand the effectiveness of past actions (Fiol & Lyles, 1985) and a guide for present organizational actions (Levitt & March, 1988). Inquiries into data are influential as a habit of mind as much as for a source of organizational information.

The onslaught of data raises a host of new challenges for educators. It is hard to use data efficiently and effectively. Are we asking the right questions? Do we have the right information to answer those questions? Are we making the right interpretations from the data we have? Are we sure that we have reached the right conclusions? What actions do we take as a result of what we conclude?

A synthesis of the vast literature on the purposes and uses of data, from research conducted both within and beyond education, can be decomposed into four essential spheres:

1. To provide feedback to teachers and students in order to facilitate the learning of individual students.
2. To hold individuals or groups accountable for their performance.

3. To monitor the implementation and impact of programs in order to make decisions about maintaining, modifying, or eliminating them.
4. To facilitate the learning of organizations so they can improve their support for members and spread knowledge across the system in order to produce better systemwide decisionmaking.

Let me say a little more about each of these fundamental purposes.

USING DATA TO FACILITATE STUDENT LEARNING

One of the primary purposes for using student performance data in education is to inform teachers about the present knowledge level of their students. This enables them to make informed decisions about what content and instructional strategies to apply in their lessons in order to move student understanding forward. This concept goes back to Vygotsky's learning theory of the Zone of Proximal Development (Vygotsky, 1987; Tharp & Gallimore, 1988), in which highly effective teachers are able to identify each student's current skill and knowledge level and teach appropriately to that level so that all students can make maximal progress. Lessons that are constructed regardless of student capacities are likely to be unchallenging for some students and mystifying to others.

Student performance data gleaned from formative assessments are essential for informing teachers' instructional practices. Formative assessments evaluate student performance and provide information so teachers can modify their practices in order to enhance student learning (Black & William, 1998a; Shepard, 2000; Wolf & Reardon, 1996). These assessments may be locally constructed activities undertaken by teachers and students or externally developed assessments that are used formatively within classrooms. In their seminal book *How People Learn*, Bransford, Brown, and Cocking (1999) emphasize the essential role of formative assessments in designing of learning environments to make student thinking visible in order to scaffold learning opportunities. "Feedback is most valuable," Bransford et al. assert, "when students have the opportunity to use it to revise their thinking as they are working on a unit or a project" (p. 129). In this way, assessments become part of the process, rather than just its product.

There is much evidence that formative assessments and associated techniques are powerful learning aides. Multiple randomized experiments and several meta-analyses of studies of formative assessments have documented their strong influence on student learning (Black & William, 1998b; Crooks, 1988; Natriello, 1987). In the most recent research summary, Black and William (1998b) concluded that there is substantial evidence that assessments "designed to strengthen the frequent feedback that students receive about their learning yield substantial learning gains" (p. 7).

Yet effectively employing assessments formatively raises a number of challenges for teaching. Teachers must learn not only to assess students appropriately but also to manage their classes in ways that allow them to make more individualized use of the ensuing information and to translate what they learn about students into effective instructional interventions. As Black and William (1998b) note, "Formative assessment is not well understood by teachers and is weak in practice [because] implementation calls for rather deep changes in both teachers' perceptions of their own role in relation to their students and in their classroom practice" (p. 17). While student performance data are a useful tool for diagnosing where students are on the learning continuum, they are not in themselves a treatment.

USING DATA TO HOLD INDIVIDUALS OR GROUPS ACCOUNTABLE

A second main purpose of data is to provide the means to appraise the effect or result of a program or policy in order to hold individuals or groups accountable for their performance (Fuhrman & Elmore, 2004). Rewards or penalties are often attached to these judgments (Ladd, 1996). Since the mid-1990s, policymakers have increasingly adopted what Elmore, Ablemann, and Fuhrman (1996) call "the new accountability," a focus on student performance outcomes rather than educational inputs as a primary source of evidence to judge the efficacy of programs or policies. In this vein, large-scale assessments of students have been used increasingly to hold teachers and schools accountable for the performance of their students (Hamilton, 2003). In the current policy environment, accountability is on the rise. The prime example is the No Child Left Behind Act (NCLB) of 2001. NCLB mandates that states begin testing all children annually in grades three through eight in reading and mathematics by 2006 and hold schools accountable for adequate yearly progress toward the goal of having all students at the proficient level or above by 2014.

The theory underlying accountability is that individuals will be motivated by both positive and negative intrinsic and extrinsic rewards and sanctions (Mohrman & Lawler, 1996). While most discussions of accountability focus on the external pressures associated with state testing, Abelmann and Elmore (2004) made the crucial distinction between internal and external accountability. Internal accountability, they argue, comes from both responsibility we feel to ourselves and collective expectations of our local communities. They contend that constructive responses to external accountability only come from environments that have strong internal accountability.

Researchers have identified both the constructive and harmful implications of the use of assessments for external accountability purposes (see Hamilton, 2003, for a comprehensive summary). At the classroom level, positive effects include more teacher focus on achievement (Stecher & Chun, 2001; Wolf, Borko, McIver, & Elliott, 1999) and increased teacher effort (Bishop & Mane, 1999). Several positive effects have also been documented at the school level. For example, principals report increasing teacher professional development opportunities, providing additional instruction to low-performing students, and revising curriculum programs (Stecher, Barron, Chun, & Ross, 2000; Stecher & Chun, 2001).

The negative implications of high-stakes testing include a narrowing of the curriculum (Firestone, Mayrowitz, & Fairman, 1998), a deemphasis on nontested subjects (Koretz, Barron, Mitchell, & Stecher, 1996; Shepard & Dougherty, 1991), and decreased attention to nontested areas within subjects (Corbett & Wilson, 1988). Several studies have also found high-stakes testing to be corrosive to teacher morale (Koretz, et al., 1996; Pedulla et al., 2003; Taylor, Shepard, Kinner, & Rosenthal, 2003).

USING DATA TO MONITOR PROGRAM
IMPLEMENTATION AND EFFECT

Data are also frequently used to evaluate the implementation and impact of educational programs and policies (Rossi, Lipsey, & Freeman, 1999). While student performance data may be one measure of a program's impact, program evaluations typically rely on a much broader array of informative data, including observations, interviews and surveys of participants, and the review of relevant documents.

Careful monitoring of program implementation is of particular interest to district leaders who wish to spread particular practices across a system. Implementation monitoring is multifaceted, including the spread of norms and beliefs about practice, the depth of changes in classroom instruction, shifts in ownership of reform practices, and longevity of reform (Coburn, 2003). Because of the complexity of implementation research, educators often lack a clear, detailed, and timely perspective on what is happening in schools and classrooms as a consequence of their reform initiatives (Leithwood & Aitken, 1995). If program effects are weak or mixed (as is often the case), leaders typically lack the data to distinguish between ineffective reform ideas and poor implementation exactly because they lack an accurate picture of the depth of implementation. Argyris and Schön (1974) embodied this idea in their distinction between *theory of action*—the logic advanced by advocates of reform to explain how an initiative is supposed to bring about intended results—and *theory in use*—the ways programs or policies are actually carried out. In essence, in order for reformers to advance understanding of the efficacy of their reform ideas, they must map their theory in use against their theory of action. This mapping process reveals to what extent problems are due to dubious assumptions about the way reforms are conceptualized, or whether weak implementation, the *theory in use*, is the source of weak or mixed effects.

USING DATA TO FACILITATE ORGANIZATIONAL LEARNING

Data are also a crucial component for organizational learning. Although there are many ways to conceive of what it means for an organization to learn, one longstanding view is the deliberate capturing and dissemination of knowledge such that the organization is able to learn from its actions and adjust its strategies and systems in order to increase efficiency and effectiveness (Easterby-Smith & Lyles, 2003). Researchers of organizational learning contend that organizations that are structured to collect, critique, and make use of data are more likely to show sustained growth and improvement (Davenport & Prusak, 2000). Critical examination of organizational performance data is seen as a cornerstone of the development of an organization that continually grows and improves (Mohrman & Wohlstetter, 1994; Senge, 1990). Collins (2001) stressed the need for critical examination of performance indicators as one key facet of organizational excellence. Organizational systems that coordinate disparate learning and develop systems to disseminate it throughout the system can turn tacit knowledge into explicit knowledge (Nonaka & Takeuchi, 1995).

There are several mechanisms to facilitate organizational learning, and data and information play a key role in all of them. Systematic inquiry, for example, is the process by which organizations focus on an important problem, devise a strategy to collect data to identify the particular source of the problem, analyze the data, take action based on what is learned, and collect data to see if the action taken has influenced the identified problem (Smith & Ruff, 1998; Preskill & Torres, 1999). This process is almost always interactive and recursive. Rarely are relationships obvious and clean. Questions often lead to more refined questions rather than definitive answers. Shulman (1981) used the term "disciplined inquiry" to characterize a more systematic pursuit of the relationship between educational interventions and teacher and student outcomes. He was a particularly passionate advocate of using inquiry as a means of knowledge growth in teaching.

Each of these four areas—individual learning, accountability, program implementation monitoring, and organizational learning—is one that all educational organizations, in some manner or another, are struggling to improve. Data are the lifeblood of each. Particularly in the past few years, as the reauthorization of federal support to high-poverty schools increases the frequency of testing, data analysis has gotten more sophisticated and regularized. Increased technological capability makes the collection of data more feasible. A rash of external providers offer a variety of data solutions, ranging from test-preparation materials, software, and analysis to district data warehousing and distribution functions. Yet few if any districts conceive of the range of data functions in the concept of *a districtwide system of data use*. In a districtwide system of data use, each of the four data functions is clearly articulated and integrated with the others, and the range of data systems and concomitant-capacity building tools form the basis for engagement with the fundamental barriers to wide-scale organizational improvement. While Duval County does not have a fully conceptualized system of districtwide data use, many of these pieces are in place and such a system is beginning to emerge in the district. For this reason, Duval County is a useful model to begin to explicate the components and meaning of a districtwide system of data use.

In this chapter I describe several key components of the data systems used in Duval County. I do not claim that the elements discussed in this chapter are an exhaustive list, as I am sure they are not, but they are a starting point for a discussion of what a system of districtwide data use might look like. Components of such a system include (1) providing school faculties with a variety of data easily organized in ways that can be used for instructional guidance; (2) establishing training so that school faculties become fluent not just with the systems for analyzing data, which is the relative easy part, but with strategies for taking what they have learned from the data and applying it to instruction; (3) building a system to monitor implementation of district reform strategies that is both a way to build capacity to implement and a way to gauge the depth of implementation. To illustrate these themes, I discuss several innovations from Duval County. At the end of the chapter I will lay out a framework for district leaders to conceptualize their own data systems to facilitate organizationwide improvement.

THE DEVELOPMENT OF DISTRICT DATA SYSTEMS
IN DUVAL COUNTY

The evolution of data use in Duval County provides a useful example of how districts can begin to think more holistically about the systematic use of data to serve multiple, interrelated purposes. While many of Duval County's efforts are models of systemwide data use in action, the integration and coordination of data and the maximization of its utility is still a work in progress.

Examining data has consistently been one of Duval County's major emphases. As Superintendent Fryer explained in September 2002, "We are focused on the data here. I've asked schools to really mine the data. [We want them] to develop expectancy tables for kids in the lower performing levels and to find out what specific things are driving the performance of kids. Then from the district level we're going to roll in and help them the best we can." Using data formatively in schools was one of Fryer's three major emphases that year. "If schools work on anything this year, its got to be using their data to get to know their kids, find out where they are, and provide them with the educational services to become proficient," he said.

The accountability context in the state of Florida provides a backdrop for the data efforts of Duval County. Florida is considered a high-stakes state because it holds both schools and students accountable for their performance (Carnoy & Loeb 2003; Goertz & Duffy, 2001). Since 1999, when Florida governor Jeb Bush introduced the Florida A+ Accountability Plan, Florida has tested students in reading and math each year in grades three to ten, writing in grades four, eight, and ten, and science in five, eight, and ten. Using a complex formula that includes participation, performance, and growth, the state assesses each school's performance and gives it a letter grade from A to F. A school that receives a D or F is called a Challenged School, and then receives additional school improvement funds and state monitoring. If a school receives two Fs over any four-year period, the school district is required to provide students access to a higher performing public school or a voucher to transfer to a private school. Because of the high-stakes nature of the Florida context, Fryer and his leadership team have focused their efforts on gleaning useful data that they can use to inform the actions of district and school leaders.

At the district level, Fryer sought to develop a "dashboard" of indicators akin to the control panel that he once relied on as an Air Force fighter pilot. Fryer used the metaphor of a dashboard to advocate for increasing the district's use of data for decisionmaking. He established a "mission control center" in a room on the third floor of the school board building, where staff from the district's research office tracked progress on its five strategic goals (academic performance, safe schools, high-performance management teams, learning communities, and accountability). The room was used to hold strategic improvement meetings and show community and business leaders the progress of the district. Informally called the war room, mission control became visual proof of both the progress of district performance and a metaphor for its commitment to evidence-based policy.

Taking Fryer's cue, many principals have fabricated similar rooms in their own schools. The enduring image from one middle school where I conducted fieldwork, for example, was of several large posters that plastered the walls of the principal's conference room, where the leadership team and other groups met. Adjacent to the main office but behind the school secretary's desk, the room was off limits to students and the general public, thus protecting the confidentiality of the data. Organized by grade level and subject, each poster listed students who did not meet the state standard in English, mathematics, or both. The posters supplied such information as special status (special education, English language learner); reading, writing, and mathematics scores on the previous year's state test; the number of books read by quarter; and space for comments. In the comments column, grades on more recent assessments were listed, along with support programs students were assigned to, and even the names of adults who were responsible for encouraging and monitoring those students' progress. The columns were cluttered with entries and notes in different handwriting, indicating that these were not wall decorations but tools in daily use. These posters served as an ongoing diary of the school's focus on pushing for learning by all students.

Duval County leaders also began to develop systems to deliver a range of individual-level student performance data to school leaders and teachers. The process was evolutionary; district leaders began to build a system and then persistently improved on it. Starting in 2001, under the direction the district's director of research and evaluation Tim Ballentine, schools began regularly receiving an electronic data file called Research Data Affects Change (RESDAC). The RESDAC file, updated quarterly, contained test scores, grades, discipline data, and demographic information on every student in that school.

A few savvy and technologically capable principals were able to cull useful information from the RESDAC file. For example, one middle school principal and his vice principal used the RESDAC data to track student progress toward three central school goals (students reading twenty-five books, receiving no grade lower than a C, and receiving no disciplinary referrals). By manipulating the RESDAC data, the vice principal was able to run quarterly reports that identified which students had not met one or more of the three school goals. School leaders and teachers targeted those students to find out why they were not meeting the goals and then designed intervention strategies to support them. The school administrators felt that attention to data, facilitated by the RESDAC file, provided them with a means to familiarize themselves with the large student population of the school. "I think it has caused me to look at every child," explained the school's vice principal. "I see them out on the breezeway and I don't know one from the other. But I know every name. I've gone through and I know these names and it is helping me find a way to reach all the kids" (quoted in Supovitz & Klein, 2003, p. 28).

Yet RESDAC was not for the faint of heart. The file was cumbersome, with multiple rows, or records, for each student. As one elementary principal recalled, "While the RESDAC reports had valuable information, mine was a five hundred-page spreadsheet. It was difficult to find the time to sort through the data, know what to look for, and how to use the information in order to improve instruction and achievement" (quoted in Grossman, Honan, & King, 2004, p. 6).

One principal in particular, Jill Budd of Duncan Fletcher Middle School, began to dig into the possibilities of the RESDAC file for instructional improvement. In 2003, she began working with Patrick Barr, a director of regional operations for the district who provided administrative technical support to schools. "Ms. Budd would constantly ask me questions about data, so I did some things for her," recalled Barr. "And one day we were sitting there and she said, 'If somebody could make sense of this they could make a million bucks.' So I started writing an application," Barr continued.

The result of the collaboration between Budd and Barr is a menu-driven management tool called the Academic Interpretation & Data Evaluation System (AIDE). AIDE provides principals with a user-friendly, interactive Web-based tool to examine student performance data. Using the data available from the district previously only through the cumbersome RESDAC file, AIDE for the first time allows principals to easily access from their desktops a variety of data on students, including grades, FCAT performance (by subject and strands within subject), and student biographical data. With a few mouse clicks, principals could aggregate student-level data in a variety of ways: by individual student, class, teacher, subject, course, or school. Simple color-coded reports show which students scored low on the FCAT and which students had solid previous FCAT performance. Students at risk of not meeting state standards were identified, as were "bubble students," those who scored ten points above or below the FCAT level 3 score in reading or mathematics.

Barr also created versions of AIDE for regions to provide school-by-school comparisons, a school-type version (high, middle, and elementary) to provide district staff analysis of the curriculum, as well as a district version to provide overall analysis of district performance.

Barr also provided some strategic consultation to principals. "I make data work for them instead of against them," he said. "So let's look at the data

. . . which groups to target that give you more value in terms of passing the FCAT. This is how you can make the data look better. Another thing I would show them is, don't try to do everything in one day and never take on the strong point, always take on the weak point, that way you get the biggest increase in your data. Yet most support for AIDE has come through training organized by Budd and provided either through the Schultz Center or during the summer principal institutes."

In a Harvard Business School case study featuring how school leaders have learned to manage using data in the Duval County Public Schools (Grossman et al., 2004), principals talked about the influence of AIDE. One high school principal in that study noted, "The data is very friendly now, and now it's color-coded, you can pull it up and people see exactly what the data is saying. It's like a traffic light. Anything that shows up in red means that you're in trouble and you really need to look in those areas. If it has yellow, it means that you're cautious, and green means you are ok. It's really useful when you have conferences with teachers, parents, and students." A principal in a low-performing elementary school noted the influence of AIDE and data use on changing teacher beliefs in her school. "The data showed that some teachers who always believed they were the best in the school actually weren't making the highest gains, which devastated some teachers but also motivated them to learn new techniques," she commented. The data also dispelled the belief that some students just cannot learn at high levels — they can improve, they just need effective and differentiated instruction. Other principals felt overwhelmed by the press to analyze data. "My education did not prepare me to be a data analyst. And if I cannot understand the data or figure out the next steps, how can I expect that of my teachers?" said one principal (quoted in Grossman, et al., 2004, p. 6)

In response to principal requests to make more use of AIDE, Barr created an overlay on AIDE called management of academic progress, or MAP, which gives principals the capability to produce over eighty detailed reports for a variety of administrative and instructional actions. These include letters to parents that document student grades and FCAT performance, goal sheets for students to see their current performance levels and identify ways to improve their reading and mathematics skills, class profiles for teachers, and performance summaries for leadership team strategic planning. Barr explained: "We created an evaluation task for everything they need to do, so if they implement safety nets, they ought to know how good they are doing with that, so they can run a report which assesses their effectiveness. The next thing they need to know is their weak and strong points from an instructional point of view, so we provide an analysis for instructional improvement. And to keep parents in the loop . . . the computer can generate letters for parents."

In 2004 the district added a set of FCAT preparation assessments, making the results available through AIDE. The FCAT practice tests were administered in August and December to all students in grades three to ten in reading and mathematics. The assessments added, according to Ballentine, the director of research and evaluation, "a couple of more sweeps to the superintendent's radar screen." The benchmark assessments were initially developed by another Florida county, Broward, from publicly available FCAT items and were adapted by Duval County to become, as Ballentine put it, "as close to a full version of FCAT as possible." The district administers, collects, scores, and returns the results in seven to ten school days. The purpose of the benchmark assessments is to provide feedback to schools and teachers about students' strengths and weaknesses in the areas that would be assessed on the state's high-stakes test. Thus the benchmark in mathematics, for example, breaks student scores into the same categories as the FCAT: number sense, measurement, geometry, algebraic thinking, and data analysis. The district also produces a "likelihood score" of the probability that the student will score a 3 or higher on the high-stakes FCAT.

In spite of the increasingly refined tools provided by the district to school leaders and teachers that facilitate their use of data, the challenge continues to be using the data to develop more effective instructional interventions that improve the quality of teaching and enhance student learning. As Ballentine said, "The thing we find is teachers are the weakest at understanding what the different kinds of data are and what they mean. . . . So a lot of what we do is we try to teach them what each of those things are, where they're best used, what they mean, and what you can do with them." An elementary principal found that examination of the data led to a diagnosis of a problem but not necessarily to an effective intervention. "You can have all the data in the world," she said, "but the real challenge is finding the right instructional strategies to address the needs that the data identifies" (quoted in Grossman et al., 2004, p. 7).

In response, through its professional development and subject matter networks, the district has tried to provide resources and strategies. As Ballentine said, "I think that probably the biggest weakness in that area is, okay, now I have this information. How does it relate to teaching strategies? So I know that students are weak in the area of multiplication of fractions. All right, what do I do now? And that's where we try to provide resources for them, or at least we tell them where they can get the resources. . . . And the academic programs people are trying to . . . teach them strategies they can use."

Implementation Monitoring

With 150 schools, monitoring reform implementation is a major challenge for Duval County leaders. The district is structured into five geographic regions of about thirty schools each (with a smaller sixth one added in 2004 to specifically focus on the district's low-performing schools). Each region is led by a superintendent and director. A major component of the regional superintendents' and directors' jobs is to monitor the implementation of the district's reform efforts in the schools in their regions. As one regional superintendent said in 2003, "For the past several years, our biggest focus has been to monitor the progress of schools in implementing the district's frameworks, to examine the data and work with schools to improve their performance." This monitoring takes many forms. The regional superintendents and directors work individually with principals to craft meaningful school improvement plans; they monitor schools' progress in meeting their identified goals; they help principals develop action research plans to satisfy the district's principal evaluation system; and they review relevant data with school leaders to help identify changes designed to improve student outcomes.

Two particular district initiatives highlight Duval County leaders' emphasis on monitoring the implementation of its reform initiatives and structuring learning opportunities for school and district leaders. The first initiative is called the Standards Implementation Snapshot System. The snapshots are intended to assess the degree to which schools are implementing key elements of the district's frameworks and provide opportunities for school and district leaders to examine each others' work.

The second initiative is a detailed biannual assessment of each school's implementation of the district's frameworks on detailed rubrics. The implementation rubrics were introduced in the 2004–05 school year. The rubrics, organized around the five components of the district's framework, provide detailed guidance for schools in implementing standards. Each of the five global targets in the implementation rubrics has a series of subcategories in which implementation at different levels (getting started, initial implementation, formative implementation, and full implementation) is described in some detail. Each subcategory contains detailed statements of what principals, leadership teams, teachers, and students will do that are associated with different levels of implementation. Whereas the snapshots provide a broad picture of implementation across the district, the implementation rubrics are designed to go deep, providing detailed guidance to school leaders as to what are district expectations for organizational and instructional emphasis and practice.

Starting at the end of the 2004 school year, the regional superintendents and directors began conducting intensive full-day visits to each school in their region to assess implementation across the implementation rubric. There are really two parts to the implementation rubric process. The first part is more informal, the byproduct of the conversation between school personnel and regional administrators. More formally, the regional superintendents and directors began scoring school-level implementation on each component of the implementation rubric in 2005 and analyzing the results for patterns both within and across schools, levels, and regions. Because these developments are relatively recent in the district leaders' efforts to spread their vision, they were not present when most of the analyses of this study were conducted.

District leaders view the snapshots and the implementation rubrics as ways of looking broadly (rubrics) and deeply (snapshots) at district, school, and teacher implementation of the district's vision. Ed Pratt-Dannals, the associate superintendent for curriculum and instruction, has developed a way to see how the implementation rubrics and snapshots fit together (see figure 5.1). According to Pratt-Dannals, "These are two really powerful ways that [let us] see how things are proceeding in our schools. With the implementation rubrics we can look at individual schools at a broader level, and with the snapshots we can go deeper to see the bite of what we are doing."

Below I describe the district's development of the snapshots as an example of how district leaders can develop a system to monitor program implementation. Such a system can serve multiple purposes, including a way to

FIGURE 5.1

Integration of Implementation Rubric and Snapshot

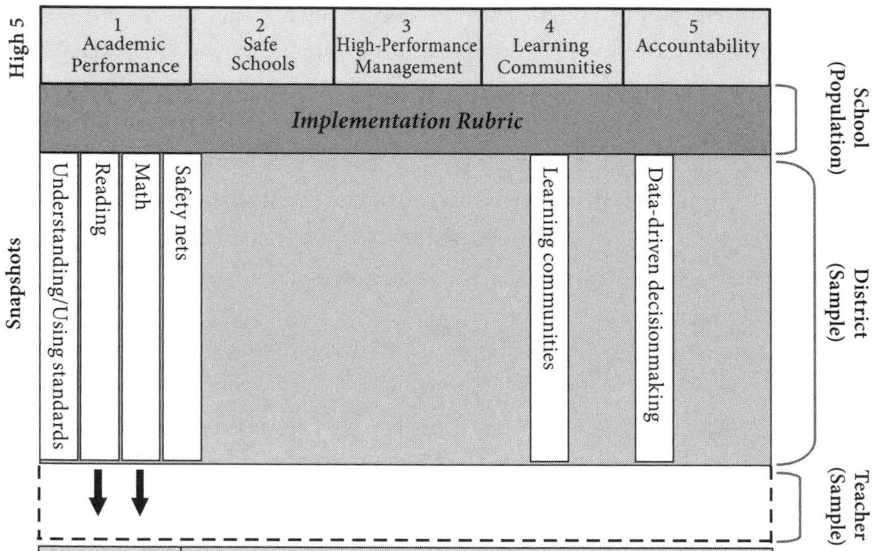

	1 Academic Performance	2 Safe Schools	3 High-Performance Management	4 Learning Communities	5 Accountability	
High 5						School (Population)
	Implementation Rubric					
Snapshots	Understanding/Using standards Reading Math Safety nets			Learning communities	Data-driven decisionmaking	District (Sample)
	↓ ↓					Teacher (Sample)

Year Introduced	Snapshot
2002–03	Understanding/Using Standards; Connecting Student Work to Standards; Safety Nets
2003–04	Data Use; Reading (Teacher-Level)
2004–05	Math (Teacher-Level); Learning Communities
2005–06	Science (Teacher-Level)?; Safety/Discipline?; Distributed Leadership?

track progress of initiatives, deepen understanding of district reforms, provide cross-school learning opportunities, and develop a sense of collective responsibility for implementation.

Snapshots

Like the district's technology delivery system for providing schools with student performance data, the snapshot system has evolved over several years. In both cases, district leaders tenaciously refined the concept and aligned it with the district's vision and needs. The antecedent to the snapshot system lay in the regional leaders' attempts to systematically capture what was happening in schools.

In 2001, the regional directors began conducting focus walks in the schools in their regions and discussing the trends they observed in their weekly meetings. These walks were modeled after a tool that America's Choice cluster leaders regularly used to get a handle on the level of implementation at their schools. Dissatisfied with the impressionistic quality of their observations, the regional directors began working with Barbara Vandervort, a longtime district employee and part-time America's Choice employee who was one of the original America's Choice cluster leaders in Duval County, to define the purpose and activity of these focus walks more carefully. I soon joined the regional directors as they began to explore ways to develop a more formal system for monitoring schools' implementation of the district's standards-based reforms.

One regional director, Steve Hite, took leadership of the project. Hite and I proposed to Superintendent Fryer that the process become more formalized throughout the district. The snapshot system was so named because it seeks to capture a "snapshot" of the depth of implementation of the district's standards-based reform initiatives. The system was conceived in the summer of 2002 and started in earnest in the fall of 2002.

Here is how the snapshot system is designed to work. Snapshots are structured visits conducted by teams of principals and district administrators who are trained to use highly specified rubrics to gauge the implementation of a particular component of standards-based reform on particular topics across the district. In this sense, snapshots are pictures taken at a particular point in time of the depth to which schools in Duval County are implementing key elements of the district's reform vision.

Each year, the superintendent's leadership team develops a list of three to five topics that are candidates for snapshots for the upcoming year. The topics are carefully chosen to reflect key elements of the district's vision for standards-based reform and reflect the district's priorities.

Next, a team from the district who are experts on that particular snapshot subject develops a rubric. Snapshot topics in Duval County have included understanding and using standards, connecting student work to standards in reading, connecting student work to standards in mathematics, safety nets, data-driven decisionmaking, and learning communities. The rubric development team specifies the characteristics at the school, classroom, and student levels that comprise different levels of implementation. The team also constructs an evidence form, which is a short list of questions for school leaders, teachers, and/or students, as well as a list of artifacts the data collectors should look for. These questions and artifacts are carefully designed to provide opportunities for respondents to supply evidence of implementation as represented on the rubric. The rubrics are then circulated throughout the district and vetted. (An example of a snapshot rubric and evidence form is provided in Appendix C.)

Before using the snapshot system, the principals and district administrators who make up the snapshot data collection teams attend a half-day training session in which they "practice" the snapshot in a small number of schools, trying out the rubrics and evidence forms in larger teams. After the training, they return to a central location for a debriefing and clarification session. On the basis of this and other collaborative feedback, modifications to the rubric and evidence form are made.

Snapshots occur monthly throughout the school year. A cadre of trained principals and district administrators visit a representative sample of schools in the district to collect data on a particular element of the district's reform efforts. The data collectors visit a cross-section of schools in the district. The schools they visit are carefully chosen to represent the district in terms of prior achievement, reform experience, grade ranges, and region. The sample can, therefore, be regarded as representative of the district as a whole.

Teams of two or three snapshot data collectors (depending on school size) visit each school in the sample for approximately three hours. As previously described, the visit is focused on a particular topic that is central to the district's reform efforts. Each snapshot team is equipped with a rubric specifying different stages of implementation of that particular element of the district's reform efforts, a list of people to talk to (who could be principals, leadership team members, teachers, and/or students, depending on the focus of that particular snapshot), a prespecified set of questions to ask, and a defined set of artifacts to examine.

Meeting first with the school's principal, the team develops a sample of individuals and classrooms to visit and talk to in particular grades and subjects. From this sample, the principal and snapshot team together select a sample of teachers that is representative of the school. Team members then spread out and collect the data on which the snapshot is based.

After completing their data collection, the team assesses the school on the rubric, using the evidence they collected during their interviews, observations, and examination of artifacts. After coming to a consensus, they meet to debrief and provide constructive feedback to the school's principal. Reliability of the snapshots is enhanced by the fact that judgments of school-level implementation are arrived at by the snapshot team. It is well known to the snapshot data collectors that the substance of their visit is confidential and should not be discussed after they leave the host school. A snapshot is completed within approximately two weeks, which allows the data collectors and the host school to schedule a visit time that is convenient for all. After completing their visit, a member of each snapshot team enters their ratings and comments onto a password-protected website. The results of the snapshot are aggregated to produce a picture of implementation of that particular topic across the district. More important, the aggregation provides anonymity to teachers and schools, reinforcing the stated aim of the snapshots to capture districtwide depth of implementation of elements of the district's framework.

The snapshot results are produced in time for monthly principals' meetings. During regional breakout sessions at these meetings, the regional directors facilitate a conversation with their principals, seeking to identify areas where the district is implementing strongly, barriers to implementation, and areas where implementation could be deepened, and to cross-germinate and capture innovative strategies that schools are using. Suggestions are compiled across the five regions and fed back to all principals and district training developers. (To learn more about snapshots, see Supovitz and Weathers, 2004)

Thus, the distinguishing characteristics of the snapshots are:

- *Snapshots provide a picture of systemwide implementation of district reform efforts.* The snapshot system is designed to capture the depth of implementation of reform efforts *across the district* at a particular point in time. No individual teachers or schools are identified when results are produced. In this sense, this is a district accountability mechanism.
- *Snapshot topics are carefully aligned with district reform strategies.* The topics for snapshots are carefully chosen to reflect district leaders' priorities.

- *Snapshot results are reliable and valid.* Careful attention is paid to producing highly reliable and valid results. The sample of schools for each snapshot is chosen to represent the district in terms of prior achievement (previous year's state accountability grade), reform experience (prior participation in the major school reform programs in the district), grade level (elementary/middle/high), and region. In each school, classrooms are randomly sampled to provide a fair representation of particular grade levels and subject areas. Common protocols are used so that data collection is as uniform as possible. Data collectors are trained in advance of the snapshots and conduct their data collection in teams so that assessments of implementation reflect consensus among team members.
- *Snapshot results are timely.* Each snapshot team enters its results onto the district's website. The results are then aggregated in time for discussion at the next monthly principals' meeting.
- *Snapshots are developed and interpreted collaboratively.* The snapshot rubrics are developed and refined with wide input. The snapshot results are discussed and explored for meaning and implications each month by school and district leaders, rather than simply reported. This structure and process are designed to reinforce a districtwide learning community that focuses on supporting and improving instruction.
- *Snapshots focus on intermediary outcomes.* While many monitoring systems emphasize the impact on student test results, this system deliberately focuses on the link between a reform initiative and student outcomes, which may shed light on the success of professional development designed to roll out reform initiatives. Through this system, the district seeks to understand the degree of implementation of its reform efforts as an important complement to examining the impact on student test performance.
- *Snapshots facilitate the building of a districtwide learning community.* The design, implementation, and analysis of the monthly snapshots constitute a collaborative process that involves members from all levels of the district in substantive conversations around the core processes of schooling (teaching and learning) and the necessary structures to support these core processes.

The snapshots have had tremendous influence on a school and district leaders in Duval County. Supovitz and Weathers (2004) documented the range of effects the snapshots have had on both those data collectors who are part of the system and principals and district administrators from across the system. First, the snapshots provide an invaluable picture at a particular point in time of what implementation of a specific element of the district's standards-based reform looks like. Second, the snapshots have provided the opportunity for principals and teachers and district administrators to deepen their understanding of the key components of the district's reforms. Third, the snapshot activities have acted as a reminder to principals and teachers of the larger framework within which they are operating and of the priorities of district leaders. Fourth, the snapshots have created a form of informal accountability whereby practice is made public and shared across schools, and members of the district community feel a sense of collective responsibility for reaching high levels of implementation. Fifth, the entire snapshot experience—from the scrutiny of the snapshot rubrics to the visits to schools with colleagues to the examination of the snapshot results—has provided a powerful alternative learning opportunity for both data collectors and the school faculties at the sites they visit. Finally, the snapshots have become a way to share ideas across the district.

INTEGRATING DATA ACROSS DIFFERENT LEVELS OF THE SYSTEM

Embedded within the matrix of Duval County's strategies for delivering student performance data to schools and collecting implementation data to monitor the breadth and depth of its reform efforts lies the nucleus of a *districtwide system of data use*. Architects of a districtwide data system gather, integrate, and disseminate streams of disparate yet relevant data in order to inform decisionmakers at various levels how to best support the delivery of instructional services to children. A complementary yet underlying use of the data is to encourage reflection by decision-makers so they get continually smarter at what they do.

In such a system, the primary purposes, and hence consumers, of the product of districtwide data systems are twofold. First, data collection and dissemination needs to be directed toward teachers and school leaders in order to improve the targeted delivery of instructional services and school-level support for this mission. This involves not only delivering useable data to teachers and school leaders, but building and exercising their skills so they can act intelligently upon their enhanced knowledge. Second, district administrators need data to inform their strategic and policy decisions. This generally means producing customized data that addresses, and even anticipates, a range of questions about the effectiveness and allocation of resources across the system.

Underlying these pragmatic uses of data are two more intangible but potentially even more powerful benefits. First, the collecting and wide-scale scrutiny of data creates a potent sense of collective accountability within the organization, because the measures system leaders choose to monitor become focal points for the attention of actors within the system who feel responsible for making improvements in the monitored areas. With the snapshots, even though there was no formal way to connect performance to what was being monitored, people still felt individually and collectively responsible for their behavior and performance on those indicators. Second, raising important questions and the candid and public inspection of the resulting data foster a culture of inquiry in which the organization demonstrates that it is willing to identify, investigate, and attempt to improve upon the very real yet difficult challenges that impede broadscale improvement. By building systems for collecting and disseminating information gained from data and a culture that can constructively use them, leaders are creating the conditions for sustainable organizational learning.

Districtwide data systems bring together the various functions of data into a coherent and conceptually unified system. Figure 5.2 depicts a model of what a system of districtwide data use might look like. The three main columns of the figure show the major functions for which data should be collected, analyzed, and used by school districts. The first major function should be the collection and dissemination of individual student performance data for the purpose of informing the actions of individual teachers and their support by school leaders. The second major function involves the collection of data on programs and policies in order to inform the strategic decisionmaking of district leaders. The third major function is what I call "accounting for accountability," which fulfills the formal data collection and dissemination functions traditionally carried out by district assessment/evaluation/accountability offices. This provides the standard reports and documentation that are required to fulfill state and federal requirements.

FIGURE 5.2
Model for Districtwide Data System

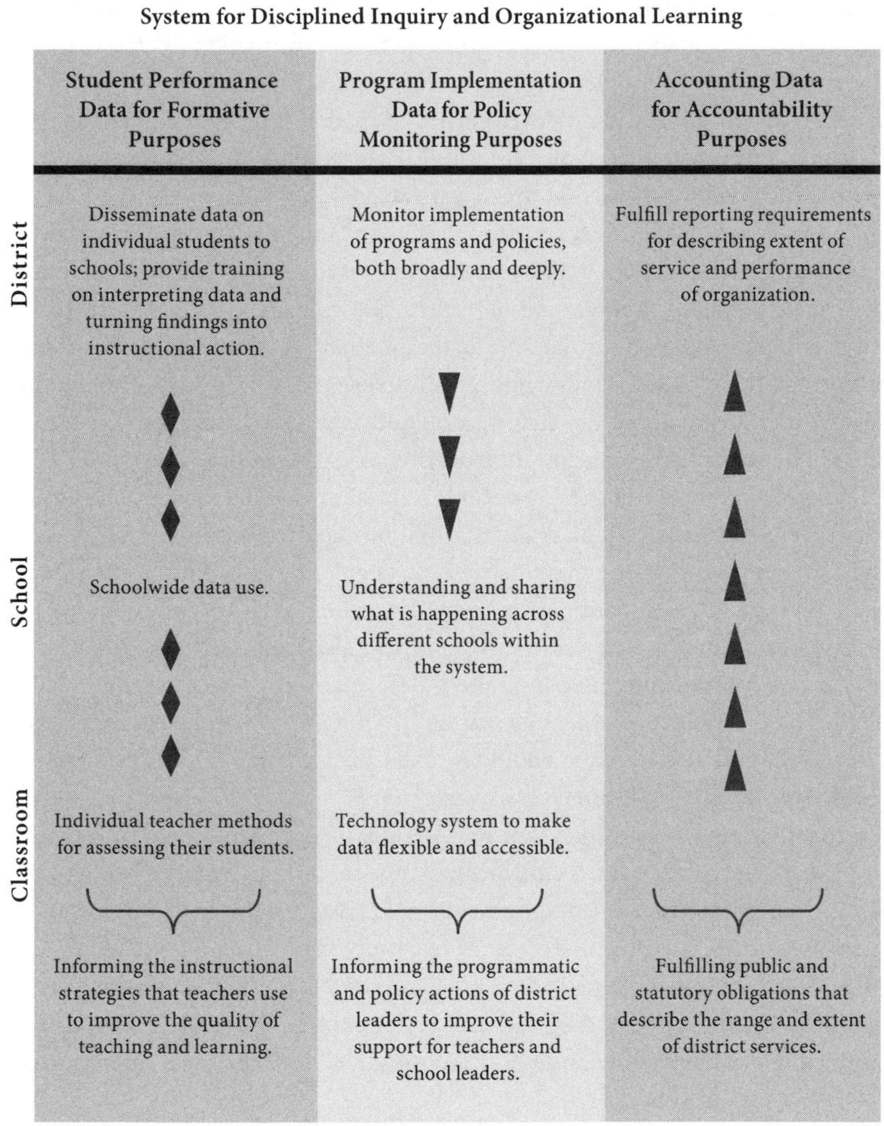

System for Disciplined Inquiry and Organizational Learning

	Student Performance Data for Formative Purposes	Program Implementation Data for Policy Monitoring Purposes	Accounting Data for Accountability Purposes
District	Disseminate data on individual students to schools; provide training on interpreting data and turning findings into instructional action.	Monitor implementation of programs and policies, both broadly and deeply.	Fulfill reporting requirements for describing extent of service and performance of organization.
School	Schoolwide data use.	Understanding and sharing what is happening across different schools within the system.	
Classroom	Individual teacher methods for assessing their students.	Technology system to make data flexible and accessible.	
	Informing the instructional strategies that teachers use to improve the quality of teaching and learning.	Informing the programmatic and policy actions of district leaders to improve their support for teachers and school leaders.	Fulfilling public and statutory obligations that describe the range and extent of district services.

These three key functions of data use are driven by the three primary reasons that district and school leaders use data, which are represented at the bottom of the figure. Data are useful to district and school leaders only if they (a) inform the instructional strategies that teachers use in their classes to improve the quality of their teaching and the learning of their students; (b) help district and school leaders improve the quality of the support, in terms of curriculum, professional development, etc., that they provide teachers to enhance their instruction; and (c) fulfill requirements and demonstrate the extent of service and reach of the organization.

The rows of figure 5.2 represent each of the primary layers of district organization: district, school, and classroom. A district system of data use must provide feedback to individuals at each of these levels. As the district's role in developing systems for data use is the primary purpose of this chapter, I emphasize this top layer in the figure. However, it is important to understand the nested hierarchy of district, school, and classroom, and the important role of data in connecting and informing each of these three layers.

First, let me focus on the district role in systemwide data use in support of instructional improvement. A district that has developed a districtwide system of data use will have great capacity to regularly collect and disseminate data on individual student performance at various levels of aggregation (i.e., school, class, grade, teacher, subgroup, individual) to teachers and school leaders to provide guidance in making decisions about instruction and instructional support. In a flexible system in which data can be aggregated at any level, these data can and should be examined at school, level, and region by district-level decisionmakers as well.

Developing a system that can provide flexible, updated student performance data to schools is a technical challenge that is increasingly being overcome by larger school districts and external assistance providers. Within the next five years, we will likely see increasingly sophisticated and effortless technical solutions that provide a range of student performance data in an array of forms. But providing the data is not enough; a corollary district responsibility is to provide targeted training for each of the consumer groups of data.

Training teachers and school leaders on how to capitalize on the latent power that resides within the data is a more daunting challenge. The challenges of training teachers and school leaders to use data intelligently should not be underestimated, because it requires teachers and school leaders to not only become proficient at using the data analysis tools but also to obtain meaning from the data, and then to turn that meaning into instructional action and support. For teachers, the data provide a means to diagnose student skill levels and needs; but any ensuing intervention requires that teachers be able to convert that diagnosis into an appropriate intervention and that they can draw from a repertoire of instructional strategies to address to a range of problems. School leaders face the same challenge at a more systemic level, that of identifying patterns within data and converting them into meaningful professional development, programmatic student support, or some other systemic response. The more data are used formatively, the greater their likely influence on interactions between teacher and learner, which lies at the heart of pedagogy.

The second component of a districtwide data-use system is a mechanism for district and school leaders to monitor the breadth and depth of the implementation of their programs and policies. District and school leaders need some reliable way to understand the extent to which their programs and policies are being applied in classrooms. The tendency is to visit a small sample of classrooms, or hear testimonials from committed individuals, or hear the scattered impressions of well-intended lieutenants, and then to consider this imperfect picture representative of the level of implementation across the system. There is a high risk of misinterpreting these data-based impressions, which can lead to erroneous action. Disciplined inquiry leads to gathering data on implementation more systematically, which presents a more accurate picture of the level and variety of implementation. A chief challenge is to avoid making data collection more resource consuming (mainly time) relative to the value of what it produces. Thus, such a system must find the right balance between sample, accuracy, burden, and utility. One way to assist with this calculation is to turn data collection into a learning opportunity for actors within the system. By doing this, both the *process* and the *product* become valuable. In this way, necessary professional development and practice in using data are provided in the service of collecting and analyzing information useful to decisionmakers.

The third component of a districtwide system of data use is one already likely being carried out by districts because it is required by federal and state funders. All districts must report a variety of information about their students, employees, and services. These reports describe the array and extent of district programs, services, and functions. They fulfill a set of requirements and obligations of the district, and the information proves useful in a variety of ways.

While this chapter focuses on the district's role in using data, the school and classroom levels are also represented in figure 5.2 because there must be a schoolwide system of data use nested within the district system. At the school level, leaders and teachers face their own challenges in using data effectively for instructional improvement. In a 2003 study I conducted with Valerie Klein, we collected data from sixty-one schools adopting America's Choice and conducted an in-depth exploration of the data practices of five of these schools (three elementary and two middle) that were identified as innovative users of data.

Putting the different practices together, we developed a model for schoolwide data use (Supovitz & Klein, 2003). A school that was using student performance data systematically practiced many of the following common practices: (a) teachers would use student performance data to identify lesson objectives, focus instruction, and align lessons with standards; (b) teachers and school leaders used it to identify students in need of additional assistance, to develop assistance plans for those students, and to monitor the effectiveness of the assistance plans; (c) school leaders used the data to plan professional development; (d) teachers and school leaders used the data to set ambitious and reasonable annual improvement goals; (e) school leaders used it to celebrate the measurable progress and achievements of faculty and students; (f) teachers and school leaders used it to communicate with parents; and (g) school leaders used the data to visually express school priorities and focus. The regular occurrence of these practices across the school did not impinge upon individual teachers' creative uses of data inside of their own classrooms. In fact, in many of the classrooms we observed, teachers had evolved their own specialized systems of data use that were idiosyncratic to their styles of instruction.

Technology must play a key role in making data useful to teachers, school leaders, and district administrators. In order to use data effectively, it is necessary to construct systems that deliver data in flexible and accessible ways, while minimizing the technical expertise necessary to cull evidence to support or refute questions. Decisionmakers must be able to inquire easily into the data in order to explore hypotheses about the relationships between what they do and the results their actions produce. Technology offers the promise of being able to do this like never before. In Duval County, AIDE and the snapshot system are examples of fruitful ways to use technology.

Data are just unexploited tools if leaders do not develop ways to put them into the hands of those who can use them and provide them with the training, support, and frames of thinking to use the data to inform actions. Data are the "crude oil" of educational improvement, having only raw potential in their unrefined form. In order to fuel improvement, data need to be refined (via a data system) and then processed (via the instructional improvement process). A truly effective organizational data system is proficient at all three of these steps: collecting the data in the first place, processing the data with some system that sorts and selects data as the user wishes, and then transforming this processed data into action. The process is self-generating in that the action produces more data.

Structured inquiry and organizational learning are means to maximize the value of data and to justify the energy that is expended in collecting and organizing them. Cyclical inquiry—in which groups follow the progressively spiraling process of identifying questions worthy of exploration, conducting investigations that bring data to bear on those questions, taking action based upon hypotheses generated by the investigations, and evaluating the effect of those actions, which in turn generates more refined questions—is theoretically a catalyst for continuous improvement. In the next chapter I turn more thoroughly to the concepts of organizational learning as I explore issues of deepening and sustaining reform.

6

Sustainability and Organizational Learning

I shall be telling this with a sigh
Somewhere ages and ages hence:
Two roads diverged in a wood, and I—
I took the one less traveled by,
And that has made all the difference.
—*Robert Frost, from "The Road Not Taken."*

If district leaders are good and lucky—mostly good, but a little bit lucky, too—they arrive at a crossroads where they must develop a plan to spread, deepen, and sustain their instructional improvement efforts. Down one road beckons the siren's song of a completely different reform program. As Hess (1999) has documented, the allure and rewards of introducing new ideas into a system generally outweigh the incentives to stick with something that has lost its sheen. And sometimes there are good reasons to take the organization off in another direction. The road less traveled however, leads into the thickets of sustainability. This is the road we are taking in this chapter.

Scale-up, or sustainability, is the holy grail of educational reform (Hatch, 2000). Those who have searched for the holy grail know that there are few clues as to how to find it. If you have instituted a set of ideas that you think are promising, how do you keep them going? How do you spread them across the system and instill them deeply in the culture and practices of the organization? How do you encourage employees to grapple with them, understand them more deeply, and use them with greater care and precision? How do you learn what ways these ideas are working and adjust the organizational systems accordingly? These are the questions of sustainability.

Part of the challenge of sustainability in education is that it has rarely, if ever, been accomplished. Heifetz (1994) distinguishes between technical and adaptive challenges. Technical challenges are those that, while difficult and perhaps even daunting, have been solved before. Adaptive challenges, by contrast, are problems whose solutions lie outside current knowledge. Improving student test performance is a technical challenge; having all students meet standards is an adaptive challenge. Improving minority student performance is a technical challenge; eliminating the achievement gap is an adaptive challenge. Sustainability is the ultimate adaptive challenge (Fullan, 2005).

The term "sustainability" is itself misleading. The dictionary definition of the word is "to keep in existence; to maintain." If educational leaders view sustainability as just maintaining changes they have already made, then they are likely lost. There is no such thing as treading water when leading educational reform. Ground gained can be quickly lost for a host of reasons, including high mobility rates and the very human tendency to wander on to new things. Innovation diffusion follows a typical pattern of slow progress at the outset, followed by a critical period where the phenomenon either accelerates or fades away (Degenne & Forse, 1999). Leaders who use the same strategies to entice stragglers to participate as they did early adopters are unlikely to increase participation beyond around 60 percent (Supovitz & Goerlich-Zief, 2000). People periodically need new and fresh ways to engage with the same problems.

Educational leaders must remember that what they are sustaining is reform or change, not the status quo. Thus the concept of sustaining reform means that an organization builds something different and then figures out ways to continually improve upon what it is doing. Sustaining should not be viewed as the glide after reaching a certain altitude. Nor should it be viewed as keeping the machine well oiled after building it. While these are powerful images, they are the wrong way to think about achieving excellence. They are wrong because they imply that continuing to do the same thing is the ticket to prolonged excellence. The challenge of sustaining reform is to find new entry points into already identified problems, to continually dig deeper into the intransigent but worthy challenges that are inherent in pluralistic educational opportunity.

There are many takes on the challenge of sustainability. Some view sustainability as the challenge of taking strong instructional practices to scale. In a 1996 article in the *Harvard Educational Review*, for example, Harvard professor Richard Elmore reviewed the historical failure of large-scale reform efforts to penetrate the status quo of teaching. Elmore distinguished between "fundamental changes in the conditions of teaching and learning for students and teachers" and more superficial changes in the organization and management of schooling. He argues that "schools might be 'changing' all the time—adopting this or that new structure or schedule or textbook series or tracking system—and never change in any fundamental way what teachers and students actually do when they are together in classrooms" (p. 3). As evidence, Elmore examined the disappointing trajectory of the reform ideas of the progressive educators of the early part of the twentieth century and the large-scale National Science Foundation curricula of the 1950s and 1960s. In both cases, Elmore concludes "innovations that require large changes in the core of educational practice seldom penetrate more than a small fraction of U.S. schools and classrooms, and seldom last for very long when they do" (pp. 1–2). For Elmore, the challenge reformers face is to maintain the meaning of reform ideas as they spread across classrooms, schools, and systems.

Cynthia Coburn (2003) sought to expand understanding of the problem of scale by conceptualizing it as a four-dimensional task of depth, spread, shift, and sustainability. First, Coburn argues, reforms must be deep; for instance, they must "effect deep and consequential changes in classroom practice" (p. 4). Akin to Elmore's definition of the problem, Coburn contends that for reforms to be scaled, they must be meaningful and go "beyond surface structures or procedures to alter teachers' beliefs, norms of social interaction, and pedagogical principles" (p. 4). Second, simply put, reforms must spread to a great proportion of the whole. Third, dominion over reform must shift from the introducer to an "internal authority" that takes ownership for the reform. This may be the transition from an external provider to the district, as was the case with NCEE and Duval County or, more intimately, from a district to teachers. Fourth, consequential changes must be sustained over time such that original and later adopters exhibit the reform practices over time. Coburn's four-dimensional conceptualization, of which sustainability is just one element to the challenge of scale-up, is useful in that it provides a way to think about the task of infusing a reform idea into the fabric of an educational organization. But it doesn't speak to *how* leaders might do so.

In *Leadership and Sustainability* (2005), Michael Fullan digs into the challenge of how education leaders might tackle the sustainability task. Fullan believes that that sustainability requires unprecedented coordination within the tri-level system of states, districts, and schools. He develops a complex formulation of what he contends are the essential elements of sustainability in education. These include what he calls "moral purpose" around both equity and excellence and a respectful and positive social environment around that purpose; "lateral networking" as a means of sharing information across units and levels of the educational organization; the blending of internal and external accountability into what he terms "intelligent accountability"; persistent improvement and collective problem-solving through candid and continuous assessment; cyclical energizing to keep the people invigorated across the long haul of change; and the development of leadership at all levels as the "primary engine" propelling continued improvement. Fullan's characterization takes us deeper into the underlying dynamics of individual psychology and organizational theory that produce the differing bonds between organizational elements and the individuals who construct and implement them.

Latticed within Fullan's (2005) framework is the core challenge of building learning into the routine work of the organization. Similarly, Elmore (1996) views the creation of "structures that promote learning of new practices" as a key solution to the problem of scale. Like Fullan and Elmore, organizational theorists often frame the core challenge of sustainability as one of organizational learning. In essence, this theory contends that if leaders can construct their organizations to tackle big challenges, continually learn from their experiences, capture this learning, and infuse that learning back into the institutional knowledge of the organization, then an organization can sustain reform. Organizational learning is the engine of sustainability.

In the business world, organizational learning is considered necessary to maintain competitiveness, something of a Darwinian imperative. According to Peter Senge (1990), the influential director of the Systems Thinking and Organizational Learning program at MIT's Sloan School of Management,

"The organizations that will truly excel in the future will be the organizations that discover how to tap people's commitment and capacity to learn at all levels in an organization" (p. 4). Organizational theorist Ikujiro Nonaka (1991) defines organizational learning as "the creation of new knowledge, dissemination of it throughout the whole organization, and embodiment of it into new technologies, products and services" (p. 98). Organizational learning is a necessary strategy for continuous improvement.

The development of an ethos of learning within an organization is therefore seen as the solution to the problem of how to deepen reform beyond the intellect of a few. By embedding the values of improvement into the regular practices and cultural fabric of an organization through learning deeply, its leaders can sustain reform through inevitable leadership turnover. To educators this seems particularly important, given the short terms of many superintendents. According to the Council of Great City Schools (2003), the average tenure of urban superintendents is 2.75 years. Given that meaningful reform seems to take at least that long, organizational learning is a promising means to sustain reform beyond the term of its initiators.

DIMENSIONS OF ORGANIZATIONAL LEARNING

There are three central views about the concept of organizational learning that are important to distinguish here. These are (1) fostering individual learning for the purposes of the organization; (2) using social interactions as a means of fostering and sharing learning across individuals and groups; and (3) embedding learning in the rules and routines of the organization. Each of these perspectives has implications for the construction of learning opportunities within organizations and the way organizational leaders structure their organizations to capture and spread knowledge in order to improve performance over time. I will explain each of these briefly, focusing most on the last, which is a key mechanism for sustaining reform in education today.

The first view of organizational learning is the notion of the learning of individuals who are nested within the organization. In this view, individual learning may be initiated, motivated, and stimulated by the organization, but learning essentially resides within the individual's cognitive functioning. In this conception of organizational learning, many authors have examined how individuals learn in organizational contexts and how that learning is transmitted through organizations (see, e.g., Hedberg, 1981; Levitt & March, 1988; Weick, 1979). Meredith Honig (2004) provides a useful definition of this aspect of organizational learning, saying that "organizational learning at root is a theory of how individuals in organizational setting manage information from internal and external environments to guide individual and organizational practice" (p. 532). In another frequently cited example of framing organizational learning as the cognitive action of individuals for the improvement of the organization, Argyris and Schön (1978) explored the ways errors are detected within firms, and they defined the distinction between single-loop and double-loop learning. Single-loop learning is the individual act of identifying and correcting mistakes within an organization's production processes; in other words, through a process of learning, an individual or group identifies and corrects specific problems within the processes of the organization. This is said to be the more common level of learning. Double-loop learning, according to Argyris and Schön, is the deeper and rarer facility of identifying and correcting flaws in an organization's assumptions, policies, and objectives. Despite the distinction between the two types of learning, both are fundamentally based on the cognitive learning power of individuals. In this tradition, views of organizational learning are largely based on individual learning that occurs on behalf of the organization. Most types of formal professional development, in which the organization seeks to improve the job performance of individuals, would fit this conception of organizational learning, which holds that organizations learn through cumulative individual learning.

The second conception of organizational learning rests on the notion that learning arises from the social interactions between individuals within the organization. In this view, people make meaning through discussions with peers and deepen their understanding through a social process. Setting up communities of practice, or professional learning communities, is viewed as a potentially powerful mechanism to spread learning across an organization. The concept of the team-based work organization has a long heritage in industry, becoming particularly prevalent in increasingly competitive knowledge-based sectors (Galbraith, 1994; Mohrman, Cohen, & Mohrman, 1995). The group practices that underlie organizational learning are seen as a means of producing more effective organizations. Deming (1986), in his work on total quality management, argued that organizations achieve quality through constant incremental improvement and that teams, including cross-functional teams, facilitate the necessary communication and feedback for ongoing organizational improvement. Senge's (1990) influential work focused on five "disciplines" that are characteristic of highly effective businesses. These include team learning, shared organizational vision, systems thinking, individual mastery, and mental modeling. Virtually all of these attributes required the close coordination and engagement of individuals into groups, a fact not lost on other organizational theorists. For example, Mohrman, Mohrman, and Lawler (1992) noted that organizations that excel in learning have a rich constellation of teams and networks that span parts of the organization and connect knowledge and perspectives. In education, professional learning communities are perceived as a powerful catalyst for improvement (McLaughlin & Talbert, 2001; Roberts & Pruitt, 2003). According to DuFour and Eaker (1998), "The most promising strategy for sustained, substantive school improvement is developing the ability of school personnel to function as professional learning communities" (p. xi). In this view, an organization learns through the social interactions of its members.

The third dimension of organizational learning is that people collectively learn through the institutional systems that surround them and guide their everyday routines. This "structural" view of organizational learning is based on the idea that an organization can "learn" as a distinct entity—that is, apart from the learning of individuals within the organization. This perspective goes back to Cyert and March's (1963) book that sought to explain the behavior of firms. In their view, organizational learning was imprinted into the rules, procedures, and routines of the organization that shaped its decision-making parameters. This view, rooted in the tradition of Frederick Taylor's (1911) scientific management and the assembly-line organization, essentially considers organizational learning as a function of the information transmitted through their bureaucracies. In this vein, Levitt and March (1988) explain how organizations learn from their experience by "encoding inferences from history into routines that guide behavior" (p. 517). They argue that an organization can be said to have learned only insofar as ideas are embedded in its rules, conventions, and standard operating procedures. Any time an organization dictates ways of doing things through standard operating procedures with the purpose of spreading knowledge, they are enhancing the probability of learning within the organization. In this view, organizations learn by expressly capturing improvement techniques and methods and infusing these more desirable ways to function into their rules, procedures, and regulations.

The cognitive, social, and institutional dimensions of facilitating learning within and by organizations are certainly not mutually exclusive. Most organizations have, to some extent, strategies based on all three of these ideas, and they are often commingled. The emphasis and distribution for enhancing learning across these three strategies are also dependent on leaders' conceptions of learning and how it occurs. Spillane (2002) adroitly demonstrated this point in a study of the relationship between school district leaders' personal views about learning and the professional development systems they constructed within their districts. Interviewing leaders in nine Michigan school districts in the early 1990s, Spillane mapped leaders' views about teacher learning and instructional change onto the way professional development was constructed in their districts. Spillane found that most leaders viewed learning in a traditionally behavioristic notion of the direct transmission of knowledge from teacher to learner without interpretation, and this approach to teacher professional development predominated. Although Spillane's study focused on the alignment of the method of delivery of professional development and personal beliefs, it could equally apply to connections between leaders' understanding of the mechanisms for delivering learning to employees and learning opportunities within organizations.

ORGANIZATIONAL LEARNING IN DUVAL COUNTY

Visitors entering the superintendent's office on the sixth floor of the Duval County School Board building could not fail to notice a large bronze plaque to the right of the doorway that read, "John C. Fryer, Jr. Superintendent of Schools, 'Chief Learner.'" This message from the top symbolized Fryer's intention to turn the district into a learning organization. Throughout his tenure, Fryer repeatedly communicated the message that he sought to imbue the organization with a mentality of continuous learning and improvement.

The signs were everywhere in conversations with Fryer between 1999 and 2005 that this notion of building an organization that valued and attended to its own learning was foremost in his mind. His interviews were riddled with references to his desire to develop a learning organization and his belief that this was the path to sustainability. As Fryer expressed in a January 2000 interview, "If you create that exciting, dynamic learning organization where everybody is just hungry, the results will come out."

Fryer believed that one of the chief impediments to improving the district's educational system was that school faculties lacked the intellectual engagement that was necessary for organizational improvement and to stimulate student learning. Fryer often complained that schools lacked what he called "a culture of learning," or the academic emphasis that spurred students and teachers to engage in learning. As he explained in a 2003 interview:

> We have to find a way to meet that challenge, because in many of our schools you can walk in and tell that's the culture is bad, the kids don't want to learn. It's not a culture of learning, it's a culture of get[ting] by with the least you can. And you know when you go to a higher-performing magnet school, the culture is one [where] it's cool to learn and it relates very much to that first principle of learning that we've been talking about a lot, that effort drives performance.

In fact, Fryer chose America's Choice as the nucleus of the district's reform in part because of its emphasis on continuous learning. Fryer saw many components of America's Choice—such as its emphasis on teacher diagnosis and judgment, study groups, and book talks and data analysis—as ways for organizational members to think more reflectively about their work. Fryer was drawn to the balance between the structured components of the program's design and the built-in encouragement of organizational learning. As he told me in a 2001 interview:

> The beauty of the [America's Choice] design, unlike so many others that are sort of a cookie cutter, is that . . . half of the design is the structure, the training that goes with it, and the rituals and routines that gives an order to what you're doing. The other half is the catalytic effect that it has. It is a catalyst for continuous learning. And so if you go to schools . . . you find teachers are reading lots of books and discussing ideas and growing in a very purposeful way.

A great deal of the effort district leaders made was to encourage this kind of activity down to the school level. Many of the district's strategies were focused on trying to foster and facilitate sustained inquiry and persistent learning on the part of teachers and school leaders.

Over time, Fryer began to point to examples of adult engagement that indicated to him that school leaders and faculties were beginning to engage in learning as well as teaching. As he commented in 2002, "When I first came here I would go around to schools and suggest things to teachers, and now I go to certain schools and teachers tell me what I ought to be reading. That is good news. That tells me that they are on fire for their own learning now. There was not that intellectual inquiry when I got here. I want to measure how that is taking hold, because that is the real, ultimate capacity-building capability."

Duval County leaders' strategies to foster learning within their organization can be organized along the lines of the individual, social, and institutional views of organizational learning. In most school districts, individual learning opportunities predominate. Professional development offerings, although often insufficient, are usually the key component of virtually any district's efforts to enhance the capacity of teachers and other employees. The organization of professional development in Duval County, including direct training of teachers and school and district standards coaches and leadership development, was discussed in detail in chapter 3 and therefore will not be emphasized here. In this chapter, the focus is on systems developed by leaders to share and spread instructional knowledge across the system. For this reason, this chapter emphasizes the social and institutional aspects of the development of learning across an organization. Rather than catalog each of the district's social and institutional learning efforts (because many initiatives have both social and institutional elements embedded within them and it becomes difficult to disentangle them), I will focus on one example of each.

The remainder of this chapter is organized into three parts. First, I say a few words about persistence as a strategy for sustainability. Since most reform tends to have relatively short cycles, we should not underestimate the power that persistence plays in deepening change. Second, I examine the social aspect of organizational learning, as embodied in Duval County's efforts to develop professional learning communities at multiple levels across the organization. Professional learning communities were a major part of Duval County leaders' efforts to encourage school and district personnel to engage with the district's reforms and deepen the implementation of standards. Third, I describe the institutional aspect of organizational learning through further analysis of the Standards Implementation Snapshot System, which was introduced in chapter 5 as a means to collect data on implementation. The snapshot system was designed to embed both individual and organizational learning opportunities into the fabric of regular work in the district. The chapter concludes with a discussion of the challenges associated with social and institutional strategies as mechanisms for scaling and sustaining reform.

Before proceeding, I must acknowledge that the frame I am putting on Duval County's efforts in this chapter is very different than how Duval County leaders themselves viewed the challenges of scale and sustainability. The integration of social and institutional strategies under the heading of organizational learning is my interpretation of a promising solution to the problems of scale and sustainability. Duval County leaders had a less developed perspective on these concepts of organizational learning. They clearly viewed the deepening of reform as a challenge to increase the value of learning in the culture of the organization, and they used the concept of enhancing adult learning in the organization through individual and social mechanisms as a means to both build capacity and change the culture of the district to infuse a higher valuation of learning into the organization. But they were less familiar with the institutional learning concept that I introduce here and did not view the three perspectives on learning—individual, social, and institutional—in an integrated way. Hopefully, by examining the strengths and shortcomings of Duval County's strategies for sustainability, other district leaders can build upon their efforts.

SUSTAINABILITY THROUGH PERSISTENCE

Persistence is one important form of sustainability. In some ways, Duval County leaders sustained their reform merely by being consistent and relatively stable in their advocacy and support for the instructional direction of the district. While their support for standards-based reform undoubtedly became more refined and sophisticated, and they developed and supplemented the core instructional ideas with different components over the seven years that Fryer led the district, much of what they supported stayed stable over that time. It is a simple and often overlooked fact in this age of fast food and immediate gratification that reform takes time to wend its way through an organization, and therefore time is a critical factor in (but not sufficient for) the spread and sustainability of reform.

When Fryer took over the superintendency in Duval County, he found the system distracted and dispersed. In an early 2000 interview, for example, Fryer assailed the lack of focus in the district and described his attempts to keep efforts centered on the instructional vision. "I have tried to focus things here," he said as he described the first year of his tenure. "It is amazing how distracted people are. For example, the IDEA legislation [the federal Individuals with Disabilities Education Act of 1997] is a good example of how a little money gives external people huge leverage at both the state and federal level. There is a potpourri of programs within the district. This is very distracting. I am keeping people focused on the High Five. Ultimately I am rallying interest in academic performance."

Charles Cline, the associate superintendent for curriculum and instruction and a veteran of over thirty years of reform efforts in Duval County, attributed the district's strong progress to its unprecedented commitment of resources at the school level. "This may sound funny to you," he told me just before Christmas in 2002, "but I think with this reform we have put more resources into actually implementing it at the school level beyond just documenting and planning. . . . That's so much different from other reforms. [The superintendent is] willing to put the resources in the academic area to see that the programs are actually implemented."

On the one hand, it is easy to see that concentrated, persistent attention and continued resources would have a positive effect on the implementation and longstanding attention to reform. On the other hand, Cline's analysis reveals a disturbing proclivity toward the standard practice of short-term cycling of reform. This reform bunny-hopping is counterproductive to the success of any intervention. No matter how potentially powerful a reform may be, if it is not given a chance to take root, it is unlikely to flower.

Other district leaders attributed the sustained attention to the district's reforms to evidence that the reforms were producing results. John Thompson, one of the five regional superintendents in the earlier days of the reform noted, "In thirty years, I've seen lots of initiatives come through and they have not sustained themselves. I think this one is different because I've seen results. I can see a distinct movement between teachers and principals toward getting student-focused instruction. One veteran kindergarten teacher told me, 'This is it. I've taught for twenty years. I am getting kindergarteners to write in January, whereas before I would be doing well if I could get them to write in May.'"

In fact, after five years, many principals assessed that the district's reforms had only reached about 50–60 percent of the teachers in the district. The principal of one of the first cohort of America's Choice schools, a thirty-year education veteran with eight years as a principal, estimated in the spring of 2003 that only about 60 percent of the district's schools had really embraced the reform. "If Mr. Fryer were to leave tomorrow and the district were to shift gears, as so often happens, I think this reform would wash away," he said. "Bits and pieces would remain, as far as using standards-based reform and all, but I think most of it would wash away, just like all other reforms do." A high school principal had a similar estimate of overall spread, but felt that elementary schools had much deeper levels of adoption than high schools.

Indeed, persistence was a strategy that Duval County leaders discussed when I asked several of them in the winter of 2004 how they were working to sustain their reform efforts. One overriding theme of those conversations was bringing the efforts and strategies they had used to effect change in their elementary schools to the high schools. They acknowledged that high schools had very different challenges, particularly around students' motivation and belief in their own abilities to learn, but they insisted that many of the instructional approaches to reading, writing, and mathematics that they had refined in the upper elementary and middle schools could be applied to high schools. Thus they viewed their high school work as replicating the careful change efforts in the upper grades that they had developed in the lower grades. They saw the replication of their efforts over the previous five years in the district's elementary schools as the major task of the next five years.

Persistence is a cudgel for sustaining reform, in that it relies on the brute-force method of doing the same thing over time. It does not account for either the need to identify new strategies for reaching people that have not been reached before or for identifying which instructional strategies are working and which are not, and then finding new and better ways of doing those things that are not effective. This calls for a more refined mechanism than unmitigated persistence.

Two themes underlay Duval County's efforts to sustain their reforms over time. The first involved developing a culture of learning in the district, which was embodied in two central efforts. District leaders sought, first, to develop professional learning communities at multiple levels within the organization and, second, to use institutional structures to expand and deepen the culture of learning. The latter involved the development of systems for learning. The snapshot system, described in the previous chapter, is a prime example of the district's initial efforts to systematically capture knowledge about its practices in order to inform next steps and spread best practices across the system.

CREATING SOCIAL LEARNING OPPORTUNITIES THROUGH PROFESSIONAL LEARNING COMMUNITIES

The central Duval County strategy for engaging school faculties and sustaining the district's reform ideas was to create a web of engagement and critical dialogue about teaching and learning through the development of professional learning communities at different levels across the organization. Initially, professional learning communities grew out of NCEE's notion that teachers should regularly meet in study groups to discuss the key instructional concepts of the design and their application in the classroom. Professional learning communities have important cultural connotations because they create norms of open dialogue and shared practice across the organization. The concept is well accepted in the education field and has been introduced in numerous venues. Yet, there is no consensus as to what professional learning communities are, how they should function, and what contribution they can make to organizational improvement.

DuFour and Eaker (1998) identify six central characteristics of professional learning communities in education. These are (1) shared understanding and common values; (2) collective inquiry into questioning the status quo, seeking and testing new methods, and reflecting on the results; (3) collaborative teams organized around a common purpose; (4) an orientation toward action; (5) an emphasis on continuous improvement; and (6) an understanding that the purpose of the community is to improve results. Research on district efforts to create small learning communities suggests that while it is relatively easy to develop the structures that allow groups of educators to meet and there are positive cultural benefits to these arrangements, a more difficult challenge is to focus groups on problems of practice (Supovitz, 2002). In a synthesis of the findings of professional learning community initiatives in Philadelphia and Cincinnati in the late 1990s, researchers found that such initiatives are not specific enough to guide teacher communities through the difficult work of critically exploring the relationship between what and how they teach and the student learning this produces (Supovitz & Christman, 2005).

Superintendent Fryer saw learning communities as a mechanism to spread promising practices both within and across schools. In a 2003 interview, Fryer talked about how teachers were sharing instructional ideas with each other. "We are sharing best practices in a lot of ways," he said. "We're now developing learning communities within the schools that are causing teachers to study practices, best practices, constantly." Fryer viewed teacher study groups and book talks as central mechanisms for sharing and deepening practice.

Duval County leaders sought to develop professional learning communities both within and across multiple levels of the organization in order to develop a culture of ongoing learning. The belief in learning communities as a mechanism for identifying and distributing promising practices was broadly shared among Duval County leaders at both the district and school levels. Leaders saw this as a way to deepen and sustain reform in the district. As one regional superintendent said about the importance of professional learning communities, "That's the only way this is going to sustain itself, because otherwise, in a few years, it's all going to crash."

From early in Fryer's tenure, the notion of learning communities was central in expanding and sustaining the district's reforms. Learning communities, one of five areas of focus that were codified in the district's Framework for Implementation of Standards, was a major emphasis of the work of school leaders and faculties. The framework listed four components under the learning communities target:

- Create a comprehensive professional development plan aligned with the school improvement plan.
- Develop and maintain a cohesive, positive, professional, and constructive school culture.
- Establish smaller learning communities for teachers and students.
- Facilitate parent and community involvement and education.

From this list, it seems apparent that district leaders had an expansive notion about what it meant to develop a professional learning community and only a fuzzy sense of how the different components fit together. The first bullet of the learning communities target focused on individual learning within the school through professional development. The second bullet emphasized the more generic notion of attention to the cultural aspects of the school environment, which can certainly influence the culture of learning in the organization but in this case seems to be more generally conceived. The third bullet stressed regrouping teachers and students into smaller learning groups, which is a related but still distinct idea from that of a professional learning community. The fourth bullet points to the notion of parental and community involvement, but it is unclear why this is related to a learning community. These components of learning communities come across as a list of loosely connected ideas that fail to coalesce into a coherent concept of a learning community that could guide the actions of school leaders and faculties.

Perhaps as a consequence, the organization and activities of professional learning communities in Duval County took many shapes and forms. Groups of teachers, school leaders, and district leaders convened under the guise of learning communities in a variety of ways. These included the development of distributed leadership teams in schools, the modeling and promoting of study groups and book talks at a variety of organizational levels (grade level, leadership team, schoolwide, principal, district), and the discussion of snapshot results at principal leadership meetings.

Perhaps as a consequence of leaders' emphasis on the term "learning communities," many activities were referred to as occasions for professional learning. At the district level, weekly meetings with the superintendent and his leadership team to discuss and plan district strategies were called professional learning community activities. The nature of monthly principal meetings changed from being largely for information dissemination to having more emphasis on discussions about the implications of districtwide data patterns, discussions about professional literature that all were asked to read, and breakout sessions to discuss the implications of district strategies. At the school level, professional learning communities focused on principals and coaches facilitating conversations with faculty about the meaning of standards and how to see their evidence in student work, on book discussions to foster conversations about learning, and on study groups to examine student work and its implications for instructional practice.

THE INFLUENCE OF PROFESSIONAL LEARNING COMMUNITIES ON PRINCIPALS AND TEACHERS

Evidence from surveys and interviews suggests that school principals and teachers at least picked up the larger district message of the learning emphasis. District leaders' focus on professional learning communities also succeeded in engaging principals, and to a lesser extent teachers, in the district's reform efforts. However, the evidence suggests that the concept of the professional learning community was insufficiently focused to achieve the larger goal of spreading instructional knowledge across the system.

Surveys of the population of district principals in 2003 and again in 2004 asked them about their agreement with several statements related to the concept of a professional learning community. The first question asked principals about their agreement with the statement, "I feel part of a district learning community." The second statement asked principals about the extent of their agreement with the statement, "I feel prepared to cultivate a learning community in my school." The results of principals' responses to these two statements are shown in figure 6.1. In 2003, 77 percent of the principals either strongly (35%) or somewhat (42%) agreed that they felt part of a learning community. In 2004, this percentage increased to 96 percent, with 52 percent strongly agreeing and 44 percent somewhat agreeing with the statement. Principals also reported that they felt high levels of preparation to cultivate a learning community in their schools. In 2003, 90 percent of principals somewhat agreed (50%) or strongly agreed (40%) that they were prepared to cultivate a learning community in their school. In 2004, this overwhelming percentage remained the same, although the proportion who strongly agreed with the statement increased from 40 percent to 49 percent.

In interviews, principals were similarly positive about the district's emphasis on adult learning. One middle school principal, for example, emphasized how learning communities were an external catalyst that allowed her to encourage her staff to continue to develop their teaching skills. An elementary principal who had recently arrived from a school district in another state noted the contrast in district emphasis on adult learning:

Nobody required me to do anything like that in my old school district. You go to a workshop once in a while, but that was it, you know. I mean we had a principal's academy . . . which was just great. But no one has really said to me that [I] have to keep learning. Now I know that for myself, because I would read journals and leadership journals and magazines and the principal's magazine, all this kind of thing, but I didn't realize what depth you really need to go to if you're going to impact students. To get them ready for future we need to keep learning. So what I want to foster here in the schools is to let the teachers know you have to keep learning.

The book talks in the monthly principals meetings were a reminder of how difficult it was to shift from an action orientation to a reflection orientation that underlies the concept of participating in a professional learning community. In 2002, a Duval County regional director observed, "When we break up into regions we are supposed to do a book talk, and the book talk is supposed to be a conversation about a book, right, that is supposed to foster a learning community. But too often it ends up being a presentation of one person telling everybody what the book was about with a couple of hasty comments from people. It's just hard to get out of the mode of sharing information, because that is important. But it can't be all that is done if you are really going to have engagement."

Interviews with school leaders and faculty members revealed just how diverse local understanding of the concept of learning community was at the school level as well. In each of the ten schools I visited during the 2002–03 school year, I asked principals, school coaches, and teachers if they had a professional learning community at their school and what it meant to be a "community of learners."

One of the most frequently mentioned strategies for building a learning community was the idea of conducting book talks with faculty. An elementary principal said, "We read and share professional articles and books in our team meetings." Another elementary principal described how she was using professional books to stimulate conversations among her faculty: "What we're doing is having book talks with the teachers. We did that last year and we're doing that again this year, and we'll try to make sure that we have a reading resource room, not just for students but for teachers."

In another school the principal and standards coach developed a learning community through public presentations of practice by teachers. They asked

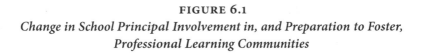

FIGURE 6.1

Change in School Principal Involvement in, and Preparation to Foster,
Professional Learning Communities

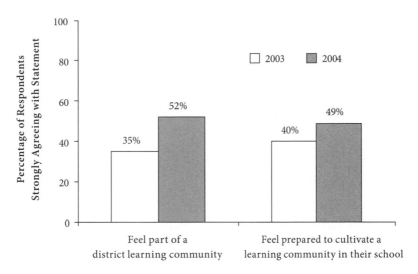

teachers to take turns facilitating professional development sessions at which they were asked to demonstrate an instructional technique; for example, in science, how they would reinforce math skills, or reading skills, or writing skills. Then people were asked to give feedback on what they might have done differently. In this way, the standards coach commented, they were able to create a more open climate for sharing techniques and approaches across the faculty.

Cross-school visitations were also mentioned as a way to develop a learning community. A few principals talked about allowing teachers to visit other schools and conduct focus walks in order to bring ideas back to try out in their classrooms. "We allow our teachers to go out and visit other schools, conduct focus walks, and come back and debrief the faculty, and set up those things they learn in their classrooms," said an elementary school principal.

When I asked school leaders what it meant to be part of a community of learners, I got a diversity of responses:

- "A community of learners, especially in this school, means that we speak the same language."

- "A community of learners is, first of all, empowering people to have a sense of parity within the system where they will have equal input into that process."
- "Continuous, continuous, continuous contact, continuous involvement, continuous dialogue, continuous problem-solving, continuous identifying strengths and weaknesses. It is continuity of effort."
- "We engage in conversations with teachers about instruction and refuse to allow them to be lulled into those debasing conversations which have existed in our profession for years about students' behavior or the students' parents or the students' parents' poor choices. So our focus is always on instruction."
- "Teachers get a chance to share ideas through their work—best practices, instructional practices."

The amorphousness of the concept of a learning community in Duval County reflected both the benefits and limitations of the leaders' strategy. On the one hand, the general nature in which the concept was introduced led to increased attention and multiple ways to encourage learning communities that allowed school leaders to interpret it in a range of creative and contextually appropriate ways as they sought different leverage points to strengthen their faculties' engagement with each other and with instructional concepts and approaches. On the other hand, poor understanding of the concept led to generally thin enactment.

From interviews with teachers and the random opportunities that I had to observe various professional learning community activities, it appeared that the implementation of this concept was often different than the descriptions offered by school leaders. For example, in one book talk described by a middle school coach, copies of the book were not available for teachers. Instead, the coach passed out some photocopies of a few pages and tried to get a conversation going about the material. Consequently, the coach admitted, the book talk was more of a presentation than a conversation. Many coaches had the sense that their role in fostering learning communities at their school was to offer training and workshops for teachers at faculty meetings, rather than an opportunity for discussion and reflection. In another school, the coach talked about the difficulties of starting a book study. She only managed to convince six of the twenty-two teachers on the faculty to participate.

Notably, teachers' responses to questions about the learning communities in their school were distinctly different from those of school principals and coaches. Teachers generally had a much vaguer conception of what made up a professional learning community, if they had heard of it at all. While this could be a matter of language, teachers could not distinguish between the development of professional learning communities and more traditional in-school professional development.

Of the twenty-nine teachers who were interviewed, nine, or roughly one-third, did not know what I was referring to when I asked them whether they had a professional learning community in their school. "I am not familiar with that" was a typical response. Twelve other teachers, or about 40 percent of those interviewed, immediately referred to book talks in response to my questions about professional learning communities. Sometimes the book talks they described were ongoing, and in other cases were an introduction to the school year. "We usually start off our year with a book talk," explained one teacher. "This year it was *Fish,* and last year was *Who Moved My Cheese.* And in each faculty meeting once a month there is some kind of discussion or an activity or something that ties it back to the theme," she said.

Several other teachers talked about in-service workshops as their schools' expression of a professional learning community. "In our faculty meetings we discuss things that are going on, our principal tries to bring us up to speed on things that are required," explained an elementary school teacher. "In our grade-level meetings, our principal and standards coach share with us so we can be on the same page about what's expected, what's not expected. I think it is so we can be all on the same page about what's working for us and what is not working for us. I think that in that way, we can all learn together," she said. Teachers' confusion about professional development and professional learning communities raises interesting questions about the distinctions and overlap between the two. I would say that professional development contributes the larger concept of developing a professional learning community, but is in itself not a professional learning community.

The picture that emerges from the interviews and survey data about the development of professional learning communities in Duval County is a complex one. The concept of learning community clearly entered into the district's lexicon and expanded interest and engagement in professional learning across the system. The responses of school and district leaders indicated that they felt part of a learning community in the district, which contributed to their sense of membership in the collective. Principals also felt empowered to support the development of professional learning communities in their schools, which seemed to foster a greater emphasis on individual and organizational learning than had existed previously. This emphasis seemed to create some excitement for both individual and collective learning and started to introduce the idea of ongoing professional growth into the expectations of the organization.

Yet the possibilities created by professional learning communities—rigorous inquiry into the problems and challenges of instructional practice and the support of that practice—seemed to be occurring only in pockets in the district, if at all. The power of the idea of a professional learning community is that the members of the group (whether defined as a teacher team, school leadership team, school faculty, school principals, district leadership, etc.) engage together in challenges of practice so that their understanding of those challenges grows deeper and is more unified. Through their investigations, proposed solutions emerge that are then tested to see if they help alleviate the issues they seek to address. Through such a repeated process, practice grows more sophisticated and powerful and the group develops a tighter sense of camaraderie and common purpose. As a result, they can construct common understanding, share knowledge and experience, and develop common goals. This form of professional learning communities was largely absent from the district, and the examples Duval County faculty members did provide were too diffused and unfocused to have a strong influence on their practice. Activities like book talks and in-school professional development sessions were too sparse and diffused to fulfill the particular goals promised by professional learning communities.

Encouragement to engage in professional learning and growth should not be confused with the intention of a professional learning community. Such activities may or may not facilitate the dialogue, interactions, and connections that foster learning communities. Some communities are merely social, while others focus on activities peripheral to instructional improvement. In the absence of structures to guide the development and engagement of professional learning communities, models of how they can be used, and facilitators to guide them, it is unlikely that they will develop into the powerful mechanisms for improvement that is their potential.

EXPANDING LEARNING THROUGH INSTITUTIONAL STRUCTURES: THE SNAPSHOT SYSTEM

Institutional learning is the third dimension of organizational learning. It can be distinguished from strategies of individual and social learning in that it is an explicit leadership strategy to decompose key organizational processes, capture areas of strength and concern, determine corrective actions for problematic areas, and spread these "learnings" across the organization.

Architects of organizational learning systems must think about processes and structures that are distinct from, yet connected to, both individual and social professional learning opportunities. According to Harvard Business School professor David Garvin (1993), institutionalized organizational learning can be defined as "the creation, acquisition, and transfer of knowledge, and the skillful modification of the organization's behavior to reflect new knowledge and insights." From this perspective, some of the strongest signals by which people within organizations learn to perform their jobs are routines and regularized procedures that are set up by organizational leaders to create common understanding and spread desired ideas and practices. These structures and routines become even more powerful if they are intentionally designed to capture and spread improvement ideas about the organization's central processes. Such systems can be used to identify effective practices and transmit them across the organization. The regularized structures of institutional learning systems signal to organizational members, either explicitly (through rules and requirements) or implicitly (through cultural preferences), the priorities, behaviors, and practices that leaders think people should adopt. In these ways, institutional structures contribute to shaping the behaviors and practices of individuals across the organization and enter into the organizational culture as the accepted "way we do things around here." Institutional learning strategies represent an approach to increasing learning by and within organizations that is distinct from either individual or social learning opportunities.

The use of institutional structures to push learning forward throughout an organization is not a well-understood strategy to facilitate learning within organizations and to sustain reform. But it should be recognized that organizational members invariably receive signals from the routines and procedures of the organization, and these communication paths therefore represent a powerful way to influence the way people carry out their daily work and the expectations that they have. The messages sent through organizational systems and procedures are always being transmitted, whether system leaders are explicit about influencing those messages or not. Therefore, the challenge for system leaders is to thoughtfully and meaningfully control and channel the learning that occurs in the organization through these reservoirs.

In retrospect, it is easy to overidentify institutional learning mechanisms. Organizational leaders can usually point back to communication mechanisms that have influenced the activities and performance of people in the organization. But I am talking about something distinct in the important sense that these systems must be instituted proactively and explicitly to have an influence on the things that people learn and the way they operate. The secret to facilitating institutional learning is to design and implement such systems with forethought.

In this section, I use the example of the snapshot system to describe one way Duval County leaders embedded learning opportunities into the everyday rhythms and routines of the district with the express purpose of enhancing understanding of their reforms. The snapshot system set up an organizational routine by which the district articulated what different levels of implementation of its instructional initiatives looked like, communicated them broadly across the organization through both the snapshot rubrics and the snapshot visits, collected extensive data on implementation, and used those data to both spread best practices and make organizational adjustments (Supovitz & Weathers, 2004).

Duval County's snapshot system, described in detail the previous chapter, is one mechanism for institutional learning. As you will recall, the snapshots are efforts to collect data on the level of implementation of key district reform components. Snapshot topics focus on the key instructional and support components of the district's reform efforts, including the use of standards, literacy and mathematics instruction, and safety nets for academically at-risk students. The system was designed to involve large numbers of leaders at all organizational levels in data collection and interpretation. Each month, a large group of trained principals and district administrators conducts site visits in a sample of district schools where, using a specified data collection protocol and rubric of the standards of evidence, they assess the school's level of implementation in a specific area. Although the sites of visits are confidential, data collectors are asked to identify and share best practices with their colleagues. The results are aggregated into a districtwide picture of implementation and used for discussions about the barriers to deeper implementation and strategic planning.

At one level the snapshots are a way to collect data on the levels of implementation of key elements of the district's reform efforts. But in another important way, the system is designed to create opportunities for organizational learning. The snapshot system can be viewed as a mechanism for institutionalizing learning because it is designed to specify high-quality practice and communicate it across the organization, capture a picture of prevailing practice across the organization, encourage conversations about both best practices and the reasons for prevailing practice, and inform strategic decisionmaking. By doing so, district leaders are developing an empirical means of assessing levels of practice across the organization, fostering learning opportunities through structured school visitations, creating a culture of inquiry around instruction and related practices, and developing a means of providing feedback to the organization to help it shape future support.

Several key tenets are fused into the way the snapshot system is designed. The snapshots contain at least five features that make them an important example of how to facilitate organizational learning. First, the snapshots are specifically linked to the organization's vision. Second, the snapshots infuse shared learning opportunities into the design of the system. Third, the snapshot system fosters a common understanding of the district's reforms. Fourth, the snapshots are a way to spread ideas throughout the district. Fifth, the knowledge accrued from the system contributes to the strategic direction of the organization. In these ways, the snapshot system represents the enactment of the idea of institutionalized organizational learning.

Linking to the strategic vision of the organization. The snapshot topics are carefully chosen to reinforce the central emphases of the district's vision for reform. The snapshot topics are all focused on the key components of the district's framework for the implementation of standards, which embodies the reform vision. Through 2005, snapshots have covered at least some part of all five framework topics, with the heaviest emphasis on academic performance. By explicitly connecting the snapshot topics to the areas of interest in the district's framework, district leaders were emphasizing their priorities. One regional superintendent explained his perception of the effect of the snapshots on principals' attention to standards: "I think for the first time, we've got principals that have started paying attention to [standards]. I think some maybe thought that this too was going to go away. But I think once you start creating a vehicle that is going to be consistent in the monitoring piece, people then respond because they know this is important." Thus, the snapshots raised the level of awareness of and attention to the district initiatives, signaling the district's priorities to school leaders and faculty members.

Infusing shared learning opportunities into the design of the system. Adults learn in many different ways and in many different situations. When we think of professional development, we tend to limit our attention to formal professional development occasions, as opposed to nontraditional yet powerful learning experiences. Shared learning opportunities that are part of regular work but outside the formal professional development structures are also powerful mechanisms for both individual learning and the shared experiences that create common understanding. These "noncanonical learning opportunities" (Brown & Duguid, 1991) gain some of their power through the complex integration of individual, social, and institutional learning. One of the most persistent findings from interviews with the snapshot data collectors was the extent to which the entire snapshot experience—from the scrutiny of the rubrics to the school visits to the examination of the snapshot results—provided a powerful learning opportunity for those involved.

The snapshots created three very different but mutually reinforcing and purposeful learning opportunities for organization members. First, the training sessions for new rubrics became important professional development opportunities for the snapshot data collectors. In advance of using a rubric new to the district, the data collectors would get together, review the rubrics and evidence forms, break out to practice their application in a small group of three to four schools, and then reconvene to compare ratings and discuss how the snapshots went and make suggestions for fine-tuning the rubrics and evidence forms. Many of the data collectors lauded the value of the training sessions and how they deepened their understanding of the snapshot topics. "The training sessions really helped me to understand what the district was trying to get at with its emphasis on standards and student work," said one snapshot data collector, an elementary school principal. "I never thought of this [the snapshots] as professional development, but I found those trainings so much more valuable than the other district training sessions," said a middle school principal.

Second, the cross-school visitations that occur as part of the snapshots became valuable professional development opportunities for both the visitors and the visited. These visits created the opportunity to share ideas about how to help improve instruction and provided direct observation of different approaches to teaching and learning that served as points of comparison and reflection on how to improve one's own leadership. One principal said she felt the visitations gave her a perspective on how other schools were approaching similar issues: "You come back to your building after you've done a visitation like that and you learn from that experience, and so, okay, I know I need to do this or don't need to do that, or I've not done that very well . . . but certainly you come back and you do realignments—that's what the process is about."

The analysis of the snapshot results at monthly principal meetings presented a third learning opportunity. One of the regional directors commented on sharing information facilitated by the snapshot visits: "I think it is especially valuable to hear conversations between principals from different regions about what they saw and what their understanding was and what their training has been and how they have accomplished things, especially with moving their teachers, because I think really the most difficult part is not the presentation of information, it's having staff to adopt it, and how do you get that to occur. So it's been helpful to see principals exchange information."

Fostering a common language and shared understanding across the district. A key component of organizational learning is the development of a shared language and commonly held set of beliefs across an organization (Daft & Huber, 1987). According to Strata (1989), organizational learning grows out of shared insights, knowledge, and "mental models" that build on past knowledge and memory. Ginsberg (1990) had a similar cultural conception of organizational learning that involved "the synthesis of a diverse set of assumptions or beliefs into a commonly shared understanding."

The snapshots acted as a means to spread the language of reform across the district. Through the rubrics and the visits Duval County leaders were giving teachers and school leaders a vocabulary with which to develop a common meaning and deeper understanding of reform. Developing a common vocabulary to discuss current and desired practice is a large reform step in itself because it creates a foundation for problem-solving interactions.

Given the size of Duval County (150 schools, about 7,500 teachers), developing a shared understanding both within and across schools is particularly challenging. And yet, this is what the snapshot process seemed to have facilitated. Several participants described how the snapshots had provided a common language with which to engage each other about the district's reforms. One district administrator, for example, discussed how the snapshots provided a mechanism for spreading what he called a "common platform" across the district:

> It certainly now gives a common platform for discussion. For example, the next piece dealing with safety nets. Now we have been talking about safety nets and encouraging schools to do safety nets, but now I think we can take those particular questions [referring to rubrics and evidence forms] as I work with and visit other schools to talk about safety nets. This allows us to have the same kind of dialogue and conversation with principals across our region. I think that's very helpful to me. Now we have the same platform and I'm not on one platform with one principal and on another platform with another.

The snapshot rubrics in particular created a means of disseminating a common language for the district's reforms across the schools in Duval County. As one district administrator commented, "The snapshot rubrics have been very helpful as talking points when I go talk to administrators, principals. And I think they've helped teachers. It's been helpful to teachers as any rubric would . . . be in learning what we're looking for. It has given us a common theme, a common goal."

Cross-pollinating ideas. Organizational theorist George Huber postulated that an important component of organizational learning was "the processing of information in order to change the range of potential behaviors" (1991). Another theme that emerged from analyses of the snapshot design was how the system became a means for sharing ideas across the district. Discussions of the snapshot results at the district's monthly principal meetings were designed to facilitate conversations rather than to simply present results to principals. The district's five regional directors were coached to facilitate an examination of the results with principals in their region in order to arrive collaboratively at conclusions about the meaning of the results and to brainstorm actions based upon their findings.

These debriefing sessions between the data collectors and the principals of the visited schools became a catalyst for professional conversations. One district administrator said,

> I noticed there was a lot of talk about best practices between the administrators, what's working what's not working, what I've tried. They get off subject of the snapshot a little bit because they're saying, "Well, how did you get them to do that? What do you say when they say this?" A lot of powerful talk goes on in those that's not really about the snapshot. It creates a moment for more collegial conversations.

Principals also reported that they learned from the experiences of other schools. One regional director explained, "The most positive thing that happened was they connected with a school that has two or three more years of training, and they will visit and do some together. So I think it was a very positive thing to connect one school with the other for them to support and help each other." An elementary school principal saw the experience of visiting another school as tremendously beneficial in terms of gathering new ideas: "The snapshot has been an amazing learning experience. It is so eye-opening to visit schools with other principals and see how they are implementing standards. I have learned so much and am able to take this back to my faculty and work on our own implementation efforts."

Influencing strategic direction. Finally, the snapshots are an important illustration of institutionalized organizational learning in that the findings emerging from them influence the district's strategic direction. As district leaders examined the snapshot results in their own meetings, they began to see implications for district professional development and sought to align the snapshot findings more closely with the sequences of principal leadership training and teacher training. One district administrator, for example, described how the snapshot results have increased the coherence of the district's training designs. She said that the results gave "information for what we need to do [in terms of] training." The district's leadership development designers also began to align the snapshot topics with leadership training, so that snapshots were conducted one to two months after topics were examined and discussed in leadership professional development sessions. Thus the snapshots acted as follow-up training and implementation for district reform strategies.

The snapshot results also influenced professional development decisions at other levels of the district. A few principals told us that they used the results of the visits to their schools to guide their within-school professional development decisions. "It [the snapshot system] is also creating or identifying the need for training," an elementary school principal told us. "A number of people haven't adopted [standards] because they need systematic training and assistance in getting there," she said. School coaches also reported that they were examining snapshot results for indications of what they should emphasize in their trainings with teachers in their schools.

District leaders also reported that the snapshot results gave them a better understanding of the extent to which the district's reform ideas were being practiced in schools and classrooms. Initial snapshots revealed, for example, that the implementation of some reform efforts had not taken place to the degree that district leaders would like. "We talk about standards, safety nets, and student work all the time, but I am always a little surprised to learn how superficially they are understood and used in some schools," said one regional superintendent. "So this is a reality check to see if what we think is happening is really happening and, if not, then to have policy discussions about what we should do about it."

THE INTEGRATION OF ORGANIZATIONAL LEARNING STRATEGIES TO SUSTAIN REFORM

It is ironic that American public school systems, the central societal means for educating the next generation of our citizenry, should have such a thin conception of their own learning. Most districts today are very staid in their attitude toward their own learning, growth, and change. Few give serious attention to the challenges of building the organization's capacity to continually improve its processes and outcomes. Perhaps this is because mature bureaucratic organizations tend to become set in their ways. This is tragically short-sighted because organizations that wish to sustain improvement efforts must contend with the challenges of improving their own learning.

In this chapter I have argued that the best hope for sustaining reform is persistent, targeted, multifaceted efforts to continually improve the ways to deliver and support instruction. As reforms start to mature in school systems, the inevitable problem leaders face is how to encourage teachers and school and district leaders to continually examine the efficacy of their work and to develop, refine, and reinvent systems for ongoing improvement. In the sustainability stage, the challenge for reformers moves from building an initial commitment to keeping people energized and focused on the work they have started. How do leaders encourage teachers within schools and the organization itself to continually grow and build its expertise so that reform becomes a catalyst for deeper, broader, and more penetrating change? The development of a culture of learning is one such potential perpetual motion machine.

To transform a school district into one that understands the value of its own deep learning in its organizational bones requires a profound cultural shift. Over time, any organization will produce its own rutted ways of doing things because of both the demands of production and the traditions and standardized procedures that produce entrenched practices. To shake people and organizations out of patterns of complacency and rote compliance, leaders must instill pride and excitement through the search for ever better ways of performing people's work. It is through this engagement with the challenges of improvement that people maintain excitement and pride in their work.

One way to consider the challenge of deepening and sustaining reform through organizational learning is to view the organization's task as threefold: disseminating, constructing, and creating knowledge. Knowledge dissemination consists of spreading knowledge about effective practices from a few with special expertise to members across the organization. Knowledge construction entails facilitating opportunities for employees to develop and test their own approaches to addressing challenges they face. Knowledge creation involves either developing or otherwise identifying new ways to address important issues and spread them across the organization. I contend that these levels of organizational learning are progressively more difficult to enact, but that sustained improvements are roughly related to how well organizations are able to address these three functions.

The first component of organizational learning is dissemination of the knowledge of a few to a broader group of people. This involves taking known information about effective practice and spreading it throughout the organization so that it broadly influences everyday work. This type of learning usually occurs through formal professional development opportunities in which deeply knowledgeable individuals work with participants so they can understand and implement particular approaches, use particular skills, or adopt particular practices in their worksites. There are also other avenues that can be used to disseminate knowledge across an organization, beyond formal professional development. In Duval County, for example, the snapshot rubrics were used to specify different levels of practice and were broadly distributed across the organization. In business, knowledge management tools such as Yellow Pages or intranet sites that give employees access to others with particular expertise (Pawlowsky, Forslin, & Reinhardt, 2001). Even though this is the first level of organizational learning, it is still challenging because there are no widely accepted and foolproof ways to transfer knowledge and expertise between individuals, particularly such complex tasks as instructional practice in loosely coupled organizations, such as education systems.

The second component of organizational learning is knowledge construction, which involves creating opportunities for groups of individuals with similar jobs to grapple with the challenges and implications of their work in order to develop a deeper, shared understanding of their craft and to identify and experiment with solutions to common problems. The constructed knowledge may or may not be new knowledge to the organization, but it is new and meaningful to those that constructed it. The knowledge construction component of organizational learning is based on the theory that valuable and meaningful knowledge is constructed by individuals, abetted by interactions among peers in groups, rather than simply transferred through knowledge dissemination activities (Wenger, 1998). Knowledge construction is a disciplined activity that must be organized and facilitated, at least initially, so that groups can identify important problems, develop reasonable solutions, and suggest ways to test those proposed solutions. Knowledge construction activities can be conducted within professional learning communities that have a particular purpose. These learning communities are tightly structured to identify particular problems of practice and develop hypothesized solutions that can be tested through structured inquiry and experimentation. These are distinguishable from the more general activities of professional learning communities, like the book talks that were described by Duval County faculty members. While professional learning communities that are focused on particular problems of practice may read and discuss books together, the books will be selected with a particular purpose that is connected to the task of the community inquiry.

The third element of organizational learning consists of the creation of new knowledge that is spread across an organization. New organizational knowledge is those ideas and practices that are distinctly new to the organization and that help members carry out their work more efficiently. Created knowledge can come from within the organization or from the outside. The structured sharing of new knowledge and new ways of practice across an organization is what makes created knowledge organizational and what distinguishes knowledge creation from knowledge construction. Whereas constructed knowledge may be new to the small group from whence it emerged, it does not become created knowledge until it is commonly shared across the organization. Thus, ideas that grow out of knowledge constructed by the inquiries of professional learning communities can become created knowledge if that knowledge is understood and used across the organization. It is the challenge of organizational leaders to identify new knowledge and create mechanisms to distribute it across the organization and to ensure that it is applied effectively. The snapshots in Duval County provide one small example of knowledge creation, in that best practices were identified across schools and then disseminated through conversations at monthly principals' meetings and infused into district professional development. Well-designed institutional learning mechanisms can surface new knowledge within an organization, and foster both individual and social learning opportunities.

The path to sustaining educational reform is undoubtedly the road less traveled. It takes prodigious effort and persistence to get enough meaningful instructional change rolling across a school system to even get to the gates of sustainability. But once there, engaging members of the organization in their own learning is the most promising path to creating the energy for change over time. By disseminating, constructing, and creating knowledge through interconnected individual, small group, and institutional learning activities, educational leaders can make all the difference.

7

The Role of the School District in Instructional Improvement

The challenge of this book thus far has been to organize and distill the lessons from Duval County's experience in order to reveal the implications of the school district acting as the central support organization for widespread instructional improvement. In this penultimate chapter, I seek to move beyond Duval County's particular circumstances to consider more generally what role, if any, the school district should play in public education in the twenty-first century. Is the district an anachronistic white elephant in the face of today's formidable educational challenges? Would some of the district's traditional support functions be delivered more effectively by other types of education support organizations, or even by being left entirely to schools? Or, should the district continue to play a fundamental role in educational reform, and if so, what should that role be? If the goal is to provide high-quality learning opportunities for all students, regardless of the economic circumstances of their parents or community, then the questions are, how can educational support organizations best facilitate reaching that goal, and what role is the school district best suited to play in meeting this challenge? This chapter is dedicated to answering these questions.

This chapter is organized into four parts. It begins by framing the problem facing today's school districts: the inherent frictions associated with the simultaneous roles of authority, support, and brokerage that districts must attempt to balance. Then, in order to begin to reconceptualize the district's role, I divide the dimensions of school support for instructional excellence into eleven essential functions. Discussion of these functions illuminates the intertwined political, organizational, and instructional challenges that districts face. I consider next whether schools are best served by centralized support or whether they are better off operating independently. And finally, after organizing the functions of education support into three convenient categories—managerial, political, and instructional—I briefly discuss each, considering whether districts, as traditionally constituted, are able to provide exemplary support for schools across this array of functions. I conclude that there are some functions for which districts are essential, others for which they are interchangeable with other types of support organizations, and still other functions for which they are fundamentally inadequate. Focusing further on the instructional functions, I break instructional support down further into the tasks of service and orchestration. I contend that service tasks are best done by districts in partnership with other education support organizations, which have greater resources and the expertise to develop the necessarily sophisticated curricular and training interventions for teachers. School support however, cannot be completely outsourced; local support organizations must assume the essential role of orchestrating the many components of instructional reform that coalesce in schools and classrooms.

TENSIONS INHERENT IN THE CURRENT DISTRICT ROLE

The tangle of organizational responsibilities that districts currently shoulder make their role in the effective functioning of schools a formidable one. Perhaps the main reason districts have such a challenging time supporting schools is because of the diversity, ambiguity, and incongruity of their multiple roles. By laying out the assorted array of functions that districts commonly undertake, and considering all that goes along with each of these functions, one can more readily see the challenge of excelling in delivering this set of responsibilities.

At the heart of the district's challenge is the difficulty of finding an appropriate stance on its multiple roles of authority, support, and brokerage with the external environment. Each of these roles requires the districts to assume a different relationship with schools and the wider world, at times putting these roles in conflict. As the authority with the power to hold schools accountable, districts may tend to control and rule on schools' efforts. In a supporting role with the responsibility to help schools improve, districts must take a different position, encouraging and nurturing the efforts of school faculties. As brokers between schools and external providers, intent on introducing new ideas into schools and classrooms, districts must play the part of the matchmaker and chaperone. These roles often conflict with one another and require different, often incompatible, skill sets for district leaders.

The uneasy relationship between authority and support is particularly prickly. Much has been written about districts becoming more customer-oriented and supportive of schools (Clement, 2002; Conyers, 2002; Olebe et al., 1992), thereby changing the dynamic of the traditionally hierarchical, often bureaucratic relationship between the two. But this proposed adjustment underemphasizes the incongruity of the difficult interactions between authority and support. It is often difficult for authority figures to provide support because of the antithetical mindsets between ruling (authority) and serving (support). Furthermore, by taking responsibility for providing support, an authority becomes partly responsible for performance, thereby putting itself in the awkward position of being both the *target* and the *agent* of accountability. By distancing itself from the target of its support an authority may clarify its accountability role, but doing so reduces the quality of its support. Alternatively, the stronger the bond created through a support relationship, the more responsibility is shared, which makes it more difficult to maintain authority.

The dual roles of authority and support also have a confounding effect on the level of relational trust between districts and schools. Relational trust is the level of respect, regard, integrity, and perceived competence one party has toward another, and it is the mainstay of productive work in schools and a key resource for reform (Bryk & Schneider, 2003). The hierarchical authority relationship between schools and districts reduces levels of relational trust. As long as districts hold the power to enforce sanctions on schools, it is in a school's interest to withhold problems from the district for fear of reprisal. The support relationship, on the other hand, encourages schools and districts to candidly discuss performance and implementation problems so that the district can provide, and schools can take advantage of, the most targeted assistance possible.

When districts act as brokers between external providers and schools, they may find themselves in the awkward position of diminishing their authority. This is the effect that some leaders in Duval County felt as America's Choice began working directly with schools to implement instructional reforms. In this situation, expertise traveled directly from the outside provider to the schools, bypassing the district. Yet the district remained in the awkward position of maintaining responsibility for monitoring implementation and holding schools accountable. In order to enforce accountability, districts must gain the expertise to monitor implementation effectively. The credibility of any authority resides in both its formal position and its knowledge and expertise. District expertise may be undermined by relying on an external partner to deliver reforms to schools. If districts are to monitor implementation, support school improvement, and hold schools accountable for their progress, they must have the expertise necessary to distinguish between different levels of implementation. In the traditional model, where districts control intervention and training, they have the expertise, and schools are the recipients of that expertise. But in situations in which expertise comes from external providers, the district can potentially lose credibility in that it has responsibility for implementation yet lacks the expertise to evaluate the level of implementation.

Brokerage may also create confusion as to the district's support role. The concept of outsourcing is a bad metaphor for a productive transaction between a district and an external provider. Implicit in the concept of outsourcing is that the one initiating the outsourcing (in this case the district) steps back and lets the vendor take over the task. But if the item being outsourced is a service, as it largely is in the case of instructional support, then the outsourcer needs to remain intimately involved because of the ongoing nature of the transaction and the need to sustain the support. The introduction of instructional innovation into schools really requires ongoing support that must be provided in concert between an external provider and a local entity. Therefore, the act of brokerage may give districts a false sense that they need not play a supportive role. Where they do provide support, there may be problems of clarity between their support efforts and those of the external provider. Districts cannot step aside because they would be abrogating an important component of the orchestration function. Nor can they supplant the external provider because, while they may be able to support the introduced set of practices, they are not in the position to commit

TABLE 7.1
Contrast among Three District Roles

	Authority	*Support*	*Brokerage*
Flow of Power	Top-down	Bottom-up	Lateral
Source of Legitimacy	Formal position	Assistance and expertise	Effective search
Implications for Trust	Discourages trust	Encourages trust	Trust neutral
Level of Required Expertise	Moderate	High	Moderate

the resources to research and development that gave the external provider a competitive advantage in the first place.

Some of the differences that arise from districts trying to play the simultaneous roles of authority, support provider, and broker are encapsulated in table 7.1. First, the flow of power is distinct for each of these roles; as an authority, the district's power stems from its high position in the hierarchy. From a support perspective, the district's power flows from a peer relationship with schools. As a broker, the district's influence flows laterally to both schools and providers.

The source of district legitimacy also differs depending on which of the three roles it is enacting. As an authority, district legitimacy comes from its formal position of power. As a support provider, district legitimacy arises from the expertise and usefulness of what it provides. As a broker, district legitimacy relies on identifying and bringing in programs and services that are perceived as useful and productive. These roles also have distinctly different effects on the trust relationships between schools and districts, as hierarchical relationships based on authority tend to reduce trust, while support relationships tend to encourage trust. Finally, playing a support role requires that districts develop a high level of expertise to provide meaningful assistance to schools, while authority and brokerage require far less.

These tensions in the district's current role suggest that we might increase its effectiveness by reconceptualizing its responsibilities. After all, there are many models for education support organizations available today, the traditional district being just one possible formulation. Education support in the future might come in combinations, ranging from single program deliverers to comprehensive support organizations. Education support organizations could include curriculum and professional development organizations, like those providing mathematics and science materials and training; comprehensive school reform providers, like America's Choice or Success for All; intermediary organizations, like the Boston Plan for Excellence or the El Paso Collaborative; subject-matter networks, like the National Writing Project; or other nontraditional educational organizations equipped to deliver instructional and organizational products and services. Any of these could reasonably be considered as an alternative to some component of the prevailing school district. Schools of the future may be supported by an array of education support organizations, with the school district being just one of several.

Because I seek to take a fresh look at the merits and shortcomings of the traditional school district, I will curtail my use of the term "school district" for the rest of this chapter and focus instead on identifying the central tasks of education support organizations. Education support organizations may be local or not, education specialists or not, but they all provide support to schools in some important way. I will refer to districts only when describing what existing districts do. When I want to depict what a district-like organization might do in the future, I will refer to it as a local support organization.

A LAYER AWAY

While it may be legitimate to debate *what* students ought to learn in school, it should be indisputable that the mission of schools is to maximize that learning. The primary responsibility of teachers is to enhance student learning directly. The school district and its nonteaching employees are a layer away from direct service to students, but they play an important role nonetheless. Their job is to design, support, and facilitate the services that are provided directly to students. Just as many lawyers may never see the inside of a courtroom, many employees of a sports franchise are never in uniform on the playing field, and many military personnel may never step onto the battlefield, district personnel may rarely see the inside of classrooms. This does not diminish their importance, for teachers could not deliver instruction nearly as well without the support provided by district employees. Teachers need support to deliver high-quality instruction. The point of these analogies is to emphasize that the delivery of education, like any complex endeavor, requires substantial organizational support. Thus, the question is not whether support is necessary, but how that support should be organized.

School districts grew out of certain historical circumstances that have helped to shape what they are today. Historically, districts evolved from having a political to an administrative emphasis. According to education historian David Tyack (1974), city schools before 1890 were dominated by school board politics. Districts at that time were essentially led by politically minded individuals who distributed patronage and provided political platforms for aspiring public servants. Progressive reformers of the early twentieth century tried to change the procedures of district decision making so that "expert managers" could run schools more efficiently and effectively. As Tyack notes, "The administrative progressives were notably successful. . . . Their success so framed the structure of urban education that the subsequent history of these schools has been in large part an unfolding of the organizational consequences of centralization" (p. 127). Districts thus became increasingly bureaucratic organizations intent on imposing professional management and institutional routines on the cottage industry of schooling.

Now is the time to rethink these well-trodden district roles and question the assumptions they are based on. Instead of accepting the district's historic role, we ought to take a step back and ask what supports are currently needed to enhance broad-scale improvement of the quality of teaching and learning, and then see to what extent the district merits a role in this endeavor. To do this we need to consider the dimensions of assistance to teachers and schools. Instead of thinking about school districts as monolithic entities, we should think of them as providers of the array of services and functions that schools need to deliver high-quality learning opportunities to students. District reconceptualization, therefore, would be derived from maximizing support to schools.

One way to consider school districts in a fresh light is to unpack the functions they ought to provide in the best of circumstances, and then to consider how those functions might be provided most effectively. To do this, we need to ask questions about support from the perspective of the schools and their constituencies, for it is the needs of the school and community that should drive what support for schools looks like. What they need may be quite different than what is currently provided. If we can identify the things that schools need to best serve students, then we can ask what types of organizations can best provide those services.

As we enumerate the elements of support needed by schools, keep a few questions in the back of your mind. Are schools better off functioning independently and providing or contracting out for their own support services, or are they better off coalescing under a single or an array of support organizations? If schools are better served by one or a group of support organizations, then what should the supporting entity or entities look like? These are questions I will return to later.

THE MAJOR FUNCTIONS OF EDUCATION SUPPORT ORGANIZATIONS

There are eleven major functions that one or more education support organizations must provide to schools in order to facilitate teaching and learning. To varying degrees, many of these are currently provided by school districts. It is also important to note that while these things are necessary to support high-quality schooling, they are not sufficient to ensure student learning. School faculties must still directly deliver learning opportunities to students to produce higher levels of performance. The following are roles to support excellent, not just basic, school functioning.

1. Manager of payroll and benefits for faculty and staff. A major task of education support is to oversee payroll and benefits for school employees. Typically, districts receive funding via local property taxes, as well as state and federal funding, the bulk of which goes to employee payroll, benefits, and associated costs. Education is a heavily service-oriented industry, and much of its funding is allocated to personnel and related costs. On average, money for salaries, employee benefits, and materials accounts for about 65 percent of school budgets (School Matters, 2005). Districts typically provide this service for schools so that they do not have to replicate this inefficient function.

2. Coordinator of materials, supplies, and resources. Schools require a vast number of materials to function properly. These include supplies for building construction and maintenance and for transportation, and smaller supplies ranging from furniture to photocopy machines to books to paper and pencils. Districts often coordinate, purchase, and deliver these resources. Much of the argument for centralizing these tasks has to do with economies of scale and efficiencies associated with education management. Having a single entity coordinate and provide these services for schools is more efficient and cost effective than having every school purchase and manage these things individually.

3. Representative of (and accountable to) the local community. Former speaker of the House of Representatives Tip O'Neill once famously observed that all politics are local. When it comes down to it, education is a similarly local enterprise and the school district plays a vital political role in our system of public education. Schools and districts derive their legitimacy and support from attending to local needs and preferences and serving constituents from their community. In doing so, they marshal political support for public education and affirm the importance of universal schooling that is the foundation of a democratic society (Gutmann, 1987). As many political scientists have noted, the school district serves as the bedrock of democratic representation and is one of the foundational institutions of our society. More pragmatically, districts are also fiscally accountable to local community members, since a substantial portion of their funding comes from local property taxes or other local funding sources. Even in the growing number of urban districts where school board members are mayoral appointees (see Kirst, 2002), school boards are immersed in the politics of the local community. Therefore, a major function of education support organizations is to respond to local preferences.

4. Fulfiller of state and federal education policy requirements. Districts commonly serve as the major conduit between state and federal policymakers and schools. There are several dimensions to this role. First, districts are often called upon to fulfill stipulations that are attached to state and federal funding, which accounts for anywhere from 38 percent to 98 percent of the income of local districts (National Center for Education Statistics, 2005). In twenty-four of the fifty states, more than half of funding comes from the state, with 59 percent the national average. Since other levels of governance have the responsibility to ensure that their funds are used appropriately, someone must track this, and it usually falls upon personnel from the district central office. Therefore, the completion of regulations and certification of participation in state and federally funded programs becomes part of the district's responsibility. Districts usually have one or several employees whose job it is to track and monitor school compliance with requirements attached to state and federal funding streams.

Second, districts are often called on to enact certain components of state and federal policy and, by doing so, themselves become a unit of accountability for state and district policymakers. Some states explicitly include districts in their accountability systems, while others do not (Carnoy & Loeb, 2003; Goertz & Duffy, 2001), but even in looser state accountability systems, districts feel responsible for the performance of their schools (Weinbaum, 2005). Since the purpose of external accountability is to monitor the performance of an entity and provide rewards or sanctions depending on performance, it would seem that districts, because of their role in supporting schools, should be included in local educational accountability. However, there is nothing inherent in accountability that would preclude states from holding schools directly accountable for performance or transferring accountability to a different support organization.

Third, districts interpret policies from above. Policy researchers have long noted the "translation" role of districts in local enactment of state and federal policy. Cohen and Hill (2001), for example, found considerable variation in districts' interpretation and enactment of California state policies around mathematics reforms. Spillane (2004) examined nine Michigan districts and found that district leaders played a major role in the interpretation and implementation of state standards, assessments, and curriculum frameworks. The "sense-making" of local actors has a major effect on the enactment and influence of state and federal policy initiatives.

5. Developer of curriculum and related materials. Districts have a long history of developing the materials that teachers use in their classrooms and defining the sequence by which those materials are used. While there are many definitions of curriculum, there is an established set of materials and documents that districts commonly compile to provide guidance and resources to teachers. These often include such things as objectives for teachers; identification and recommendation of best practices; the scope and sequence of lessons within units; and the array of materials, which includes textbooks, tasks and kits, lesson plans, pacing guides, and assignments. The ubiquity of state standards has somewhat transformed the district's role, detailing a set of things children should know and be able to do. But there is a lot of space between state standards and the daily activities of teachers in classrooms. This is the realm of curriculum.

6. *Provider of professional development.* Building the capacity of teachers and school leaders to deliver powerful instruction is a major need of schools, as demonstrated in chapter 3 of this book. Currently, teachers participate in relatively little professional development. While districts typically spend anywhere from 3–7 percent of their budgets on professional development for teachers (Miles, Odden, Fermanich, & Archibald, 2005), district professional development only amounts to a handful of days each year. A 2000 survey of a nationally representative sample of mathematics and science teachers, for example, found that 81 percent of teachers of grades 5 through 8 and 65 percent of teachers of grades 9 through 12 participated in fewer than fifteen hours of in-service professional development in their subject area annually (Smith, Banilower, McMahon, & Weiss, 2002).

These numbers no doubt mask the complexity and variation of the professional development situation in districts across the nation, but it is clear that districts remain the predominant deliverers of professional development for teachers. A spring 2005 statewide survey of a random sample of New Jersey teachers, for example, found that 91 percent had attended at least five hours of district professional development in the previous year. By contrast, only 52 percent had attended a workshop outside of their district (Firestone & Hirsh, 2006).

The provision of high-quality, aligned professional development for teachers and school leaders raises a number of issues for education support organizations. Professional development is becoming more sophisticated and connected to particular programs and curricula, less generic. Professional development is increasingly being embedded in the fabric of school life through such ongoing and intensive activities as coaching, lesson studies, and study groups. Some entity needs to plan and facilitate these activities.

7. *Searcher for ideas, high-quality materials, and effective practices to bring into the system.* Organizational improvement is built on the infusion of new ideas and better ways of doing things. Even in situations where there is a clear need for external materials, support, or different strategies, school personnel often do not have the time or perspective to scan the educational landscape in search of programs, materials, or resources to address their need (Gross, Kirst, Holland, & Luschei, 2005). This challenge is made more complex by the inherent difficulties in the education industry; namely that good information is difficult to come by and measurement problems often obfuscate the true merit of educational interventions. While there are several efforts underway to consolidate information about program quality (i.e., the What Works Clearinghouse, Comprehensive School Reform Quality Center), this is an endemic problem in education and will continue to be for the foreseeable future. Therefore, education decisionmakers will have to be highly skilled in their abilities to distinguish among differing levels of program quality, have a broad perspective on the educational landscape, and the time and resources to scour that landscape. These qualities are not likely to be found in schools, and some support entity that knows the schools well will have to provide it.

8. Monitor of program implementation. When school or district leaders identify a practice that they believe to be effective and invest in materials and resources associated with that practice, they should be interested in understanding the extent to which those practices are being adopted in schools and classrooms and the extent to which the programs and practices are contributing to student learning. This requires a monitoring and evaluation function. Because of the technical skills associated with credible monitoring and evaluation, this function will likely have to be carried out by members of an organization external to schools.

9. Facilitator of networks between schools as a mechanism for spreading and sharing knowledge. The task of education is time consuming for school leaders and faculties, and schools can become isolated in their efforts. For this reason, schools can benefit from structured opportunities that allow teachers and leaders to share with and learn from the experiences of their peers. According to Fullan (2005), "We can't change the system without lateral (cross-school and cross-district) sharing and capacity development" (p. 66). Schools can benefit from some external organization facilitating cross-school interactions that enable educators to share ideas and practices.

10. Organizer and deliverer of student performance results and other data to inform instructional and strategic decisionmaking. The collection and disaggregation of student performance data is becoming increasingly prevalent (Herman & Haertel, 2005). Teachers and school leaders are increasingly being asked to make decisions based on a range of data (Earl & Katz, 2002). Furthermore, the imperfect alignment between assessment for accountability purposes and for formative feedback to teachers is giving way to a host of formative and interim benchmark assessments that provide finer-grained information to teachers. Yet schools do not have either the resources or technical expertise to coordinate the increasing amounts of data available to them (Supovitz & Klein, 2003). The demands associated with the emphasis on data-driven decisionmaking raise a host of issues for education support organizations. First, someone must organize the data so that decision-makers have access to what they need in a usable form. Many districts are working with external groups to provide data management and warehousing functions (Wayman, Stringfield, & Millard, 2004). Second, increased technical capacity requires an increase in the human skills necessary to turn data into actionable knowledge. Both schools and support organizations need to build their skill in asking the right questions and making appropriate use of data to improve organizational performance.

11. *Coordinator of programs and resources,* Finally, but not least important, is the entity that coordinates the range of activities, resources, and policies that engage schools. One of the chief findings that came out of decades of programmatic research on educational reforms is that individual reforms are likely to be ineffective if they are implemented in isolation amid other incompatible efforts (Fuhrman, 1993). Somebody must consider the "fit" between programs and policies to encourage compatibility and synergy and ensure philosophical alignment. Therefore, a crucial role of an effective education support organization is to orchestrate among particular programs and to provide coherence across them.

These eleven elements represent the core functions of support for schools. Any attempts to assess the effectiveness of school districts or education support organizations must consider the effectiveness of the delivery of these functions. The reader should also recognize that there is no importance attached to the order of this list, nor to their relative scope and emphasis. Some of these functions are less time and resource intensive than others, while others are more strategic and therefore may require targeted attention rather than a high level of fiscal resources. As presently implemented by school districts, there is also considerable variability in the attention and emphasis paid to these functions. Some districts devolve instructional authority to schools and attend more to the administrative functions. Others attend heavily to their local communities and therefore emphasize the civic aspects of these functions. The data management function seems relative to district size, as many smaller districts lack the capacity to manage and manipulate student data. Precedent, priorities, culture, and personalities influence district emphases.

THE RATIONALE FOR CENTRALIZED SUPPORT FOR SCHOOLS

Now it is time to turn back to the question of whether schools are better off operating autonomously and procuring or contracting out individually for their own support services or whether they are better served by coalescing under some sort of support umbrella. Should schools throw off the district's protective but sometimes smothering cover and operate independently?

There are no doubt disadvantages for schools operating within a central framework. Many of the arguments that are put forward by charter school advocates summarize the restrictions that are often associated with centralized school systems. These include constraints on the hiring and firing of teachers, restraints on creativity that are connected with operating within a bureaucracy, and lack of parental choice as to what school their children attend (Bulkley & Wohlstetter, 2004). Schools would gain some flexibility by controlling their own support.

Yet, the eleven functions described above provide abundant evidence of why schools receive substantial benefit from the services that are provided by an effective education support system. Districts and other support organizations can provide multiple fiscal and maintenance services, such as payroll system management, supply procurement, and building maintenance, more cost efficiently than schools could individually. Districts and other support organizations can also give schools access to an array of instructional resources that they have the wherewithal and expertise to coordinate more effectively than schools can independently. Furthermore, a district can act as a buffer between the state and local political arenas and schools, thereby protecting schools somewhat from political turbulence. Thus there are clear economic, political, and knowledge benefits that accrue when schools operate within a system that provides them with information and services.

Support organizations also provide important equity benefits for schools. The centralized implementation of many of these functions contributes to a more equitable distribution of resources to schools than might result if they were on their own. The more resources and expertise are spread across a system, the more equitable education in the community is likely to be. In sum, the benefits of centralized support outweigh the constraints. While the disadvantages of centralized systems must be addressed, education support organizations on balance help to produce higher quality and more equitable education for all students in a community.

THE SHAPE AND FORM OF EDUCATIONAL IMPROVEMENT

Having established the importance of some centralized education support organization assisting schools in their efforts, I next explore what type of entity is best suited to play this role. One convenient way to reorganize the eleven central education support functions is to group them according to Larry Cuban's (1988) three dominant images of the superintendency. Cuban studied the historic roles of district leaders and identified three dominant responsibilities: administrative chief, negotiator-statesman, and instructional supervisor. Administrative chiefs were primarily committed to directing organizations that were dedicated to achieving the highest levels of productivity and efficiency. Negotiator-statesmen considered community relations and the political dimensions of their jobs to be especially integral. Instructional supervisors emphasized themselves principally as "teachers of teachers" (p. 112) and therefore viewed classroom support as a primary function. Extrapolating these roles out to the organization, the eleven central functions can be grouped into the managerial, political, and instructional, as shown in table 7.2.

Now, having simplified these eleven functions into three general areas, we confront the central questions of this chapter. First, what type of organization is best suited to deliver them? Second, what are the implications for the form of present day districts?

The managerial functions of education support organizations. The managerial functions are largely matters of efficiency and effectiveness. These are

TABLE 7.2
*Managerial, Political, and Instructional Functions of
Education Support Organizations.*

Managerial Functions of Education Support Organizations
- Manager of payroll and benefits for faculty and staff
- Coordinator of materials, supplies, and resources

Political Functions of Education Support Organizations
- Representative of (and accountable to) the local community
- Fulfiller of state and federal education policy requirements

Instructional Functions of Education Support Organizations
- Developer of curriculum and related materials.
- Provider of training and professional development.
- Searcher for ideas, high-quality materials and effective practices to bring into the system
- Monitor of program implementation
- Facilitator of networks between schools as a mechanism for spreading and sharing knowledge
- Organizer and deliverer of student performance results and other data
- Coordinator of programs and resources

by no means simple tasks, but they could just as easily be carried out by the current entity we call the school district as by any number of fiscal organizations. There are clearly economies of scale and organizational advantages to doing these tasks centrally for groups of schools, but what type of organization performs them is open to consideration. The organization that enacts them must be well versed in the functioning of schools, but the school district does not have to be the one delivering paychecks, coordinating employee benefits, and ordering supplies for schools. If it is more efficient and effective to outsource them, then there are no reasons not to. Whether this is conducted by a public or private organization seems largely a matter of quality of service and cost effectiveness.

The political functions of education support organizations. What I am calling the two political functions of local education are somewhat distinct from each other, so let us consider them separately. First is local political representation. As the local representative of public education, the school district plays an integral role in marshalling public support for education and instilling the values of civic involvement in both the community and students. The roots of local political involvement in education run deep in American political and civic tradition and are one manifestation of how communities imbue their values and priorities into society. There are long-established precedents for local control of education, and school boards have an enduring history as both the local expression of community preferences and a bedrock component of America's system of democratic institutions. Because values are inevitably instilled in children through their education, communities have both the right and the duty to help shape their children's educational experiences. The school board, whether elected or appointed, is the voice of that local expression. While the line between board policy and the superintendent's managerial responsibility is often fuzzy, which contributes to the uneasy relationships that often exist between district leaders and school board members, the purpose of the school board is to express community preferences. Removing the district from this equation would dilute the community's voice and weaken the public influence on the education of children. There seems to be no legitimate alternative to some form of local support organization as the expression of the local community.

The second aspect of the political function of education support organizations is as an accountability mechanism for state and federal policy. There is a managerial component of this task that, much like payroll, could be handled by any type of education support organization. Fulfilling the requirements and protocols that document the appropriate use of state and federal funding, for example, could be done by any type of education support organization. Yet once it is involved in and becomes responsible for some aspects of this chain, the support entity also becomes an interpreter, and thus an enactor, of policy. In the current system, the school district is identified as a target of accountability precisely because of the influential role it plays in supporting schools. If the district's responsibilities are reconfigured, then whatever organization is playing the support role is likely to become a target of accountability.

The instructional functions of education support organizations. In decomposing the functions of the education support organizations, I have identified seven functions that I have categorized as instructionally related. These are (1) searching the complex external environment to identify new programs, materials, and ideas that match need, beliefs, and local context; (2) developing curriculum materials; (3) providing high-quality and aligned professional development to teachers and school leaders; (4) monitoring fidelity of program implementation; (5) organizing and presenting an array of data for schools to use to inform teaching and improve performance; (6) facilitating constructive interactions and engagement across schools; and (7) coordinating the range of programs and offerings that are available to schools so that they reinforce, rather than contradict, each other.

These are not always cleanly and obviously instructionally related. While some of them are directly connected to instructional emphasis, others may be in support of instruction. So, for example, consider a school's need for a student discipline program. You may or may not call this an instructionally related issue. Student behavior certainly influences the learning environment of schools, and a code of behavior is a necessary precursor to instruction—if classrooms and schools are not safe and secure learning environments, then teaching and learning cannot take place. But wherever you place this task, somebody must be responsible for identifying the interventions schools use. In this case, identifying the appropriate program, providing professional development, monitoring implementation, creating opportunities for school personnel to discuss their experiences, and ensuring that the selected program or approach is consistent with other initiatives at the school are crucial for effectiveness. I have already argued that school leaders are neither well trained nor positioned to coordinate search and implementation and that there are advantages to some type of support organization working with schools to identify and support such an intervention.

We can break down the seven instructional support tasks further into two sets: one set involves tasks of orchestration, the other set, service-oriented tasks. These are shown in table 7.3. The search function, program monitoring, network facilitation, and coherence are more tasks of orchestration. They require the education support organization to take a more global view of the integration of materials and supports that schools need to use their resources effectively in order to provide the best possible learning environments and opportunities for students. The development of curriculum materials, provision of professional development, and organization of student performance data, on the other hand, are more technically oriented services that need to be provided to schools. These services require a different kind

TABLE 7.3
Decomposition of Instructional Support Tasks

Orchestration Tasks	Service Tasks
1. Searching	1. Curriculum development
2. Program monitoring	2. Training and professional development
3. Network facilitation	3. Data provision
4. Coordinating program and resource coherence	

of expertise than the orchestration tasks. Service tasks require sophisticated, in-depth know-how about particular topics.

Let us return to the question of whether these instructional functions are best provided by districts or some other form of support organization. I will argue that the orchestration-related instructional functions are best delivered by a district-like local support organization, while the service-related instructional functions are best developed and delivered by external providers but supported through partnerships between external providers and local support organizations.

Orchestration tasks are best performed by a local support organization. The set of orchestrating tasks includes searching for appropriate ideas, materials, practices, and programs; monitoring program implementation for feedback and improvement purposes (not accountability); facilitating cross-school networks; and coordinating program and resource coherence. These tasks are best done by a local support organization that knows schools and the community well, and has the geographical proximity to provide nuanced and enduring support.

Of course, the implementation of these tasks presumes that the local support organization, community, and schools see them as integral. There are many current situations where school districts do not see all or even some of these tasks as their purview. Districts that have a decentralized culture may not interpret these tasks as their responsibility. And we should not assume that this is a perspective held solely by the district, because many schools do not want districts to play these roles and resist efforts to constrain their independence.

However, as I have argued throughout this book, these are essential tasks for wide-scale school improvement. Furthermore, it is hard to imagine the orchestration tasks being carried out by anything but a local support organization. The provider of the orchestration tasks must be very familiar with local schools and have connections and insight into the neighborhoods the schools are serving. The provider of orchestration must be geographically close to the schools because the tasks of orchestration require frequent, individualized, and personal interaction.

These orchestration tasks also require the local support organization to develop several distinct attributes. First, and perhaps most important, they call for a more global outlook on the education industry and the perspective to navigate the national, and even international, educational landscape in order to identify and access ideas and resources. Second, they require the local support organization to develop a close and collegial relationship with schools. Third, they call for a diverse set of skills on the part of the local support organization, including the ability to match prospective solutions with school needs, the facility to develop and nurture networks that increase opportunities for identified good practices to travel across sites, the skill to identify practices that are faithful to the program design and provide constructive feedback on practices that are not, and the perception to see in what ways and to what extent instructional ideas and conceptions fit together and complement or conflict with each other. These attributes are not always close to the types of organizational skills valued and exercised by today's school districts. However, because of the close relationship the local support organization must maintain with schools and the community, a remodeled conception of the school district is uniquely qualified to play the orchestration role.

Instructional service tasks are best performed by external provider/local support organization partnerships. I have identified three instructional service tasks: developing curricular materials for schools, providing associated professional development for teachers and school leaders, and organizing data on which teachers and school and district leaders can base instructional and organizational decisions. The first two of these, in particular, cut to the core functions of education support organizations, which are providing materials for students and teachers to interact with and improving teachers' capacity to maximize students' learning opportunities in order to enhance learning to the greatest extent possible. The data function is a more recently emphasized function but is nonetheless a crucial component of instructional support and guidance.

Who should develop and provide these three service tasks? Historically, districts have developed materials and delivered the bulk of professional development to teachers. But these service functions are becoming increasingly sophisticated, technical, and expensive for local entities to develop and provide independently, and therefore the bulk of materials are best developed externally to districts and delivered via partnerships between external providers and local support organizations.

One might even go so far as to argue that recent experiences of external providers make the local provision of these services obsolete. The last twenty years of development of large-scale programs like textbook series and associated professional development, comprehensive school reform (CSR) programs, and a range of other intermediary organizations have demonstrated that school capacity-building can be delivered effectively by external providers, which often operate nationally. These external providers serve thousands of schools and are, in some sense, "virtual school districts." They provide instructional materials, resources, training, and support to large groups of teachers and schools; the services they provide are essentially synonymous with many components of the district's traditional function.

Yet, experience has shown that there are severe constraints to completely outsourcing these service functions. School reform models introduced externally rarely have staying power in schools. For example, a study of Success For All, the most widespread CSR program, found that after five years, only four of the thirteen schools were still implementing it (Datnow, 2002). Other external providers have similar track records. So why aren't schools generally persisting with these external networks and models? In some cases this is because there is no external pressure to persist with a particular approach in the absence of the orchestration of a local support organization. Cost is another possible factor; many external reform designs are expensive for schools and come with no mechanism for longer-term sustainability. In other cases, schools simply grow out of a particular approach and are ready to search for a different approach due to shifting needs or a changing student population.

While there are good reasons not to completely outsource the instructional service tasks to external providers, there are also powerful arguments against keeping these functions entirely within local support organizations. From this and other studies, it seems abundantly clear that districts as support organizations for schools do not have nearly as much instructional expertise as many of the external providers. Districts today are just not structured or equipped to efficiently accumulate and effectively package instructional expertise as are external providers. While there was more emphasis on the development of curriculum within districts twenty years ago, movement toward cost efficiencies have forced most district spending to be allocated to the classroom, thereby cutting many district curriculum development positions. While external providers depend on the marketplace to vet the quality of their products and services, districts have no comparable development mechanism. There is a cost consideration here as well. As Duval County discovered in its materials development process, it could not produce quality instructional materials and training guides for teachers nearly as cost effectively as it could if it purchased them from an external provider. This suggests that external providers can be more economical than local support organizations in this task.

External providers are also generally better situated to develop professional development materials and deliver training, at least initially, to teachers and school leaders than local employees because they are likely to have more widespread experience and broader technical expertise. This is not to denigrate the skills and competence of local providers, but external organizations are able to attract talented people and bring substantial resources to bear on developing professional development materials and associated training.

The specialized advantages of external providers are even more apparent if we focus on the third service task, the development of data management systems that provide performance information to schools and teachers. External data system providers can capitalize on their experience and specialized technical expertise to provide sophisticated systems beyond the capacity of all but a few current districts. While Duval County was able to develop a relatively sophisticated data delivery system internally, most districts lack the capacity to do this well or efficiently. The development of data systems to deliver information to schools and teachers is a relatively replicable task (although variable across states and districts with different assessments and breakdowns of data) that external providers are better equipped to develop. The data from these systems must, of course, be interpreted and acted upon locally.

In this conception, "partnership" is the operative word, and both provider and district must approach the relationship as such. Local support organization leaders literally cannot afford to simply step aside and let an external provider work with schools to implement a program. They must start from day one to build an infrastructure to support implementation from different angles than the provider. Among the questions to consider are: How does support fit into the existing professional development structure of the local support organization? How does the existing coaching structure, if any, in the local support organization work with the provider's services and materials? How do external programs fit into program monitoring and accountability structures within the local support organization? How are leaders at different levels of the organization trained to both understand and support external programs? There is a balance to be found in the most effective delivery of the three service tasks, which is why partnerships between external providers and local support organizations are essential. These partnerships are likely the best option for supporting instructional improvement in schools most effectively.

The unique, long-lasting relationship between Duval County and the National Center on Education and the Economy has created the opportunity to explore the lessons and implications of a long-term relationship between a district and an external provider. Here are some of the lessons I take from their partnership:

1. Local/external partnerships can be productive precisely because they can bring new ideas into schools and districts. Schools and districts can be relatively insular organizations, and external providers bring fresh perspectives and different formulations into them, thereby infusing them with new ideas and practices. In this case study, America's Choice brought many new ideas about the organization and delivery of instruction into Duval County that existed only in isolated pockets, if they existed in the district at all. Many of these ideas had to do with integrating instructional practices into a coherent set, so that while some of these practices may have been familiar to teachers, their integration into an instructional system was innovative.

2. Local support organizations must match the offerings of external providers to their instructional philosophy. One of the particular challenges district leaders face if they seek to develop one or more partnerships with outside instructional service providers is to match the instructional philosophy that underlies the external provider's program with the needs of their schools and community. There are several organizational and cultural dimensions to this matching process.

First, district leaders must address coherence both across content areas and grade levels. Students who are fed formulas and rules in one subject area and asked to construct understanding in another are likely to suffer from the contrast. Similarly, students who are trained with one approach at one grade level will be less prepared to use a different approach at higher grade levels. Thus, instructional programs must "fit" together both pedagogically and temporally. Second, an external provider's instructional philosophy must be rich enough to allow for both teacher variation and growth. At any one time, teachers in a system will have widely divergent capabilities to handle a particular instructional approach and will embrace the approach differently (see chapter 4). Thus, programs must contain, and district leaders must embed, different levels of support and flexibility for teachers to use the instructional approach. The approach must also be flexible enough to allow teachers to grow into it such that they do not become bored or constrained. District leaders should not think of instructional programs as "consumables" that they try on and discard like old clothes. They should instead carefully identify programs they can grow into and wear comfortably over several years.

3. External providers are better equipped to develop materials than local support organizations. Districts should not be in the curriculum materials development business, except for supplementary materials. The development and updating of aligned instructional materials is a large and expensive undertaking. External providers, because they have both the human and financial resources, are better positioned to produce high-quality instructional materials more cost effectively than school districts. This is not to say that all materials produced by external providers are of high quality, but they are likely to be better than what is "homegrown." Furthermore, external providers can continue to refine and expand their materials, while district efforts are more likely to become static after an initial professional development push.

4. Professional development must be a joint venture between local support organizations and external providers. Since professional development is largely training on the implementation of materials or processes, external providers are initially more adept with these and therefore better suited to train teachers and coaches on their instructional applications. At the same time, external providers need real-world sites to continue to develop and refine materials, and districts that enter into deeper relationships with providers may contribute intellectual capital to that work. Over the longer term, as instructional support is an ongoing process, districts must work with external providers to develop the capacity to provide the nuanced support necessary for teachers to become increasingly skilled. This leads to the next lesson.

5. Partnerships must explicitly build local capacity to provide support to schools. Partnerships between districts and external providers need to build the skill levels of both school faculties and district personnel. Therefore, the partnership should include initial direct assistance from the external provider to school personnel, as well as capacity-building at the district level, in order to allow districts to take over at least some school support over time. Thus, from the start there must be a common understanding that support from the external provider will shift over time as an intervention matures. While the district may assume more school-based training and support responsibilities, in a long-running partnership the provider will continue to introduce refinements and produce leading-edge training for those more experienced with the intervention.

6. External providers may encounter resistance from both the community and the local support organization. The tradition of local control over education runs deep, and there may be community resistance to external providers who are too high-profile in their coordination of schools. Community members may see this outsourcing as an infringement on their influence over education in their schools. Similarly, district leaders may not want to become too reliant on external providers because it would reduce their own authority. Part of this is the capacity-building that district leaders may feel they must control within their own organization, and part of this may be their desire not to be constrained by external organizations.

7. Self-sufficiency on the part of the local support organization and schools is a myth. There is no such thing as self-sufficiency for a school district. While district leaders may feel a strong need to wean themselves away from any reliance on external providers and become self-sufficient (see item 6 above), this is a fallacy. Districts will never be able to support a program the way the developer can. While the relationship between a district and a developer can evolve and levels of support can change over time, the turnover of faculty and district-level support staff is such that longstanding relationships should become the rule rather than the exception. From the district's perspective, this means that they must choose partners carefully for both stability and depth. A major partner or program that doesn't endure does no good to a district. Likewise, a program that does not have levels of depth is also shortsighted from a district's perspective. While the relationship may change over time and the services external organizations provide may mature and change, there will always be the need for ongoing interaction. Self-sufficiency is a myth in today's complex world, if it ever was possible, and both parties should recognize the advantages to enduring partnerships as long as there are opportunities for mutual benefit.

8. Local support organizations must manage their relationships with external partners. The interests of school districts and external providers are not always the same. External providers will naturally want districts to continue using their services, although these relationships mature and commitments may change and lessen over time. Thus, districts must exert some control over the extent and form of these partnerships. In particular, districts should urge external providers to continue to push implementation deeper in sites that adopt early, even as introductory implementation continues in new sites or with new employees.

These lessons will be valuable to local support organizations that undertake deep and enduring partnerships with external providers. In sum, I have argued that some of the education support organization functions may be outsourced, others are best carried out by local education support organizations that share many of the characteristics of the modern school district, and others are most successful when done in partnership between external providers and local support organizations.

SUMMARY

In this chapter I have argued that districts play a diverse and complex set of roles in supporting schools. I began with a discussion of the inherent conflicts among the roles of authority, support, and brokerage that districts have traditionally been asked to play. Each of these roles requires a different stance on the part of the district relative to schools. Next, I laid out the eleven major functions that I believe are needed to support schools as they help students achieve at high levels. I then considered whether these functions could be effectively carried out by individual schools, and concluded that schools were not equipped to do so and that some sort of education support organization was necessary. I then grouped the eleven functions into administrative, political, and instructional categories in order to consider whether districts were best equipped to carry them out, or whether some other education support organization was better suited to do so. Administrative functions, I argue, are largely matters of efficiency and could be carried out by either districts or other organizations. The political functions are twofold, one having to do with fulfilling state and federal requirements, the other with representing local needs. The former, I contend, could be fulfilled by an entity other than a district, but the latter is a largely local function. The instructional functions consist of a set of orchestration tasks and a set of service tasks. Orchestration tasks are best performed by a local support organization, while service tasks are best provided by external providers in partnership with local support organizations. This sets the stage for a discussion of the appropriate role of the school district in the twenty-first century, which is the focus of the final chapter of this book.

8

The Twenty-First-Century School District

School districts oriented toward sustained systemwide enhancement of teaching and learning are the key to widespread educational improvement in the twenty-first century. Despite their shortcomings, local school districts are still uniquely situated to play a critical role in improving American public education. As demonstrated in the previous chapter, the school district remains a prime mechanism for coordinating and building instructional capacity in large numbers of schools so that all students, regardless of heritage or situation, have high-quality learning experiences. The alternatives pale in comparison. While states serve important functions in terms of accountability and overall goal-setting, they lack the expertise and capacity to deliver the intensive, high-quality support schools need to meet performance goals. External providers or other types of intermediary organizations, while they have some unique advantages over districts and can make important contributions to the school improvement process, lack both the broad capacity to entrench improvement and the geographical proximity to sustain it. Individual schools cannot efficiently supply the resources and expertise to support their needs. Thus, while states, intermediate organizations, external providers, and individual school leaders play important roles in classroom improvement, local districts must orchestrate the delivery of resources to schools and lead the charge for systemwide improvement. Reconceived as local support organizations, school districts remain the best hope for enhancing the quality of teaching and learning for the next generation of Americans.

What could a district of the twenty-first century look like? In this final chapter I explore a reconceptualization of the district's role to better support improvements in teaching and learning. I argue that in order to achieve broad-scale improvement in the quality of education across schools in America, school districts must rethink their internal relationships with the schools within their purview and their external relationships with the state, the broader education industry, and the surrounding environment.

The central theme of this chapter is that school districts must evolve into organizations dedicated to supporting sustained improvement in the quality of instruction. To do so, districts must move along a continuum from essentially administrative organizations to teaching organizations to organizations that learn for the purpose of improving the quality of teaching in the system. This migration is depicted in figure 8.1.

In order to become a learning for teaching organization, a district must focus on enhancing the learning of organization members for the purpose of improving teaching. The rest of this chapter is devoted to providing a more complete picture of what such an organizational journey might entail and the implications for district leaders.

MOVING FROM AN ADMINISTRATIVE ORGANIZATION
TO A TEACHING ORGANIZATION

The utility of school districts for future generations of students ultimately rests on their ability to take the next steps in their historical development. In the nineteenth century, fledgling school districts were primarily politically motivated organizations (Cuban, 1988). In the twentieth century, in response to the dramatic growth in the demand for universal education and the need to professionalize their workforce and organization, districts became managers of the local education system and were devoted foremost to administrative efficiency. Districts at the dawn of the twenty-first century must become teaching organizations intent on supporting systemwide instructional excellence. Furthermore, they must strive to become "learning for teaching" organizations in which systematic learning for the purpose of improving and supporting instruction is embedded in the culture, practices, and routines of the organization.

FIGURE 8.1
Evolution of District Organization

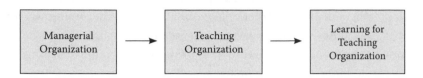

Moving from an administrative organization to a teaching organization means prioritizing instructional improvement over the managerial tasks of supporting schooling. Administration is still an important component of the district function, but it is done in the service of improving teaching and learning and does not crowd out the prominence of the latter. While leaders of teaching organizations will still attend carefully to administrative and political functions, they will not allow these responsibilities to become their primary activities; rather, they will view many administrative and political responsibilities as opportunities to reinforce their instructional priorities.

The challenges for leaders of teaching organizations are greater than for those preoccupied with administration, because they must resist the constant tug of noninstructional demands that vie for their attention. As we saw in chapter 2 with the example of the bus contract in Duval County, it is relatively easy, even for instructionally minded district leaders, for political and administrative situations to distract from instructional priorities. Leaders of teaching organizations must be constantly vigilant, skillfully preserving instructional attention and finding creative ways to refuel and redirect the organization to engage in instructional improvement. The careful decomposition and consideration of the different district functions, as laid out in chapter 7, may help teaching organization leaders think about the best way to integrate, manage, and balance the range of district responsibilities in order to develop and maintain instructional focus.

The payoff for districts that become teaching organizations is increasingly clear. There has been much evidence over the past decade suggesting that teaching organizations improve student learning. This study of Duval County is just one of a string of district-focused studies that reveal the promise and payoff of concerted instructional support. Districts such as New York's Community District #2 (Elmore & Burney, 1997); San Diego (Darling-Hammond et al., 2005), Charlotte-Mecklenberg and Sacramento (Snipes, Doo-little, & Herlihy, 2002), and Minneapolis and Aldine, Texas (Togneri & Anderson, 2003) are all documented improvement stories that hinge upon a district taking a distinct instructional emphasis; that is, becoming teaching organizations. These studies provide evidence that districts that engage in sustained instructional improvement efforts can enhance the learning outcomes for students across their systems.

The commitment to becoming a teaching organization still leaves plenty of tough decisions and challenges for school leaders. As I described in the introduction to this book, there are many ways district leaders could go about building a teaching organization. Leaders could encourage schools to adopt or create their own instructional interventions. They could promote one or multiple external providers to work with schools to implement externally developed school reform models. They could develop and specify their own instructional approach with varying degrees of coherence across subjects and grade ranges. Each of these approaches and countless others involve varying amounts of district specification as to what instruction should look like and demands different kinds and levels of district expertise in support of schools. Yet regardless of the level of instructional specification provided by the district, each of these approaches represents a vision for improving the quality of instruction. In the more centralized approaches, the district builds or adopts a particular conception of instructional quality. In the more decentralized approaches, the instructional vision may emanate from school faculties, but the district develops and implements a particular process for engaging school faculties in the challenges of instructional improvement. In either case, it is this vision for instructional improvement that distinguishes the teaching organization from an administrative one.

Regardless of how an instructional vision is formed, the challenge for leaders of teaching organizations is how to enlist virtually all schools and their faculties in the difficult work of instructional improvement. This entails providing teachers with the rationales, structures, and incentives to engage in improving their craft. In chapter 3, I described some of the particular techniques used by Duval County leaders in their efforts. Part of the success in Duval County can be ascribed to the levels of engagement they achieved across their 150 schools, as detailed in chapter 4. But even so, as we also saw in chapter 4, there was plenty of piecemeal adoption, superficial implementation, and outright rejection. Traditionally, the strategies of reform leaders have gained only partial and tentative engagement in improvement. In order to deepen reform, district leaders must make headway on a problem that has perennially bedeviled education reformers.

THE EDUCATIONAL DIALECTIC

Regardless of what tack reformers take to introduce and spread reform, they are bound to run up against what I call the educational dialectic. A dialectic is a process in which two seemingly contradictory and opposing ideas butt up against each other. The resolution, or synthesis, occurs as the two ideas are brought into harmony. The educational dialectic is the challenge of synthesizing the two prevailing yet paradoxical school improvement support strategies.

The myriad individual strategies that districts use to leverage school improvement can be boiled down into two opposing perspectives on how to design organizational systems most effectively in order to improve schools. One of these approaches, often called the top-down or control strategy, relies on the institution of a range of managerial mechanisms, including structured curricula, regimented school and classroom routines, and high-stakes accountability systems, to regulate classroom teaching and standardize student learning opportunities. The other, commonly framed as the bottom-up or commitment strategy, emphasizes the development of autonomous work arrangements for teachers who seek to support their professional judgment and increase their engagement in the tasks of instruction. Rowan (1990) called these two competing perspectives the control and commitment strategies. McAdams (2006) termed them managed instruction as opposed to performance/empowerment. Fullan (1994) identified them as the top-down versus bottom-up strategies for reform.

Each of these approaches has inherent benefits and shortcomings. The benefits of centralized reform strategies are that they allow for high-quality design because they can be shaped by a small group of knowledgeable people. They also allow for tighter quality control because they are standardized. They also can be more easily supported because they follow more predictable implementation patterns. However, the top-down or control strategy tends to spread reforms broadly but not deeply, eliciting uneven engagement and encouraging relatively superficial compliance rather than deep commitment. The imposition of reform denies participants the ownership that is necessary to build the deep engagement that produces meaningful change. The articulation of an instructional vision from the top of an organizational hierarchy or from a source external to the organization is essentially a control strategy, in that it specifies what teachers should do in the absence of their contributions and consent. Tactics that require faculties to vote on the introduction of externally introduced reforms are relatively superficial efforts to mitigate the shallow buy-in by participants in control systems.

The alternative approach, the bottom-up or commitment strategy, carries its own advantages and problems. One example of a more bottom-up approach is to encourage teachers and schools to engage in their own instructional improvement investigations and to support this process, rather than privileging any particular instructional philosophy. The merit of this approach is that it engenders faculty buy-in. This approach tends to stimulate pockets of fervent engagement, but it almost never reaches beyond those with sympathetic inclinations to engage members of the organization more broadly in a particular reform. Participants in such reforms often provide great energy and produce innovative solutions to nettlesome problems. However, this approach typically asks more of participants than can be regularized into a widespread adoption strategy. The downside of this approach is that it is difficult to support through a centralized infrastructure because it is impossible to gather the diverse instructional expertise to support a range of solutions. District leaders must choose their poison: they can go broad and relatively shallow, or they can go narrow and deep.

Duval County's reform efforts reflect an interesting mix of the commitment and control strategies. America's Choice, which later morphed into the district's standards-based reform effort, was a fairly well-specified instructional system, but one whose design required teachers to apply considerable professional judgment. The literacy program, for example, relied on the regularized approach of the workshop model yet asked teachers to structure their classes and create routines so they could confer individually with students, assess their levels of performance, and instruct them accordingly. This was a sophisticated system that created a set of specified and regular structures (i.e., control) but relied heavily on the professional decisionmaking of teachers (i.e., commitment).

The way Duval leaders chose to introduce reform into the district also suggests a combination of the control and commitment approaches. For example, there was a strong emphasis on America's Choice as the preferred system, yet district leaders stopped short of demanding that all schools in the district implement the model. However, once a school chose an approach, they were expected to implement it. Furthermore, district leaders infused into this model a series of commitment-style elements, most notably professional learning communities, which were intended to elicit the engagement of teachers and school leaders in their own improvement. A synthesis of the control and commitment strategies glimmers within this story.

There is a potential synthesis for the dialectic of the control and commitment strategies: an overall vision of instructional quality supported by structured inquiries at multiple levels of the organization that are designed to engage people to explore the implications of the guiding vision for their own work and practice. This approach encourages choice and engagement within the parameters of an overall perspective on what makes for effective instruction. An overall instructional vision is essentially a control strategy in that it specifies what instruction should look like. But within the specified boundaries, leaders can use a range of processes to encourage organizational members to incorporate the meaning of the vision in their practice. By doing this they enact a commitment strategy designed to engage teachers and others to diagnose, investigate, and resolve the problems and challenges they encounter as they seek to implement the overall vision. Through this synthesis of the commitment and control strategies, districts start to move from a teaching organization to a "learning for teaching" organization.

THE LEARNING FOR TEACHING ORGANIZATION

The resolution of the educational dialectic can be found in districts that move from having solely a district-directed instructional focus to combining it with the multiple ways to engage members at all levels of the organization in their own learning, which is characteristic of bottom-up reform. This still requires districts to develop an instructional framework that provides substantial guidance to teachers and school leaders and, at the same time, to develop a range of strategies that engage teachers and school leaders in identifying and working on the challenges that arise in their classrooms and schools as a result of their attempts to enact the instructional vision. By combining some level of district directedness with structured inquiry by teachers around the district instructional framework, districts are moving from a teaching organization to a learning for teaching organization.

This synthesis of the control and commitment strategies can be found primarily in the valuation of purposeful learning within the organization. Purposeful learning, as we shall shortly see, is structured inquiry by organizational members into what they determine are the central challenges that arise out of their work with the express goal of enhancing enactment of a larger instructional vision. In addition to purposeful learning, there are also several other qualities that distinguish learning for teaching organizations from teaching organizations. Learning for teaching organizations seek to infuse a learning ethos into their culture. They value and use evidence as a means to guide their improvement. They reorient their relationships to schools to provide better support for instructional improvement. They also rethink their relationships externally to the broader educational environment in order to improve the resources available to schools.

LEARNING FOR TEACHING ORGANIZATIONS VALUE PURPOSEFUL LEARNING

Districts that aim to build their capacity to serve as teaching organizations will almost gravitationally find that they need to expand professional development opportunities. Once a district seriously starts to bring its resources to bear on improving the instructional opportunities of all students, it will the need to expand on the learning opportunities of district employees (school faculties, school leaders, district administrators, district leaders, etc.), because efforts to improve the district's quality of instruction require people at many levels of the organization to learn new and better ways to perform their jobs. Thus, districts will likely start to experiment with the means by which they deliver learning opportunities to professional employees across the organization. Most districts do this almost instinctively, because they see professional development as the clearest way to improve the quality of instruction. Workshops, coaching, professional learning communities, inquiry teams, lesson studies—these are all mechanisms for schools and districts to increase opportunities for teachers to engage in improving their practice. However, these tend to be viewed strictly as capacity-building for teachers and leaders, rather than part of larger system of organizational learning. The lack of purposeful coherence is what distinguishes the teaching organization from the learning for teaching organization.

Leaders of learning for teaching organizations envision a larger framework, in which multiple learning opportunities are embedded into the routines of the work week. These could include a range of activities. The range of learning opportunities would be incorporated into a unified design to engage people in making meaning of and deepening their understanding of how to enact and support a uniform vision of instructional quality. Leaders would give thought to the integration of the learning opportunities, the required adjustments and implications for time allocation within peoples' work days, and the ways learning would be captured and shared across the organization. Professional learning in a learning for teaching organization is directed toward the purpose of the organization.

A central component of a learning for teaching organization is the creation of structured opportunities for teachers to deepen their craft knowledge. Within the framework of an instructional vision, districts need to encourage teachers to conduct their own inquiries into their instructional strategies and the implications for the learning of their students. Following the tenet of the commitment strategy, district leaders must facilitate the process so that the choice of structured inquiry arises out of the needs of teachers.

There are lots of entry points into the process, some more formal than others. Districts must facilitate these inquiries, whether organic or externally structured, to ensure that they produce clear learning. There are many external structures that could facilitate this process, including examining student assignments like those facilitated by the Standards in Practice process of the Education Trust; the Japanese process of lesson studies, in which teachers carefully craft, deliver, and debrief a particular lesson; the backward mapping of student outcomes to lesson planning facilitated by Wiggins and McTighe's (1998) *Understanding by Design*; or the formative assessment techniques described by Black and colleagues (Black, Harrison, Lee, Marshall, & William, 2003), in which teachers use a variety of informal feedback techniques to both understand the influence of their instructional efforts on students and to engage students in their own learning. Despite their different emphases, each of these techniques is a structured approach to engage teachers in the complexities of their craft and to facilitate their ongoing professional growth.

The critical distinction here is that no one of these programs should be imposed across an entire school system. This would be perceived as just another control strategy and would result in predictably partial engagement. It is critical, therefore, that the choice of inquiry arise out of teacher need. District leaders must facilitate the process for teachers to choose inquiries that have real meaning for them, yet still connect to the larger instructional vision. In such a system, teachers are explicitly engaged in their craft as learners for the purposes of the organization, and supported by the organization to do so.

Creating a process to engage teachers in learning that is designed to improve their craft knowledge and is aligned with the purposes of the organization is a central task of a learning for teaching organization, but such an organization also does several additional things. It also takes this concept and applies it not only to teachers but to other levels of the system. So, for example, principals might engage in structured investigations into ways to encourage student engagement and motivation or to use data to identify and support low-performing students. District administrators might inquire into different strategies for supporting school leaders or structuring and supporting teacher inquiries.

LEARNING FOR TEACHING ORGANIZATIONS MOLD THE CULTURE OF THE ORGANIZATION

There are also important cultural shifts that both accompany and propel learning for teaching organizations. The very concept of organizational culture is both abstract and elusive, because it somewhat unpredictably grows out of both direct and incidental activities of individuals and the organization. Organizational culture is both an influence on and the product of tangible actions, processes, and artifacts of the organization. According to MIT organizational psychologist Edgar Schein (2004), organizational culture is a pattern of shared basic assumptions that are both learned through past problem-solving and transmitted to new organizational members as the correct way to perceive, think, and feel. In this way, the cultural and organizational components of the valuation and regular practice of learning are symbiotic because they feed into and are dependent upon each other. Regular organizationwide purposeful learning begets the cultural valuation of such learning, just as infusing the value of purposeful learning into the culture of an organization begets deeper organizationwide purposeful learning practices.

A prime change for leaders of learning for teaching organizations is to embed the value of purposeful learning into the cultural DNA of the organization. Schein (2004) argues that one way to distinguish leadership from management is that leadership creates or changes culture, while management and administration act within a culture. The bottom line for leaders, says Schein, "is that if they do not become conscious of the cultures in which they are embedded, those cultures will manage them" (p. 23). To do so requires a high level of awareness among organizational leaders because every act has the potential to significantly influence the culture of the organization, and they must be prepared for this. In many ways, the three dimensions of organizational learning that I discussed in chapter 7—individual learning, social learning, and institutional learning—are really just three means by which the value of purposeful learning can be infused into the culture of an organization. It is well beyond my scope here to go deeply into the intricacies of forces and actions that affect organizational culture, but organizational leaders must be extraordinarily aware of the implicit and explicit messages they send when they introduce new ideas and practices.

LEARNING FOR TEACHING ORGANIZATIONS USE EVIDENCE TO GUIDE IMPROVEMENT

Another attribute of a learning for teaching organization is the way it uses data and evidence to ask questions, develop hypotheses, test assumptions, and inform decisions. The rhetoric around evidence-based practice in education is profuse, but quite different from reality. In the rough-and-tumble world of school districts, few if any have developed sophisticated data systems that regularly inform important questions. Nor have systems trained teachers and administrators widely enough to effectively use available data to inform decisionmaking. Even rarer are systems that appropriately balance regularized data collection with flexible and ad hoc systems to answer emerging questions. Even so, evidence-based practice holds immense promise as a means to improve the likelihood that selected approaches will actually improve solutions to identified problems. Increasing the data available to decisionmakers at all levels of the education system, and then providing them with the skills to draw reasonable conclusions from the data, and to take actions based on those conclusions, is bound to improve the effectiveness of the organization. Data are the wellspring of organizational learning.

This is why harnessing data to produce sustained organizational learning is so fundamental to learning for teaching districts of the twenty-first century. I am speaking specifically of building systems of organizational improvement into the regularized practices of the organization. To do this, districts need to identify testable action plans, implement them, assess their efficacy, and use these data to expand, refine, or discard ideas or strategies. This requires district leaders to think strategically about the initiatives they champion. It also requires districts to break down initiatives into testable chunks, rather than just looking at the end result of student performance. There are too many variables that go into student performance to make it a reliable short-term, large-scale indicator of program effectiveness. Therefore, districts must include implementation in the equation.

For this reason, learning for teaching organizations will place at least as much emphasis on indicators that lead to test performance as on actual test results. Formative assessment techniques are particularly valuable in this sense because they are connected to the tighter cycles of feedback that are necessary to provide teachers with the fresh data necessary to inform their instruction. Systems that collect data on implementation are similarly important because they can identify why something is or is not working, rather than whether it did or did not work.

Districts also must develop better feedback systems to provide evidence as to how introduced innovations are faring. Thus, district leaders must develop data feedback systems for three purposes: first, to collect data that teachers and school leaders need to make decisions about the instruction and support of individual students; second, to allow local inquiry groups to evaluate their hypotheses; third, to provide guidance about programmatic decisions, distinguishing between flawed design and weak implementation. As important as these three systems might be, they will only be useful if decisionmakers at all levels of the organization are trained to analyze and use their output. Finally, districts must develop systems to disseminate student data, implementation data, and the knowledge acquired by group inquiries across the system. Through the dissemination of these data and engagement with them, organizational members can capitalize on these experiences to produce better practice.

LEARNING FOR TEACHING ORGANIZATIONS REORIENT THEIR RELATIONSHIPS WITH SCHOOLS

Another conceptual shift in the transition from a teaching organization to a learning for teaching organization occurs in the relationship between the district and schools. Overall, this change must be characterized by less of an authority relationship between the two and more of a support relationship. An adjustment of this relationship is important for at least two reasons. First, as I argued in chapter 7, authority relationships discourage candor on the part of those who are being held accountable, while support relationships encourage honest discussion of problems so improvement can be tackled together. Second, since federal and state governments play a heavy authority role in schools already, there is little need for districts to duplicate this effort. Alternatively, there is plenty of school need for support and few entities readily available to provide it.

A major reorientation for districts seeking to become learning for teaching organizations is to adjust their accountability relationships with schools. The dominant model is one of external accountability, in which states hold one entity (schools or districts) accountable for external test performance through a variety of tangible and symbolic rewards and sanctions. Ladd (1996) refers to external accountability as state expectations for student performance as measured by achievement on tests in basic academic subjects. O'Day (2003) refers to such a system as "unilateral accountability" because it is unidirectional, or "top-down in design and enforcement" (p. 157). Much has been written about the organization and influence of external educational accountability systems (see Herman & Haertel, 2005, for an overview), but the inescapable fact is that such systems have evolved to play a the dominant role in shaping of education activity in public schools today. These external systems send powerful signals to schools about acceptable levels of performance and generate tremendous amounts of energy toward changing behaviors to conform to the requirements of the system. But, as currently constructed, external accountability systems provide little in terms of information or resources for improvement beyond extrinsic motivational signals.

Federal and state policymakers play the dominant role in external accountability, and there is no need for districts to replicate this role. In fact, overly rigid external accountability systems have taken on a level of importance disproportionate to their utility. This is not to say that districts should not hold schools and teachers accountable for implementation and performance, but they can counterbalance the overemphasis on external accountability in several ways. First, they can implement their own complementary set of intermediate indicators that provide feedback to schools on the road to high-stakes events. When coupled with more comprehensive systems of data use, this can provide a more multidimensional and comprehensive picture of student learning (Supovitz & Klein, 2003).

Second, districts can complement external accountability with two more constructive forms of accountability. They can develop systems of reciprocal accountability in which they help foster the capacity schools need to reach goals in exchange for performance expectations. And they can use the pressure of collective responsibility that arises in social systems to motivate individual response.

Reciprocal accountability arises from the idea that accountability and capacity are two sides of the same coin. Accountability is reasonable only if people are provided with the knowledge, skill, and resources to achieve the goals for which they are held accountable. Elmore (2002) describes reciprocal accountability for capacity: "For every increment of performance I demand from you, I have the equal responsibility to provide you with the capacity to meet that expectation. Likewise, for every investment you make in my skill and knowledge, I have a reciprocal responsibility to demonstrate some new increment in performance" (p. 5). Reciprocal accountability changes the relationship between districts and schools in that both parties have important responsibilities in trying to reach mutually desirable goals. According to Elmore, such reciprocal accountability is "the glue that, in the final analysis, will hold accountability systems together" (p. 5). By encouraging reciprocal accountability, districts can change the dynamic of their relationships with schools. They position themselves within, not above, the accountability system, shoulder to shoulder with schools, to achieve improvement.

The second form of accountability that districts need to foster is the notion of collective responsibility, which is a more informal form of accountability, but an important influence on behavior nonetheless. Collective responsibility is the extent to which members of an organization hold shared norms, values, and a sense of responsibility toward the group as a whole. Lee and Smith (1996) define collective responsibility as the collaborative nature of staff relationships and their perceived ability to influence their environment. They found higher levels of collective responsibility to be associated with higher student learning. Collective responsibility is a powerful force in shaping behavior because individuals are more motivated by peer pressure and how others they know will think of them than by external rewards and sanctions. The sense of collective responsibility taps into the very human desire to gain and maintain credibility in the eyes of one's peers.

By complementing rather than replicating the powerful influences of external accountability, districts can influence behavior and serve schools more effectively. Through reciprocal accountability they can shift the dynamic of their accountability relationship with schools toward mutual engagement in the improvement process. Collective responsibility is a more informal, but nonetheless formidable, force to motivate and direct engagement and influence the behavior of individuals toward particular purposes.

LEARNING FOR TEACHING ORGANIZATIONS REORIENT THEIR RELATIONSHIPS WITH THE EXTERNAL ENVIRONMENT

The international knowledge base of instructional improvement and school organization is growing and changing too rapidly for districts to self-generate much of the knowledge they need for improvement. Therefore, districts must increasingly look outward to bring new ideas and practices into their organization and reposition themselves to facilitate the enactment of that knowledge in schools. Hence, districts must fundamentally recast their role relative to the outside world. They must become more capable of searching the external environment, better able to judge the quality and promise of external opportunities, and able to conceptually integrate these ideas into a coherent whole. They need to make the transition from a manager of the status quo to an overseer of innovation.

This transformation demands a fundamental shift in district leaders' thinking. To play a vital role in the future of public education, district leaders must reposition their organizations relative to schools and the broader education industry. District authority can no longer rest upon its formal status as the overseer of schools, but it must rely instead on the legitimacy of carefully chosen ideas and strategies designed to bring about systemwide improvement.

Identifying, brokering, and supporting the introduction of new ideas and initiatives are a major responsibility of learning for teaching organizations. Modern districts must build their capacities to scan the broader educational environment in order to identify and incorporate ideas and initiatives that will support their quest for improvement. New ideas brought into a system must be carefully chosen, calibrated, and massaged to fit within the contextual situation of schools and their levels of development. In doing so, districts must forge productive partnerships with external providers and develop the capacity to influence those partnerships and shape them to their needs.

Districts must realize that they are always going to need partnerships with external providers and intermediary organizations and that self-sufficiency is an outdated concept. The goal of partnerships is improved delivery of instruction to students, not achievement of self-sufficiency. Rather than trying to wean themselves away from such relationships, districts must learn to manage them.

External providers are often trying to provide particular programs or interventions to districts, and these (hopefully) are a good fit for the needs of districts at that particular point in time. But as districts grow, their needs will change, and they must encourage external providers to grow and change their services to fit district needs. There is an uncomfortable dance between districts and providers around customization. Providers tend to want to deliver a standardized package to clients, while districts may have particular needs and priorities that are not perfectly suited to the provider's program. The balance here is tricky, as programs cannot move so far away from their intended design as to diminish their power, yet they must fit into the context they enter.

Powerful technical assistance to districts is a combination of program and service that changes over time to meet evolving needs. The long relationship between Duval County and the National Center on Education and the Economy was a model for district/provider relationships in that it persisted and changed as the district evolved over time. Each actor received tremendous benefit from the relationship: Duval County from the knowledge and expertise it acquired, and NCEE from the intellectual property it developed as it tested out new ideas in the field. Louis Gomez (personal communication, April 27, 2006) of Northwestern University talks about powerful technical assistance to schools as morphing a service over time to fit the needs of the client. Districts need to think similarly about their relationships with external assistance providers.

SYSTEMS LEADERSHIP

The perceptive reader will have noticed that this book has not been explicitly about leadership, yet it is all about leadership. Most stories of great accomplishment tend to focus too much on the roles and actions of the key actors. The stories thus become the tales of the personal characteristics of the individuals who play the central roles, and not the stories of what they built and how they built it.

But what is the role of individual leadership in stories of great organizational success or, for that matter, failure? Are the individuals just the necessary actors in the dramas that are unfolding, or is theirs the essence of the story? In this story, I have expressly avoided focusing on Superintendent Fryer's individual leadership style and personal magnetism, of which there are abundant examples. This is because I believe strongly that it was the ideas and the systems that he and his leadership team put into place that make Duval County's improvement story an example of powerful leadership. In this sense, I am making the case that systems leadership is a more powerful approach to improvement than individual leadership.

Stories that focus on individual leaders and not on what they build risk missing the forest for the trees. The stories of individuals are not what is important, because their goal is to build something greater than themselves. It is telling that the great companies that Jim Collins (2001) identifies in *Good to Great* were rarely led by strongly charismatic personalities. As Collins argues, such personalities tend to get in the way of building sustainable organizational success. "For these people," Collins says of ego-first leaders, "work will always be . . . about what they get—fame, fortune, adulation, power, whatever—not what they build, create, and contribute" (p. 36). Collins's work suggests that leaders' attention to self comes at the expense of building a more broadly effective organization. As soon as charismatic leaders leave, their organizations often stagnate or decline.

The message I hope to leave is that the heroes of any powerful organizational tale are the organizational systems that are built, not the individuals who build them. What *potentially* distinguishes Duval County from other districts is not only what it has been able to accomplish, but the extent to which the organization is able to sustain and expand on its success through indelible transformations of the way the organization operates. This is the legacy of systems leadership.

THE TRUE PURPOSE OF EDUCATIONAL REFORM

The true purpose of educational reform is to foster deep and lasting improvement in the quality of instruction inside classrooms. To do so requires more than the implementation of a single program. Programs are the vehicles of reform but should not be confused with reform itself. Programs are the Trojan horses that allow new ideas to enter people's minds, while reforms are the ideas themselves. Reform will have more than a superficial impact only when reform ideas are both conceptually powerful and have the chance to take root. Deep, lasting reform comes in the internalized understanding of the purpose and intent of the reform, not from implementation of programs. Regardless of the promise of their core idea, many reforms fail because the programs they are wrapped in are not powerful enough to change the complex environments in which they are introduced. For reform to flourish, therefore, requires multiple programs to introduce the same message through different entry points. Programs themselves are the outer expression, or the hooks, by which people engage with reform ideas. The real purpose of education reform is to build habits of mind, not the adoption of particular initiatives.

A case in point comes from this astute observation by a Duval County district administrator, who in 2002 predicted that the residual influence of the district's work with America's Choice would not be the program, but the ideas beneath it. "Well, the good stuff leaves behind things that become ingrained in the system, which people just don't realize," he said. "Before America's Choice there [were] certainly things that we weren't doing that are now part of the system, and that I guess is the way you'd want to think about it after it's gone. You know, if a teacher says, 'Boy, I'm glad we're not doing that America's Choice stuff anymore' . . . they don't stop to think that they're still looking at performance standards. Whether we call them America's Choice or New Standard Performance Standards or whatever, they're still looking at performance standards. That is the legacy of most good reforms."

The distinction between programs and reform has important implications for district leaders, who are uniquely positioned to orchestrate programs that reinforce the underlying ideas of reform. Programs may come and go, but reform must persist in order for meaningful change to occur. Introducing new and different programs is actually helpful as long as they reinforce the larger reform message. New programs may reinvigorate and excite people, but they must remain consistent with the essential reform ideas. A range of different programs can help with different pieces of the puzzle. Educational leaders need to think of the longer-term goal of reforming their organization, not just implementing particular programs.

This book has been an exploration of the transformation of the school district. It focuses on ways districts can reinvigorate their role in improving the quality of teaching and learning, not just in individual schools but across school systems. This story demonstrates that comprehensive systems built by committed leaders can have a powerful influence on the quality of education that all children receive. Such reforms are limited in that they cannot alleviate the fundamentally inequitable social conditions that disadvantage children in deep and profound ways. Even so, powerful organizational reforms can help transform school districts into systems dedicated to improving the quality of instruction and enhancing students' learning opportunities. Through sustained organizational learning focused on the improvement of teaching, school districts can dramatically improve the quality of the professional lives of educators and fulfill public education's mission to prepare well-educated American citizens for the twenty-first century and beyond.

APPENDIX A

—

Data Collection and Analysis

Data collection for this study occurred over a seven-year period, from 1999 to 2005. In the first two years, 1999 and 2000, the collected data were predominantly part of the Consortium for Policy Research in Education's (CPRE) national evaluation of the America's Choice program. Beginning in 2000 and running through 2002, Duval County also contracted separately with CPRE to conduct a more intensive evaluation of America's Choice in the district. The early data collection therefore had a particular focus on the implementation of America's Choice. In 2002, as the spread of the reforms began to take root and transition into a district-based reform, I began to conceive of the ideas for this book and organize data collection more specifically for these efforts.

The data collection for this book can be organized into two distinct sets: data collected from the district and data collected from schools.

DISTRICT DATA

The first set of data collected for this book was focused specifically on the district's reforms and reform strategies. These included interviews with a range of district administrators, attendance at a variety of district-level meetings and principal professional development sessions, surveys of the population of principals in the district in 2003 and 2004, examination of district documents, and tracking and analysis of district policies and activity through the *Florida Times-Union*.

The chief method of collecting data on district policy was through interviews with key district leaders. The table below summarizes the fifty-four district interviews that were conducted with district personnel from 1999 to 2005. Appendix B shows examples of protocols used to conduct some of these interviews.

Year	Number of Interviews	Person Interviewed
1999	4	Superintendent, Chief of Staff, Regional Superintendents (2)
2000	10	Superintendent, Regional Superintendents (3), Regional Directors (3), Director of Academic Programs, Supervisor of ESOL/Alternative Education, Associate Superintendent for Curriculum and Instruction
2001	10	Superintendent (2), Director of Research and Evaluation, Chief of Staff, Regional Superintendents (2), Principals (4)
2002	11	Superintendent, Associate Superintendent for Administration and Business Services, Associate Superintendent for Curriculum and Instruction, Director of Urban Systemic Initiative, Regional Superintendents (2), Regional Director, Director of Research and Evaluation, Director of Standards, Math Supervisor, Science Supervisor
2003	9	Superintendent (2), Chief of Staff, Associate Superintendent for Curriculum and Instruction, Director of Research and Evaluation, Regional Superintendents (2), Regional Director, Math Supervisor,
2004	7	Superintendent, Regional Superintendents (2), Regional Directors (2), Associate Superintendent for Curriculum and Instruction, Director of Research and Evaluation
2005	3	Superintendent, Regional Superintendents (2)

In 2003 and 2004, a survey of principals in the population of schools in the district was conducted. The survey instrument consisted of a series of items on standards-based reform in the district, the work of school and district standards coaches, leadership of reform in their schools, and the use of the snapshot system. The survey was conducted during one of the district's principal meetings in the spring of each year, and therefore response rates were high. In 2003, 93 percent of principals completed the survey. In 2004, 92 percent of principals in the district completed the survey. The survey instrument is reproduced at the end of appendix B.

Appendix A

SCHOOL DATA

In the 2002–03 school year, I set out to methodically collect data on school and teacher understanding of the district's reforms and levels of implementation through a series of site visits to ten district schools.

The sample of schools were selected as a purposeful sample that were intended to be representative of the district on a range of dimensions, including performance, student demographics, grade levels, and the reform design they were implementing. The ten schools were roughly representative of the broader array of schools in the district in terms of percentage meeting standard in reading (48% in the sample compared to 56% in the other district schools), percentage meeting standard in mathematics (47% in the sample compared to 49% in the other district schools), percentage minority (66% compared to 57%) and percentage of students receiving federal lunch assistance (50% compared to 51%). T-tests of differences between the means of these groups showed no significant differences.

The demographics of the 10 schools that were visited during the 2002-03 school year are shown in the following table. Some of the numbers are approximations to protect the identity of the schools.

Demographics of Sample of Schools Visited

School	Level	Design	2002 Grade	2003 Grade	Percent Minority	Percent Lunch Assistance	Number of Students
Johnson	Elementary	Standards-Based	C	C	70	65	750
Fillmore	Elementary	Direct Instruction	D	D	95	90	650
Hamlin	Elementary	Standards-Based	B	A	10	50	570
Tompkins	Elementary	America's Choice	C	C	90	90	275
Wilson	Middle	Standards-Based	A	A	25	20	1250
Burr	Middle	Standards-Based	B	A	50	50	750
Hendricks	Middle	America's Choice	D	D	99	80	1000
Hobart	High	Standards-Based	C	D	50	NA	2200
Sherman	High	America's Choice	D	C	30	NA	1200
Dawes	High	Standards-Based	F	D	99	NA	1600

Data collection from each school included an interview with the principal, an observation of an English language arts class, an interview with the teacher of that class, interviews with at least two other teachers in the school (one mathematics), and an interview with the school's standards coach. The principal chose both the teacher to be observed and those to be interviewed. Across the ten visits, I interviewed twenty-nine teachers, all ten principals, and coaches in eight of the ten schools, as shown in the following table.

Data Collection in Each School in Sample

School	Level	Design	Principal Interviewed	Coach Interviewed	Number of Teachers Interviewed
Johnson	Elementary	Standards-Based	1	0	3
Hamlin	Elementary	Standards-Based	1	1	2
Fillmore	Elementary	Direct Instruction	1	1	3
Tompkins	Elementary	America's Choice	1	1	4
Wilson	Middle	Standards-Based	1	1	2
Burr	Middle	Standards-Based	1	1	3
Hendricks	Middle	America's Choice	1	1	2
Hobart	High	Standards-Based	1	1	5
Sherman	High	America's Choice	1	2	3
Dawes	High	Standards-Based	1	0	2
		TOTAL	10	9	29

DATA ANALYSIS

Almost all interviews were tape recorded and transcribed. The transcribed interviews were entered into the NVIVO qualitative software program. Through a recursive and inductive process, a series of codes at the school and district levels were developed around the major categories by which the book is organized (vision, commitment and capacity building, data use, sustainability). The coding structures consisted of similar, but not identical, codes for the district and school interviews. In both data sets, codes were developed in five major areas:

1. **Vision.** In this area, the data were coded for such major categories as the clarity of the vision within the different content areas, the coherence of the vision across the content areas, connection to standards, opposition to the vision and/or competing visions. At the school level, additional codes were added to indicate how principals, coaches, and lead teachers viewed their roles in the reform and whether they thought the district had articulated a clear vision of instruction.

2. **Communication and Support of Vision.** Codes in this category included professional development at all levels of the system (Schultz Center, in-school, leadership training, etc.), tools and strategies used to explain and communicate the vision, perceptions of district support and guidance for the vision, and perceptions of the value of different district support initiatives.

3. **Monitoring.** Monitoring codes focused on the different district interventions around the use of data, including the snapshot system, Appraisal Plus system, Aide system, and other data initiatives. Other codes in this category grouped interview data on accountability, monitoring, and perceptions of district expectations around data from different actors within the system.

4. **Refining and Deepening.** Codes in this category assessed perspectives on district strategies for sustainability. These included the development of a culture of learning at the school and district levels, understanding and familiarity with the district's professional learning community initiatives, and general perceptions on sustainability and strategies for spreading and deepening reform over time.

5. **Other.** This coding category captured eclectic and emerging themes. These included the focus on high schools, the emphasis on safety nets, background information on the community, the school board and district/board relations, the union and district/union relations, perceptions of the effect of district reforms, budget issues, and a category to capture memorable quotes from interviewees.

Of course, data could be, and often were, coded into multiple categories. After initial coding, the data were printed individually by code and reorganized and reanalyzed to look for patterns within the major coding categories. With the tried and true methods of different colored highlighters and Post-it notes, I developed and tested theories and ideas against the data. From these recursive analyses, the basic chapter structure and themes within this book began to take shape.

APPENDIX B

——

Interview and Survey Instruments

The following five interview protocols were used during the 2002–03 school year for data collection at the district and school levels. After the interview protocols is a copy of the principals survey that was administered in 2004.

SENIOR DISTRICT LEADER PROTOCOL

1. What are your major goals for the district this year? How are you planning on reaching those goals? How will you know at the end of the year that you have reached your goals?
2. Please describe your overall vision for the district?
3. Please describe your overall vision for improved student learning in the district?
4. Please describe what you think good instruction should look like in English and mathematics in:
   a. Elementary school classrooms?
   b. Middle school classrooms?
   c. High school classrooms?
5. How are you holding individuals and schools accountable for implementation?
6. How do you communicate your vision to teachers and school leaders?
7. What are the major strategies you are using to improve teaching and learning in the district? Tell me a little about each one.
   Probes:
   a. How are human and financial resources allocated to support your vision?
   b. Professional development (district/principals/teachers)
   c. Incentives/sanctions
   d. Communications within district
   e. Communication outside of district

8. How do you know whether or not your message is being heard?
9. How do you know whether instruction is changing in schools?
10. What is your role in enacting the district's vision?
11. What is the schools' role?
12. What are the barriers to achieving this vision?

DISTRICT LEADER/PROGRAM ADMINISTRATOR PROTOCOL

1. Tell me about the [program] strategy in Duval County?
2. What is your job as the [position, i.e., Program Director, Regional Director]?
3. Please describe what you think good instruction should look like in English and mathematics in
   a. Elementary school classrooms?
   b. Middle school classrooms?
   c. High school classrooms?
4. How are you building a workforce to carry out this instructional vision?
5. How do you communicate your vision of instruction to schools?
6. How does the district support the improvement of instruction in classrooms?
7. What are the district's strategies for improving the learning experiences of district administrators to support the improvement of instruction inside classrooms?
8. How does the [program] work with other initiatives in Duval County?
9. How does the district build teachers' capacity to carry out the work?
10. How do you monitor whether schools are implementing the frameworks?
11. What incentives/disincentives are there for schools to implement the frameworks?
12. What are the district's strategies for improving the learning experiences of school leaders to support the improvement of instruction inside classrooms?
13. What are the district's strategies for improving the learning experiences of district administrators to support the improvement of instruction inside classrooms?
14. What do you see as the major challenges you face in improving instruction in Duval County?
15. How do you think the superintendent is doing? What is your take on the strides he has made?
16. One of the things you are encouraging schools to do is to develop a professional learning community. What is that and how should school leaders try to foster it?
17. What are the major distractions for you as you try to be an instructional leader in the district?
18. How do you see your role as an instructional leader in the district?

PRINCIPAL INTERVIEW PROTOCOL

1. How long have you been a principal at this school? In this district?
2. I'm not familiar with your school, so tell me a few things that will give me a flavor of the place? [Probes: students, teachers, community]
3. What are the district's expectations for your school?
4. How does the district communicate these expectations to you?
5. How does the district support you in reaching these expectations?

    Probe: Is the support adequate?
6. Do you agree with these expectations? Are they realistic? Do they fit your school's needs?
7. Do you have a structure in the school to foster a professional learning community?

    Probes: What does it look like?

    How does it work?

    What is its purpose?
8. What is the district's vision of good instruction? How does the district communicate this vision to you?
9. What are you held accountable for?
10. Who are you accountable to?
11. How does the district hold you accountable? Are there any incentives?
12. What do you think of the Appraisal Plus evaluation system? Is it contributing or distracting to your efforts to improve instruction in your school?
13. What are the district initiatives that are building capacity at your school? How are they working?
14. Tell me what your coach does. Do you define this work or is it defined for you?
15. How does the coach work with the literacy coaches/USI teachers/math lead teacher?
16. What do you see as the strengths/weaknesses of having a coach in the school?

    Probe: How has the coach been received by your faculty?
17. How do you see your role as an instructional leader in the district?
18. What are the major distractions for you as you try to be an instructional leader in the district?
19. What would you like to be doing more of?
20. What would you like to be doing less of?
21. How would you characterize the relationship between the faculty in the school?

TEACHER INTERVIEW PROTOCOL

1. What do you teach? What grades do you teach?
   [IF OBSERVED]
2. Tell me about the lesson I just saw/am about to see. What is/was the goal of the lesson?
3. How does it fit into the larger curriculum?
4. How did you decide to teach this lesson?
5. Was it typical? Why or why not?
   [END OBSERVED]
2. How long have you been a teacher in this school? In this district?
3. I'm not familiar with your school, so tell me a few things that will give me a flavor of the place? [Probes: students, teachers, community]
4. What are the district's expectations for your teaching?
   If response focuses on instruction:
   a. What kinds of guidance/direction do you get about the content you teach?
   b. What about the pedagogy you use?
   If response focuses on outcomes:
   c. How does the district assist you to reach those outcomes?
5. Tell me about the professional development you have participated in over the past year or so.
   a. How did you decide to attend what you did?
   b. Did you have a choice of what to attend?
   c. Are professional development decisions made at the school? By the district? By individual teachers?
   d. How was the quality? Has it changed/improved the way that you teach?
6. Tell me a little about your [whatever principal calls the professional learning community].
   Probes: How often do you meet?
   How is it organized?
   What do you discuss?
   Is it useful to you?
7. What is the district's vision of good instruction? How does the district communicate this vision to you?
8. What are you held accountable for?
9. Who are you accountable to?
10. How does the district hold you accountable? Are there any incentives?

11. Who is your standards coach? How, if at all, do you work with him/her? What else do they do?
12. How would you characterize the relationship between the faculty in the school?

SCHOOL COACH INTERVIEW PROTOCOL

1. How long have you been a coach at this school?
2. What was your job before you became a coach? In this school?
3. I'm not familiar with your school, so tell me a few things that will give me a flavor of the place? [Probes: students, teachers, community]
4. What is your job as a coach? What do you do?
5. What is the district's expectation for you as a coach?
6. How does the district communicate its expectations to you?
7. How does the district support you in reaching these expectations?
8. Tell me about the professional development you have participated in over the past year or so.

      Probes: How did you decide to attend what you did?

              Did you have a choice of what to attend?

              Are professional development decisions made at the school? By the district? By individual teachers?

              How was the quality? Has it changed/improved the way that you teach?

9. Do you feel prepared to do your job as coach? Why or why not?
10. What are the district's strategies for improving the learning experiences of teachers to improve their instruction?
11. Do you have a structure in the school to foster a professional learning community?

      Probes: What does it look like?

              How does it work?

              What is its purpose?

12. What is the district's vision of good instruction? How does the district communicate this vision to you?
13. What are you held accountable for?
14. Who are you accountable to?
15. How does the district hold you accountable? Are there any incentives?
16. How do you work with the literacy coaches/USI teachers/math lead teacher?
17. What do you see as the strengths/weaknesses of having a full-time coach in the school?

      Probe: How have you been received by your faculty?

18. What would you like to be doing more of?
19. What would you like to be doing less of?
20. How would you characterize the relationship between the faculty in the school?

2004 PRINCIPAL SURVEY

I. About Standards-Based Reform

1. Please mark the extent to which you disagree or agree with each of the following statements about standards-based reform.

	Strongly Disagree	Somewhat Disagree	Somewhat Agree	Strongly Agree
a. The role of the principal in standards-based reform is clear to me.	O	O	O	O
b. Standards-based reform is improving the quality of education that the children in Duval County receive.	O	O	O	O
c. District leadership support my efforts to introduce standards-based reform in my school.	O	O	O	O
d. District leadership have articulated a clear vision of what is effective instruction in English language arts.	O	O	O	O
e. District leadership have articulated a clear vision of what is effective instruction in mathematics.	O	O	O	O
f. District leadership have articulated a clear vision of what is effective instruction in science.	O	O	O	O
g. District leadership have articulated a clear vision of what is effective instruction in social studies.	O	O	O	O
h. My regional supervisors have the expertise to support me to improve my school's implementation of standards-based reform.	O	O	O	O
i. Standards-based reform will exist 5 years from now in the district.	O	O	O	O
j. I support the district's efforts to implement standards-based reform.	O	O	O	O

2. Please mark the extent to which you disagree or agree with each of the following statements.

	Strongly Disagree	Somewhat Disagree	Somewhat Agree	Strongly Agree
a. The Framework for Implementation of Standards is specific enough to guide the work of my school.	O	O	O	O
b. The monthly principal's meetings contribute to my efforts to implement standards-based reform in my school.	O	O	O	O
c. I feel I am part of a learning community in this district.	O	O	O	O
d. The teachers at my school support standards-based reform.	O	O	O	O
e. Implementation of standards-based reform will improve my school's FCAT scores.	O	O	O	O
f. Standards-based reform is more promising than previous reform efforts.	O	O	O	O
g. We are held accountable for our school's performance on the FCAT.	O	O	O	O
h. We are held accountable for our school's implementation of standards-based reform.	O	O	O	O
i. Instruction in literacy, mathematics, and science in this district are philosophically similar.	O	O	O	O

II. About the Work of Your School and District Standards Coaches

3. Please mark the extent to which you disagree or agree with each of the following statements about the role of the coach in standards-based reform.

	Strongly Disagree	Somewhat Disagree	Somewhat Agree	Strongly Agree
a. I have a strong positive working relationship with the standards coach at my school.	O	O	O	O
b. My standards coach and I have a common understanding of the coach's role and responsibilities within the school.	O	O	O	O
c. The strategy of having a full-time standards coach has improved teaching and learning in my school.	O	O	O	O
d. Faculty at my school think that a full-time coach takes a needed person out of the classroom.	O	O	O	O

e. When I need advice about the implementation   O   O   O   O
    of standards I consult our school's District
    Standards Coach.

f. Our District Standards Coach has been   O   O   O   O
    responsive to our school needs.

g. Our District Standards Coach has deepened   O   O   O   O
    our school's implementation of standards-
    based instruction.

III. *About Your Leadership of a Standards-Based School*

4. Please indicate how prepared you feel to do the following:	Not Adequately Prepared	Somewhat Prepared	Fairly Well Prepared	Very Well Prepared
a. Lead a standards-based school.	O	O	O	O
b. Conduct focus walks to provide feedback to teachers on their implementation of standards.	O	O	O	O
c. Assist teachers in implementing standards-based instruction.	O	O	O	O
d. Assess teachers' understanding of standards.	O	O	O	O
e. Analyze the results of the FCAT in relation to the standards.	O	O	O	O
f. Facilitate the implementation of safety nets for students.	O	O	O	O
g. Lead professional development workshops on standards with your entire school's faculty.	O	O	O	O
h. Cultivate a learning community in your school.	O	O	O	O

5. Please mark the extent to which you disagree or agree with each of the following statements.	Strongly Disagree	Somewhat Disagree	Somewhat Agree	Strongly Agree
a. There is strong evidence that Duval's standards-based reform initiative improves teaching and student performance.	O	O	O	O
b. The model classroom has been an effective tool to encourage teachers to adopt new instructional practices.	O	O	O	O
c. Teachers can use pretty much any instructional approach they want as long as their students perform well on the FCATs.	O	O	O	O

	Strongly Disagree	Somewhat Disagree	Somewhat Agree	Strongly Agree
d. Decisions about new programs should be based on a careful review of the evidence of their effectiveness.	O	O	O	O
e. The only evidence you can rely on are your own observations.	O	O	O	O
f. Endorsements by teachers who are using the program in other schools are the best source of evidence of quality.	O	O	O	O
g. Published research is the best source of evidence of effects of new programs.	O	O	O	O

IV. About Appraisal Plus

6. Please mark the extent to which you disagree or agree with each of the following statements the Appraisal Plus system.

	Strongly Disagree	Somewhat Disagree	Somewhat Agree	Strongly Agree
a. I feel prepared to write specific, measurable targets.	O	O	O	O
b. The feedback I have received from my supervisor is timely.	O	O	O	O
c. The five targets in my Appraisal Plus plan were approved before Christmas.	O	O	O	O
d. My Appraisal Plus plan is aligned with the goals of my school.	O	O	O	O
e. The Appraisal Plus website makes it easier for me to use the Appraisal Plus system.	O	O	O	O
f. I have received clear direction on Appraisal Plus from my regional office.	O	O	O	O

V. About the Standards Implementation Snapshot System

7. Please mark the extent to which you disagree or agree with each of the following statements about the snapshot system.

	Strongly Disagree	Somewhat Disagree	Somewhat Agree	Strongly Agree
a. The snapshots provide our district with valuable information about the implementation of standards.	O	O	O	O
b. The snapshot rubrics have helped me to better understand what to focus on in order to implement standards-based reform.	O	O	O	O

c. The discussion about the snapshot results at the monthly principals meeting is valuable to me. O O O O

d. The snapshot system has deepened my understanding of standards-based reform. O O O O

e. I have learned something useful as a result of participating in a snapshot. O O O O

f. I have modified a practice at my school as a result of something I learned from the snapshots. O O O O

g. The discussion about the snapshot results at the monthly principals meeting provides me with guidance as to what to focus on in my school. O O O O

h. Snapshot visits provide a valuable opportunity to learn about instructional practices. O O O O

i. The snapshot system has improved the implementation of standards in the Duval County. O O O O

8. Please mark the extent to which you disagree or agree with each of the following statements about the snapshot system.	*Strongly Disagree*	*Somewhat Disagree*	*Somewhat Agree*	*Strongly Agree*
a. The snapshot visits to my school were useful to me.	O	O	O	O
b. The snapshot visits to my school were useful to my faculty.	O	O	O	O
c. The snapshot data collectors were qualified to assess implementation of standards in my school.	O	O	O	O
d. The snapshots completed at my school were a fair assessment of our implementation of that aspect of standards-based reform.	O	O	O	O
e. The snapshots are well aligned with training.	O	O	O	O
f. The snapshot results for my school are used by district administrators to make judgments about my individual school's implementation.	O	O	O	O
g. I have disseminated the snapshot rubrics to my faculty.	O	O	O	O
h. I regularly share the snapshot results with my faculty.	O	O	O	O

	Strongly Disagree	Somewhat Disagree	Somewhat Agree	Strongly Agree
i. We are held accountable for our school's implementation of the content of the snapshots.	O	O	O	O
j. I have incorporated the snapshots into my Appraisal Plus project.	O	O	O	O
k. I talk with other principals about how to deepen instructional practice as a result of the snapshots.	O	O	O	O
l. I talk with teachers in my school about how to deepen instructional practice as a result of the snapshots.	O	O	O	O
m. The snapshots capture important knowledge about best practice.	O	O	O	O

9. Were you one of the snapshot data collectors in 2003–04?

      O No   O Yes

If you answered NO to question 9, skip to question 13. Otherwise, please continue with question 10.

10. How many years have you been a snapshot data collector?

      O 1 Year   O 2 Years

11. Please mark the extent to which you disagree or agree with each of the following statements the snapshot system.

	Strongly Disagree	Somewhat Disagree	Somewhat Agree	Strongly Agree
a. The snapshots are well organized.	O	O	O	O
b. The snapshot rubrics and evidence forms are clear.	O	O	O	O
c. I have learned a lot from visiting other schools.	O	O	O	O
d. I am comfortable making the assessments asked of me.	O	O	O	O
e. I am comfortable providing feedback to other principals at the end of the snapshot visits.	O	O	O	O
f. I have had adequate training to conduct the snapshot visits.	O	O	O	O
g. One snapshot a month is manageable.	O	O	O	O
h. I have learned a lot from other team members during snapshot visits.	O	O	O	O

12. Will you choose to be a snapshot data collector again next year?

      O No   O Yes

VI. *About Your Background and Your School*

13. Including this year, how many years have you been:

a. A principal at your school?   _____ years (including this school year).

b. A principal in Duval County?   _____ years (including this school year).

14. My school is:

      O Elementary   O Middle   O High

15. In the past three years was your school part of either of the following reform initiatives? (Mark all that apply):

      O America's Choice   O Direct Instruction

16. My position is:

      O Principal   O Assistant Principal

      O District Administrator   O Other

17. My school is in Region

      O I   O II   O III   O IV   O V   O Not Applicable

18. My school's grade last year was

      O A   O B   O C   O D   O F   O No grade

THANK YOU FOR YOUR TIME!

Snapshot Documents

Standards Implementation
Snapshot System

A system for tracking the implementation of standards in Duval County

RUBRIC: SAFETY NETS

Target 2 of the Duval County Framework for Implementation of Standards asks principals and teachers to provide safety nets for all students. This rubric describes different levels of implementation of the safety net component of the target.

Host Principal Rating:

1. Preparing	2. Getting Started	3. Moving Along	4. In Place
☐	☐	☐	☐

Your ratings (Mark all that apply, and then assess the overall phase of implementation.):

Preparing	*Getting Started*	*Moving Along*	*In Place*
☐ Principal analyzes last year's assessment data and/or beginning of the year baseline assessment data to identify and place students in need of remediation.	☐ Leadership team analyzes last year's assessment data and/or beginning of the year baseline assessments to identify and place students in need of remediation.	☐ Leadership team, as well as teacher teams of various configurations, regularly analyzes student performance data.	☐ Leadership team, as well as teacher teams of various configurations, regularly analyzes a variety of student performance data and adjusts safety net programs accordingly.

Preparing	*Getting Started*	*Moving Along*	*In Place*
☐ Schoolwide action plan identifying specific students, previous interventions, and potential new safety net services is developed.	☐ Leadership Team reviews existing programs (i.e., before school, after school, Saturday, course recovery, team-up, mentoring, tutoring, other remediation) to see if data, identified students, and safety nets are aligned.	☐ Teachers are provided with training specifically on how to support at-risk students.	☐ Student progress is monitored and assessed throughout safety net implementation.
☐ School has some programs for students who need extra time/instruction to meet standards, but options are limited.		☐ School provides a variety of programs for students to meet standards (i.e., before school, after school, Saturday, course recovery, team-up, mentoring, tutoring, other remediation).	☐ All instructors of safety net courses have appropriate content expertise.
☐ Few classroom teachers have identified at-risk students in their classes and have a plan for moving the students up to standard.	☐ Some classroom teachers have identified at-risk students in their classes and have a plan for moving the students up to standard.	☐ Most classroom teachers can identify at-risk students in their classes and have a plan for moving the students up to standard.	☐ Teacher teams regularly meet to discuss progress of at-risk students toward standards.
	☐ Remediation sessions are focused to provide intense instruction to move students closer to standards.	☐ Most instructors of safety net courses have appropriate content expertise.	☐ Students are moved in and out of safety net programs as needed to perform at standard.
	☐ School leaders are regularly monitoring student progress.	☐ There is a formalized communication system between safety net teachers and students' regular classroom teachers.	☐ All classroom teachers can identify at-risk students in their classes and have a plan for moving them to standard.
	☐ Safety nets are organized, scheduled, and focused on critical areas for improvement	☐ Teachers are provided with quarterly updated data on all students.	☐ Safety net programs are reviewed & revised for effectiveness and targets are developed to include in following year's School Improvement Plan.

EVIDENCE FORM: SAFETY NETS

Questions for Principal:

1. Please describe the safety net programs at your school?
2. What data do you use to help you identify students who are at-risk and how do you analyze the data?
3. How would you rate your school on the overall rubric (provide rubric)?
4. How do you know when safety net programs are working?
5. What training has been provided to your staff on helping at-risk students meet standards?
6. Who teaches safety net courses and what are their qualifications?

Questions for Leadership Team Member:

1. How is your school identifying and helping at-risk students?
2. What is the role of your leadership team in the school's safety net programs?
3. How do you know when safety net programs are working?

Questions for Safety Net Providers:

1. How were you chosen to provide the safety net course? What is your content background in this subject?
2. Do you talk with the students' regular teachers? What do you talk about? How regularly do you talk?

Questions for Teachers:

1. Who are the at-risk students in your class? How do you know when a student needs instructional intervention?
2. What strategies are you using to bring them up to standard?
3. Can you show me an action plan for a struggling student? Please explain it to me.
4. Do you meet with other teachers to discuss at-risk students? With who? How often? What information do you use? What do you talk about?

Questions for Students Whom Teacher Has Identified as At Risk:

1. What standards are the most difficult for you to meet?
2. What would help you to meet the standards?
3. What kind of help are you getting to meet the standards?

Possible school/classroom artifacts:

Examined	Present	
☐	☐	Safety net plans in SIP.
☐	☐	Individual student monitoring forms.
☐	☐	Safety net schedules.
☐	☐	Safety net attendance rosters.
☐	☐	Student action plans.
☐	☐	Targeted student list with data.

Other Pertinent Information:

SAMPLING OF TEACHERS

Use this form when you are picking the classrooms to be visited with the host principal. It may help you to array the possible classrooms to be visited and help you in selecting a representative sample of the school. The host principal should select one classroom and the visiting data collectors should select three.

☐ Elementary school classrooms should be in grades 3 and 4.

☐ Middle school classrooms should be in Language Arts in grades 6 and 7.

☐ High school classrooms should be in Language Arts in grades 9 and 10.

Grade	Teacher Name	Comments	Selected

Appendix C

EXAMPLE OF SNAPSHOT RESULTS

Overall Ratings of Safety Nets

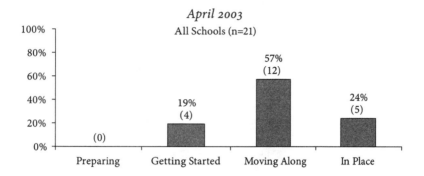

April 2003

All Schools (n=21)

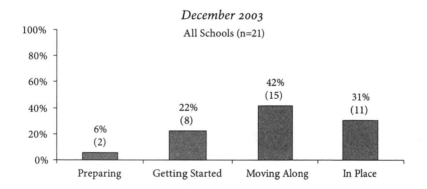

December 2003

All Schools (n=21)

Safety Net Ratings by School Level

April 2003

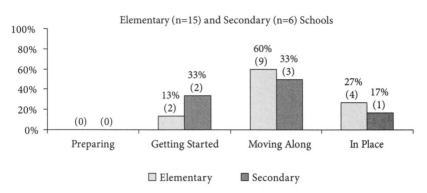

Elementary (n=15) and Secondary (n=6) Schools

December 2003

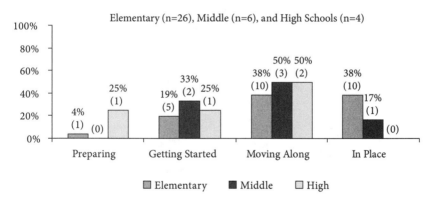

Elementary (n=26), Middle (n=6), and High Schools (n=4)

References

INTRODUCTION

Bach, A., & Supovitz, J. A. (2003). *Teacher and coach implementation of writers workshop in America's Choice Schools, 2001 and 2002.* Philadelphia: Consortium for Policy Research in Education.

Berends, M., Bodilly, S., & Kirby, S. (2002). *Facing the challenges of whole school reform.* Santa Monica, CA: RAND.

Fuhrman, S. H. (1993). The politics of coherence. In S. H. Fuhrman (Ed.), *Designing coherent education policy: Improving the system* (pp. 1–34). San Francisco: Jossey-Bass.

Hoffman, L., & Sable, J. (2006). *Public elementary and secondary students, staff, schools, and school districts: School year 2003–04.* Washington, DC: National Center for Education Statistics.

Lytle, J. (2002). Whole school reform from the inside. *Phi Delta Kappan, 84,* 164–167.

Poglinco, S. M., Bach, A. J., Hovde, K., Rosenblum, S., Saunders, M., & Supovitz, J. A. (2003). *The heart of the matter: The coaching model in America's Choice Schools.* Philadelphia: Consortium for Policy Research in Education.

Supovitz, J. A., & Klein, V. (2003). *Mapping a course for improved student learning: How innovative schools systematically use student performance data to guide improvement.* Philadelphia: Consortium for Policy Research in Education.

Supovitz, J. A., & Poglinco, S. M. (2001). *Instructional leadership in a standards-based reform.* Philadelphia: Consortium for Policy Research in Education.

Supovitz, J. A., Poglinco, S. M., & Bach, A. (2002). *Implementation of the America's Choice literacy workshops.* Philadelphia: Consortium for Policy Research in Education.

Supovitz, J. A., Poglinco, S. M., & Snyder, B. A. (2001). *Moving mountains: Successes and challenges of the America's Choice comprehensive school reform design.* Philadelphia: Consortium for Policy Research in Education.

Supovitz, J. A., Taylor, B., & May, H. (2002). *Impact of America's Choice on student performance in Duval County, Florida.* Philadelphia: Consortium for Policy Research in Education.

Supovitz, J. A., & Weathers, J. (2004). *Dashboard lights: Monitoring implementation of district instructional reform strategies.* Philadelphia: Consortium for Policy Research in Education.

CHAPTER 1

Annenberg Institute for School Reform. (2003). *The Annenberg Challenge: Lessons and reflections on public school reform.* Providence: Author.

Bach, A., & Supovitz, J. A. (2003). *Teacher and coach implementation of writers workshop in America's Choice Schools, 2001 and 2002.* Philadelphia Consortium for Policy Research in Education.

Berends, M., Bodilly, S., & Kirby, S. (2002). *Facing the challenges of whole school reform.* Santa Monica, CA: RAND.

Borman, G. D., Hewes, G. M., Overman, L. T., & Brown, S. (2003). Comprehensive school reform and achievement: A meta-analysis. *Review of Educational Research, 73,* 125–230.

Cohen, D. K. (1982). Policy and organization: The impact of state and federal educational policy on local school governance. *Harvard Educational Review, 52,* 474–499.

Cohen, D. K. (1995). What is the system in systemic reform? *Educational Researcher, 24*(9), 11–17.

Cohen, D. K., & Barnes, C. A. (1993). Pedagogy and policy. In D. K. Cohen, M. W. McLaughlin, & J. E. Talbert (Eds.), *Teaching for understanding: Challenges for policy and practice* (pp. 207–239). San Francisco: Jossey-Bass.

Cross, R. W., Rebarber, T., Torres, J., & Finn, C. E. Jr. (2004). *Grading the systems: The guide to state standards, tests, and accountability policies.* Washington, DC: Fordham Foundation.

Crowson, R., & Morris, V. C. (1985). Administrative control in large-city school systems: An investigation of Chicago. *Educational Administration Quarterly, 21,* 51–70.

Cuban, L. (1988). *The managerial imperative and the practice of leadership in schools.* Albany: State University of New York Press.

Datnow, A. (2002). Can we transplant educational reforms, and does it last? *Journal of Educational Change, 3,* 215–239.

Datnow, A., Borman, G. D., Stringfield, S., Overman, L. T., & Castellano, M. (2003). Comprehensive school reform in culturally and linguistically diverse contexts: Implementation and outcomes from a four-year study. *Education Evaluation and Policy Analysis, 25,* 143–170.

Datnow, A., Hubbard, L., & Mehan, H. (2002). *Extending educational reform.* London: RoutledgeFalmer.

David, J. L., & Shields, P. M. (2001). *When theory hits reality: Standards-based reform in urban districts.* Menlo Park, CA: SRI International.

Domanico, R., Finn, C. E. Jr., Innerst, C., Kanstoroom, M., & Russo, A. (2000). *Can philanthropy fix our schools? Appraising Walter Annenberg's $500 million gift to public education.* Washington, DC: Thomas B. Fordham Foundation.

Elmore, R. F. (1993). The role of local school districts in instructional improvement. In S. H. Fuhrman (Ed.), *Designing coherent education policy* (pp. 96–124). San Francisco: Jossey-Bass.

Elmore, R. F., & Burney, D. (1997). *Investing in teacher learning: Staff development and instructional improvement in Community School District #2, New York City.* New York: National Commission on Teaching and America's Future.

Floden, R., et al. (1988). Instructional leadership at the district level: A closer look at autonomy and control. *Educational Administration Quarterly, 24,* 96–124.

References

Franceschini, L. A. (2002, April). *Memphis, what happened? Notes on the decline and fall of comprehensive school reform models in a flagship district.* Paper presented at the annual meeting of the American Educational Research Association, New Orleans.

Fuhrman, S. H. (1993). The politics of coherence. In S. H. Fuhrman (Ed.), *Designing coherent education policy: Improving the system* (pp. 1–34). San Francisco: Jossey-Bass.

Fuhrman, S. H., & Elmore, R. F. (Eds.). (2004). *Redesigning accountability systems for education.* New York: Teachers College Press.

Hannaway, J., & Sproull, L. (1978). Who's running the show? Coordination and control in educational organizations. *Administrator's Notebook, 27,* 1–4.

Hess, F. M. (1999) *Spinning wheels: The politics of urban school reform.* Washington, DC: Brookings Institution Press.

Hoffman, L., & Sable, J. (2006). *Public elementary and secondary students, staff, schools, and school districts: School year 2003–04.* Washington, DC: National Center for Education Statistics.

Ingersoll, R. M. (1996). Teachers' decision-making power and school conflict. *Sociology in Education, 69,* 159–176.

Kerchener, C. (2001, April 18). Looking the gift horses in the mouth. *Education Week.*

Linn, R. L. (2000). Assessment and accountability. *Educational Researcher, 29*(2), 4–16.

Lytle, J. (2002). Whole school reform from the inside. *Phi Delta Kappan, 84,* 164–167.

Matthews, J. (2003, June 2). The 100 best high schools in America. *Newsweek,* pp. 48–55.

McDonald, J. P., McLaughlin, M. W., & Corcoran, T. (2000, April). *Agents of reform: The role and function of intermediary organizations in the Annenberg Challenge.* Paper presented at the annual meeting of the American Educational Research Association, New Orleans.

Mitchell, N. (1997, August 27). Education commission offers first round of findings. *Florida Times-Union.* Retrieved March 15, 2004, from http://www.jacksonville.com/tu-online/stories/082797/2a1new_c.html

Mitchell, N. (1998, May 8). Fryer: Job "just struck me right in the heart." *Florida Times-Union.* Retrieved March 15, 2004, from http://www.jacksonville.com/tu-online/stories/050898/met_2a1fryer.html

Newmann, F. M., Smith, B., Allensworth, E., & Bryk, A. (2001). Instructional program coherence: What it is and why it should guide school improvement policy. *Educational Evaluation and Policy Analysis, 23,* 297–321.

Poglinco, S. M., Bach, A. J., Hovde, K., Rosenblum, S., Saunders, M., & Supovitz, J. A. (2003). *The heart of the matter: The coaching model in America's Choice schools.* Philadelphia: Consortium for Policy Research in Education.

Rowan, B. (1982). Instructional management in historical perspective. *Educational Administration Quarterly, 18*(1), 43–59.

Skinner, R. A., & Staresina, L. N. (2004). State of the states. *Quality Counts, 23*(17), 97–99.

Smith, M. S., & O'Day, J. A. (1991). Systemic school reform. In S. Fuhrman & B. Malen (Eds.), *The politics of curriculum and testing* (pp. 233–267). New York: Falmer Press.

Snipes, J., Doolittle, F., & Herlihy, C. (2002). *Foundations for success: Case studies of how urban school systems improve student achievement.* Washington, DC: Council of Great City Schools.

Spillane, J. P. (2002). Local theories of teacher change: The pedagogy of district policies and programs. *Teachers College Record, 104,* 377–420.

Spillane, J. P., & Thompson, C. (1997). Reconstructing conceptions of local capacity: The local education agency's capacity for ambitious instructional reform. *Education Evaluation and Policy Analysis, 19,* 185–203.

Supovitz, J. A., & Klein, V. (2003). *Mapping a course for improved student learning: How innovative schools systematically use student performance data to guide improvement.* Philadelphia: Consortium for Policy Research in Education.

Supovitz, J. A., & Poglinco, S. M. (2001). *Instructional leadership in a standards-based reform.* Philadelphia: Consortium for Policy Research in Education.

Supovitz, J. A., Poglinco, S. M., & Bach, A. (2002). *Implementation of the America's Choice literacy workshops.* Philadelphia: Consortium for Policy Research in Education.

Supovitz, J. A., Poglinco, S. M., & Snyder, B. A. (2001). *Moving mountains: Successes and challenges of the America's Choice comprehensive school reform design.* Philadelphia: Consortium for Policy Research in Education.

Supovitz, J., & Snyder, B. (2003). *The impact of standards-based reform in Duval County, Florida, 1999–2002.* Philadelphia: Consortium for Policy Research in Education.

Supovitz, J. A., & Taylor, B. S. (2005). Systemic education evaluation: Evaluating the impact of systemwide reform in education. *American Journal of Evaluation, 26,* 204–230.

Supovitz, J. A., Taylor, B., & May, H. (2002). *Impact of America's Choice on student performance in Duval County, Florida.* Philadelphia: Consortium for Policy Research in Education.

Supovitz, J. A., & Weathers, J. (2004). *Dashboard lights: Monitoring implementation of district instructional reform strategies.* Philadelphia: Consortium for Policy Research in Education.

Togneri, W., & Anderson, S. E. (2003). *Beyond islands of excellence: What districts can do to improve instruction and achievement in all schools—a leadership brief.* Washington, DC: Learning First Alliance.

Tyler, W. (1988). *School organization.* New York: Croom Helm.

Wilson, B., Herriott, R., & Firestone, W. (1991). Explaining differences between elementary and secondary schools: Individual, organizational and institutional perspectives. In P. Thurston & P. Zodhiates (Eds.), *Advances in educational administration* (pp. 131–157), Greenwich, CT: JAI Press.

CHAPTER 2

Ballentine, T. (2002). *Evaluation of direct instruction in Duval County, Florida.* Unpublished manuscript.

Collins, J. C., & Porras, J. I. (1994). *Built to last: Successful habits of visionary companies.* New York: HarperBusiness.

Cuban, L. (1988). *The managerial imperative and the practice of leadership in schools.* Albany: State University of New York Press.

References

Datnow, A., Borman, G. D., Stringfield, S., Overman, L. T., & Castellano, M. (2003). Comprehensive school reform in culturally and linguistically diverse contexts: Implementation and outcomes from a four-year study. *Education Evaluation and Policy Analysis, 25,* 143–170.

Diamond, L. (2000a, June 21). Duval schools to expand rival reading programs. *Florida Times-Union.* Retrieved April 21, 2004, from http://www.jacksonville.com/tu-online/stories/062100/met_3360611.html

Diamond, L. (2000b, August 13). Choice for Duval is America's. *Florida Times Union.* Retrieved April 21, 2004, from http://www.jacksonville.com/tu-online/stories/081300/met_3788016.html

Education: An easy call. (2001). *Florida Times Union.* Retrieved April 21, 2004, from http://jacksonville.com/tu-online/stories/040401/opi_5818975.html

Hamann, M. S. (2001). *Report to the Duval County Public Schools on the first year evaluation of the direct instruction reading initiative.* Greensboro, NC: Author.

Kotter, J. P. (1998). Leading change: Why transformation efforts fail. In *Harvard Business Review on Change* (pp. 1–20). Cambridge, MA: Harvard Business School Press.

Marshall, R., & Tucker, M. (1992). *Thinking for a living: Education and the wealth of nations.* New York: Basic Books.

Mitchell, N. (1998, August 2). "I just don't quit." *Florida Times-Union.* Retrieved March 23, 2001, from http://www.jacksonville.com/tu-online/stories/080698/met_2a1Fryer.html

Pinzur, M. (2001, May 6). Politicians join fray over bus contracts. *Florida Times-Union.* Retrieved April 22, 2004, from http://jacksonville.com/tu-online/stories/050601/met_6101026.html

Resnick, L. B., & Hall, M. W. (1998). Learning organizations for sustainable education reform. *Daedalus, 127*(4), 89–118.

Richardson, M. (1998, September 11). Diverse group takes on the city's greatest cares. *Florida Times-Union.* Retrieved April 21, 2004 from http://www.jacksonville.com/tu-online/stories/091198/dsr_icare.html

Senge, P. M. (1990). *The fifth discipline: The art and practice of the learning organization.* New York: Doubleday.

Smith, M. S., & O'Day, J. (1991). Systemic school reform. In S. Fuhrman & B. Malen (Eds.), *The politics of curriculum and testing* (pp. 233–267). New York: Falmer Press.

Thurow, L. C. (1999). *Building wealth: The new rules for individuals, companies, and nations in a knowledge-based economy.* New York: HarperCollins.

Tucker, M. S., & Codding, J. B. (1998). *Standards for our schools.* San Francisco: Jossey-Bass.

CHAPTER 3

Anderson, J. R., Reder, L. M., & Simon, H. A. (1996). Situated learning and education. *Educational Researcher, 25*(4), 5–11.

Arons, A. B. (1989). What science should we teach? In the Biological Science Curriculum Study (Ed.), *A BSCS thirtieth anniversary symposium: Curriculum development for the year 2000* (pp. 13–20). Colorado Springs, CO: Biological Science Curriculum Study.

Berman, P. (1978). The study of macro- and micro-implementation. *Public Policy, 26,* 157–184.

Borko, H., & Putnam, R. T. (1995). Expanding a teacher's knowledge base: A cognitive psychological perspective on professional development. In T. R. Guskey & M. Huberman (Eds.), *Professional development in education: New paradigms and practices* (pp. 35–66). New York: Teachers College.

Bybee, R. W. (1993). *Reforming science education: Social perspectives and personal reflections.* New York: Teachers College Press.

Cohen, D. K. (1988). Teaching practice: Plus que ca change. In P. W. Jackson (Ed.), *Contributing to educational change: Perspectives on research and practice* (pp. 27–84). Berkeley, CA: McCutchan.

Cohen, D. K., & Hill, H. C. (1998). *State policy and classroom performance: Mathematics reform in California* (CPRE Research Report RR39). Philadelphia: Consortium for Policy Research in Education.

Commission on the Skills of the American Workforce. (1990). *America's choice: High skills or low wages!* Rochester, NY: National Center on Education and the Economy.

Corcoran, T., & Goertz, M. (1995). Instructional capacity and high performance. *Educational Researcher, 24*(9), 27–31.

Darling-Hammond, L, & McLaughlin, M. W. (1995). Policies that support professional development in an era of reform. *Phi Delta Kappan, 76,* 597–604.

Diamond, L. (2000, August 13). Choice for Duval is America's. *Florida Times Union.* Retrieved April 21, 2004, from http://www.jacksonville.com/tu-online/stories/081300/met_3788016.html

Duval County Schools. (2003). *Principal career path and leadership development program.* Jacksonville, FL: Author.

Elmore, R. F. (1993). The role of local school districts in instructional improvement. In S. Fuhrman (Ed.), *Designing coherent education policy* (pp. 96–124). San Francisco: Jossey-Bass.

Evans, R. (1996). *The human side of school change: Reform, resistance, and the real-life problems of innovation.* San Francisco : Jossey-Bass.

Firestone, W. A. (1989). Using reform: Conceptualizing district initiative. *Educational Evaluation and Policy Analysis, 11,* 151–164.

Fuhrman, S. H., & O'Day, J. A. (Eds.). (1996). *Rewards and reform: Creating educational incentives that work.* San Francisco: Jossey-Bass.

Fullan, M. (1991). *The new meaning of educational change.* New York: Teachers College Press.

Gonzalez, R. (2004a). *Ruben's demo video.* Retrieved January 2, 2004, from http://www.thelugeman.com/demo-video-2.htm, retrieved

Gonzalez, R. (2004b). *Motivational keynote.* Retrieved January 2, 2004, http://www.thelugeman.com/motivantional-speech.htm

Gonzalez, R. (2004c). *Ruben Gonzalez, the luge man.* Retrieved January 2, 2004, from http://www.thelugeman.com/

Hall, G. E., & Hord, S. M. (1987). *Change in schools: Facilitating the process.* Albany: State University of New York Press.

References

Hawley, W. D., & Valli, L. (1999). The essentials of effective professional development: A new consensus. In G. Sykes & L. Darling-Hammond (Eds.), *Handbook of teaching and policy.* New York: Teachers College Press.

Horsley, D. L., & Loucks-Horsley, S. (1998). Tornado of change. *Journal of Staff Development, 19*(4), 17–20.

Kennedy, M. M. (1998, April). *The relevance of content in-service teacher education.* Paper presented at the annual meeting of the American Educational Research Association. San Diego.

Lieberman, A. (1995). Practices that support teacher development. *Phi Delta Kappan, 76,* 591–596.

Little, J. W. B. (1993). Teachers' professional development in a climate of educational reform. *Educational evaluation and policy analysis, 15,* 129–151.

Marek, E. A., & Methven, S. B. (1991). Effect of the learning cycle upon student and classroom teacher performance. *Journal of Research in Science Teaching, 28*(1), 41–53.

Marsh, D. D., & LeFever, K. (1997, April). *Educational leadership in a policy context: What happens when student performance standards are clear?* Paper presented at the annual meeting of the American Educational Research Association, Chicago.

McDermott, L. C. (1990). A perspective in teacher preparation in physics and other sciences: the need for special science courses for teachers. *American Journal of Physics, 58,* 734–742.

McLaughlin, M. W. (1987). Learning from experience: Lessons from policy implementation. *Educational Evaluation and Policy Analysis, 9,* 171–178.

Mohrman, A. M. (1989). *Large-scale organizational change.* San Francisco: Jossey-Bass.

Mohrman, S. A., & Lawler, E. E. (1996). Motivation for school reform. In S. H. Fuhrman & J. A. O'Day (Eds.), *Rewards and reform: Creating educational incentives that work* (pp. 115–143). San Francisco: Jossey-Bass.

National Council for Teachers of Mathematics. (1989). *Curriculum and evaluation standards for teaching mathematics.* Reston, VA: Author.

National Research Council. (1996). *National science education standards.* Washington, DC: National Academy Press.

National Reading Panel. (2000). *Teaching children to read: An evidence-based assessment of the scientific research literature on reading and its implications for reading instruction.* Washington, DC: National Institute of Child Health and Human Development.

O'Day, J., & Smith, M. (1993). Systemic reform and educational opportunity. In S. H. Fuhrman (Ed.), *Designing coherent education policy: Improving the system* (pp. 250–312). San Francisco: Jossey-Bass.

Resnick, L, & Klopfer, L. (1989). Toward the thinking curriculum: An overview. *Toward the thinking curriculum: Current cognitive research, 1989 yearbook of the Association for Supervision and Curriculum Development* (pp. 1–10). Alexandria, VA: ASCD.

Schmidt, W. (1999, January 8). *A splintered vision: An investigation of U.S. science and mathematics education.* Paper presented at the annual conference of the National Center for Education and the Economy, San Diego.

Showers, B., & Joyce, B. (1996). The evolution of peer coaching. *Educational Leadership, 53*(6), 12–16.

Smylie, M. A., Bilcer, D. K., Greenberg, R. C., & Harris, R. L. (1998, April). *Urban teacher professional development: A portrait of practice from Chicago.* Paper presented at the annual meeting of the American Educational Research Association, San Diego.

Spillane, J. P., Reiser, B. J., & Reimer, T. (2002). Policy implementation and cognition: Reframing and refocusing implementation research. *Review of Educational Research, 72*(3), 387–431.

Supovitz, J. A., & Turner, H. (2000). The influence of standards-based reform on classroom practices and culture. *Journal of Research in Science Teaching, 37*(1), 1–18.

Weatherly, R., & Lipsky, M. (1977). Street-level bureaucrats and institutional innovation: Implementing special education reform. *Harvard Educational Review, 47*, 171–197.

Weick, K. E. (1976). Educational organizations as loosely coupled systems. *Administrative Science Quarterly, 21*, 1–19.

Wenger, E. (1998). *Communities of practice: Learning, meaning, and identity.* Cambridge, England: Cambridge University Press.

Zigarmi, P., Betz, L., & Jennings, D. (1977). Teachers' preferences in and perceptions of inservice. *Educational Leadership, 34*, 545–551.

CHAPTER 4

Cohen, D. (1988). Teaching practice: Plus ca change. In P. Jackson (Ed.), *Contributing to educational change: Perspectives on research and practice* (pp. 27–84). Berkeley, CA: McCutchan.

Cyert, R., & March, J. (1963). *A behavioral theory of the firm.* Englewood Cliffs, NJ: Prentice Hall.

Garan, E. M. (2002). *Resisting reading mandates: How to triumph with the truth.* Portsmouth, NH: Heinemann.

Ingersoll, R. M. (2003). *Who controls teachers' work? Power and accountability in America's schools.* Cambridge, MA: Harvard University Press.

Kim, T. & Kuo, W., (1999). Modeling manufacturing yield and reliability. *IEEE Transactions on Semiconductor Manufacturing, 12*, 485–492.

Labaree, D. D. (2004). *The trouble with ed schools.* New Haven, CT: Yale University Press.

Lortie, D. (1977). Two anomalies and three perspectives: Some observations on school organization. In R. Corwin & R. Edelfelt (Eds.), *Perspectives on organizations* (pp. 20–38). Washington, DC: American Association of Colleges for Teacher Education.

Macduffie, J. P. (1995). Human resource bundles and manufacturing performance: Organizational logic and flexible production systems in the world auto industry. *Industrial and Labor Relations Review, 48*, 197–221.

National Reading Panel. (2000). *Teaching children to read: An evidence-based assessment of the scientific research literature on reading and its implications for reading instruction.* Washington, DC: National Institute of Child Health and Human Development.

Sedlak, M., Wheeler, C., Pullin, D., & Cusick, P. (1986). *Selling students short.* New York: Teachers College.

References

Shulman, L. S. (1983). Autonomy and obligation: The remote control of teaching. In L. S. Shulman & G. Sykes (Eds.), *Handbook of teaching and policy* (pp. 484–504). New York: Longman.

Supovitz, J. A., & Goerlich-Zief, S. (2000). Why they stay away: Revealing the invisible barriers to teacher participation in content-based professional development. *Journal of Staff Development 21*, 24–28.

Supovitz, J. A., & LaCoe, C. (2006). *Decomposing teacher autonomy.* Unpublished Manuscript.

Weick, K. (1976). Educational organizations as loosely coupled systems. *Administrative Science Quarterly, 21,* 1–19.

Weick, K. & Roberts, K. (1996). Collective mind in organizations: Heedful interrelating on flight decks. In M. Cohen & L. Sproull, (Eds.), *Organizational learning* (pp. 330–358). Thousand Oaks, CA: SAGE.

Xiao, Y., & Moss, J. (2001). Practice of high reliability teams: Observations in trauma resuscitation. In *Proceeding of the Human Factors and Ergonomics Society* 44th Annual Meeting, 395–399. Available at http://www.hfrp.umm.edu/paperstore/papers/2001/Xiao%20Moss%20hfes%202001-camera%20ready.pdf

CHAPTER 5

Abelmann, C. H., & Elmore, R. F. (2004). When accountability knocks, will anyone answer? In Richard Elmore (Ed.), *School reform from the inside out: Policy, practice, and performance* (pp. 133–199). Cambridge, MA: Harvard Education Press.

Almeida, P., Phene A., & Grant, R. (2003). Innovation and knowledge management: Scanning, sourcing and integration. In M. Easterby-Smith & M. A. Lyles (Eds.), *Handbook of organizational learning and knowledge management* (pp. 356–371). Malden, MA: Blackwell.

Argyris, C., & Schön, D. A. (1974). *Theory in practice: Increasing professional effectiveness.* San Francisco: Jossey-Bass

Bishop, J. H., & Mane, F. (1999). *The New York state reform strategy: The incentives effects of minimum competency exams.* Philadelphia: National Center on Education in Inner Cities.

Black, P., & William, D. (1998a). Inside the black box: Raising standards through classroom assessment. *Phi Delta Kappan, 80,* 139–148.

Black, P., & William, D. (1998b). Assessment and classroom learning. *Assessment in Education, 5,* 7–68.

Bransford, J. D., Brown, A. L., & Cocking, R. R. (Eds.). (1999). *How people learn.* Washington, DC: National Academies Press.

Carnoy, M., & Loeb, S. (2003). Does external accountability affect student outcomes? *Educational Evaluation and Policy Analysis, 24,* 305–331.

Chakravarthy, B., McEvily, S., Doz, Y., & Rau, D. (2003). Knowledge management and competitive advantage. In M. Easterby-Smith & M. A. Lyles (Eds.), *Handbook of organizational learning and knowledge management* (pp. 305–323). Malden, MA: Blackwell.

Coburn, C. (2003). Rethinking scale: Moving beyond numbers to deep and lasting change. *Educational Researcher, 32*(6), 3–12.

Collins, J. (2001). *Good to great.* New York: HarperCollins.

Corbett, H. D., & Wilson, B. L. (1988). Raising the stakes in statewide mandatory minimum competency testing. In W. L. Boyd & C. T. Kerchner (Eds.), *The politics of excellence and choice in education: The 1987 Politics of Education Association yearbook* (pp. 27–39). New York: Falmer Press.

Crooks, T. J. (1988). The impact of classroom evaluation practices on students. *Review of Educational Research, 58,* 438–481.

Davenport, T. H., & Prusak, L. (2000). *Working knowledge: How organizations manage what they know.* Boston: Harvard Business School Press.

Easterby-Smith, M., & Lyles, M. A. (2003). Watersheds of organizational learning and knowledge management. In M. Easterby-Smith & M. A. Lyles (Eds.), *Handbook of organizational learning and knowledge management* (pp. 1–16). Malden, MA: Blackwell.

Elmore, R. F., Abelmann, C. H., & Fuhrman, S. H. (1996). The new accountability in state education reform: From process to performance. In H. Ladd (Ed.), *Holding schools accountable: Performance-based reform in education.* Washington, DC: Brookings Institution Press.

Fiol, C. M., & Lyles, M. A. (1985). Organizational learning. *Academy of Management Review, 10,* 803–813.

Firestone, W., Mayrowetz, D., & Fairman, J. (1998). Performance-based assessment and instructional change: The effects of testing in Maine and Maryland. *Educational Evaluation and Policy Analysis, 20,* 95–113.

Fuhrman, S. H., & Elmore, R. F. (Eds.). (2004*). Redesigning accountability systems for education.* New York: Teachers College Press.

Goertz, M. E., & Duffy, M. C. (2001). *Assessment and accountability systems in the 50 states: 1999–2000.* Philadelphia: Consortium for Policy Research in Education.

Grossman, A., Honan, J. P., & King, C. (2004). *Learning to manage data in Duval County Public Schools: Lake Shore Middle School.* Cambridge, MA: Public Education Leadership Project at Harvard University.

Hamilton, L. (2003). Assessment as a policy tool. *Review of Research in Education, 27,* 25–68.

Koretz, D., Barron, S., Mitchell, K., & Stecher, B. (1996). *The perceived effects of the Kentucky Instructional Results Information System.* Santa Monica, CA: RAND.

Ladd, H. (Ed.). (1996). *Holding schools accountable: Performance-based reform in education.* Washington, DC: Brookings Institution Press.

Leithwood, K., & Aitken, R. (1995). *Making schools smarter: A system for monitoring school and district progress.* Thousand Oaks, CA: Corwin Press.

Levitt, B., & March, J. (1988). Organizational learning. *Annual Review of Sociology, 14,* 319–340.

Mehrens, W. A., & Lehmann, I. J. (1973). *Standardized tests in education* (2nd ed.). New York: Holt, Rinehart and Winston.

Mohrman, S. A., & Wohlstetter, P. (Eds.). (1994). *Organizing for high performance.* San Francisco: Jossey-Bass.

Mohrman, S. A., & Lawler, E. E. (1996). Motivation for school reform. In S. Fuhrman & J. O'Day (Eds.), Rewards *and reform: Creating educational incentives that work* (pp. 115–143). San Francisco: Jossey-Bass.

References

Natriello, G. (1987). The impact of evaluation processes on students. *Educational Psychologist, 22*, 155–175.

Nonaka, I., & Takeuchi, H. (1995). *The knowledge-creating company*. New York: Oxford University Press.

Pedulla, J. J., Abrams, L. M., Madaus, G. F., Russell, M. K., Ramos, M. A., & Miao, J. (2003). *Perceived effects of state-mandated testing programs on teaching and learning: Findings from a national survey of teachers*. Boston: National Board on Educational Testing and Public Policy.

Preskill, H. S., & Torres, R. T. (1999). *Evaluative inquiry for learning in organizations*. Thousand Oaks, CA: Sage.

Rossi, P. H., Lipsey, M. W., & Freeman, H. E. (1999). *Evaluation: A systematic approach*. Thousand Oaks, CA: Sage.

Senge, P. (1990). *The fifth discipline: The art and practice of the learning organization*. New York: Doubleday Currency.

Shepard, L., & Dougherty, K. C. (1991, April). *Effects of high-stakes testing on instruction*. Paper presented at the annual meeting of the American Educational Research Association, Chicago.

Shepard, L. A. (2000). *The role of classroom assessment in teaching and learning* (CSE Technical Report 517). Los Angeles, CA:. National Center for Research on Evaluation, Standards, and Student Testing.

Shulman, L. S. (1981). Disciplines of inquiry in education: An overview. *Educational Researcher, 10*(6), 5–12, & 23.

Smith, D., & Ruff, D. (1998). Building a culture of inquiry: The school quality review. In D. Allen (Ed.), *Assessing student learning: From grading to understanding* (pp. 164–182). New York: Teachers College.

Snipes, J., Doolittle, F., & Herlihy, C. (2002). *Foundations for success: Case studies of how urban school systems improve student achievement*. Washington, DC: Council of Great City Schools.

Stecher, B. M., Barron, S. I., Chun, T., & Ross, K. (2000). *The effects of the Washington state education reform on schools and classrooms* (CSE Technical Report 525). Los Angeles: Center for Research on Evaluation, Standards, and Student Testing.

Stecher, B. M., & Chun, T. (2001). *School and classroom practices during two years of education reform in Washington State* (CSE Technical Report 550). Los Angeles: Center for Research on Evaluation, Standards, and Student Testing.

Supovitz, J. A., & Klein, V. (2003). *Mapping a course for improved student learning: How innovative schools systematically use student performance data to guide improvement*. Philadelphia: Consortium for Policy Research in Education.

Supovitz, J. A., & Weathers, J. (2004). *Dashboard lights: Monitoring implementation of district instructional reform strategies*. Philadelphia: Consortium for Policy Research in Education.

Taylor, G., Shepard, L., Kinner, F., & Rosenthal, J. (2003). *A survey of teachers' perspectives on high stakes testing in Colorado: What gets taught, what gets lost* (CSE Technical Report 588). Los Angeles: Center for Research on Evaluation, Standards, and Student Testing.

Tharp, R. G., & Gallimore R. (1988). *Rousing minds to life: Teaching, learning, and schooling in social context.* Cambridge, England: Cambridge University Press.

Togneri, W., & Anderson, S. E. (2003) *Beyond islands of excellence: What districts can do to improve instruction and achievement in all schools—a leadership brief.* Washington, DC: Learning First Alliance.

Vygotsky, L. S. (1987). *The collected works of L. S. Vygotsky* (R. W. Rieber & A. S. Carton, Eds.). New York : Plenum Press

Wolf, S. A., Borko, H., McIver, M. C., & Elliott, R. (1999*). "No excuses": School reform efforts in exemplary schools of Kentucky* (CSE Technical Report 514). Los Angeles: Center for Research on Evaluation, Standards, and Student Testing.

Wolf, D. P., & Reardon, S. F. (1996). Access to excellence through new forms of student assessment. In J. B. Baron & D. P. Wolf (Eds.), *Performance-based student assessment: Challenges and possibilities.* (Ninety-fifth yearbook of the National Society for the study of Education) (pp. 1–31). Chicago: University of Chicago Press.

CHAPTER 6

Argyris, C., & Schön, D. A. (1978). *Organizational learning: A theory of action perspective.* Reading, MA: Addison-Wesley.

Brown, J. S., & Duguid, P. (1991). Organizational learning and communities-of-practice: Toward a unified view of working, learning, and innovation. *Organization Science, 2*(1), 40–57

Coburn, C. E. (2003). Rethinking scale: Moving beyond numbers to deep and lasting change. *Educational Researcher, 32*(6), 3–12.

Council of the Great City Schools. (2003). Urban school superintendents: Characteristics, tenure, and salary. *Urban Indicator, 7*(1), 1–8.

Cyert, R. M., & March, J. G. (1963). *A behavioral theory of the firm.* Englewood Cliffs, NJ: Prentice-Hall.

Daft, R., & Huber, G. (1987). How organizations learn: A communication framework. *Research in the Sociology of Organizations, 5,* 1–36.

Degenne, A., & Forse, M. (1999). *Introducing social networks.* Thousand Oaks, CA: Sage.

Deming, W. E. (1986). *Out of crisis.* Cambridge, MA: Center for Advanced Engineering Study.

DuFour, R., & Eaker, R. (1998). *Professional learning communities at work.* Atlanta: Association for Supervision and Curriculum Development.

Elmore, R. F. (1996). Getting to scale with good educational practice. *Harvard Educational Review, 66,* 1–26.

Fullan, M. (2005). *Leadership and Sustainability.* Thousand Oaks, CA: Corwin Press.

Galbraith, J. R. (1994). *Competing with flexible lateral organizations* (2nd ed.) Reading, MA: Addison-Wesley.

Garvin, D. A. (1993) Building a learning organization. *Harvard Business Review, 71*(4), 78–84.

Ginsberg, A. (1990). Connecting diversification to performance: A sociocognitive approach. *Academy of Management Review, 15,* 514–535.

References

Hatch, T. (2000). What does it take to "go to scale"? Reflections on the promise and perils of comprehensive school reform. *Journal of Students Placed at Risk, 5*, 339–354.

Hedberg, B. (1981). How organizations learn and unlearn. In P. C. Nystrom & W. H. Starbuck (Eds.), *Handbook of organizational design* (pp. 3–27). London: Oxford University Press.

Heifetz, R. A. (1994). *Leadership without easy answers.* Cambridge, MA: Belknap Press.

Hess, F. M. (1999). *Spinning wheels: The politics of urban school reform.* Washington, DC: Brookings Institution Press.

Honig, M. I. (2004). Where's the "up" in bottom-up reform? *Educational Policy, 18*, 527–561.

Huber, G. P. (1991). Organizational learning: The contributing process and the literatures. *Organization Science, 2*(1), 88–115.

Levitt, B., & March, J. G. (1988). Organizational learning. *Annual Review of Sociology, 14*, 319–340.

McLaughlin, M. W., & Talbert, J. E. (2001). *Professional communities and the work of high school teaching.* Chicago: University of Chicago Press.

Mohrman, A. M., Mohrman, S. A., & Lawler, E. E. (1992). The performance management of teams. In W. Bruns (Ed.), *Performance measurement, evaluation, and incentives.* Cambridge, MA: Harvard Business School Press.

Mohrman, S. A., Cohen, S. G., & Mohrman, A. M. (1995). *Designing team-based organizations: New forms for knowledge work.* San Francisco: Jossey-Bass.

Nonaka, I. (1991). The knowledge creating company. *Harvard Business Review, 69*(6), 97–104.

Pawlowsky, P., Forslin, J., & Reinhardt, R. (2001). Practices and tools of organizational learning. In M. Dierkes, A. Antal, J. Child, & I. Nonaka (Eds.), *Handbook of organizational learning and knowledge* (pp. 775–793). New York: Oxford University Press.

Roberts, S. M., & Pruitt, E. Z. (2003). *Schools as professional learning communities.* Thousand Oaks, CA: Corwin Press.

Senge, P. (1990). *The fifth discipline: The art and practice of the learning organization.* New York: Doubleday.

Spillane, J. P. (2002). Local theories of teacher change: The pedagogy of district policies and programs. *Teachers College Record, 104*, 377–420.

Strata, R. (1989). Organizational learning—the key to management innovation. *Sloan Management Review, Spring*, 63–74.

Supovitz, J. A. (2002). Developing communities of instructional practice. *Teachers College Record, 104*, 1591–1626.

Supovitz, J. A., & Christman, J. B. (2005). Small learning communities that actually learn: Lessons for school leaders. *Phi Delta Kappan, 86*, 649–651.

Supovitz, J. A., & Goerlich-Zief, S. (2000). Why they stay away: Revealing the invisible barriers to teacher participation in content-based professional development. *Journal of Staff Development, 21*(4), 24–28.

Supovitz, J. A., & Weathers, J. (2004). *Dashboard lights: Monitoring implementation of district instructional reform strategies.* Philadelphia: Consortium for Policy Research in Education.

Taylor, F. W. (1911). *Principles of scientific management.* New York: Harper & Row.

Weick, K. E. (1979). Cognitive processes in organizations. *Research in Organizational Behavior, 1,* 41–74.

Wenger, E. (1998). *Communities of practice: Learning, meaning, and identity.* Cambridge, England: Cambridge University Press.

CHAPTER 7

Bryk, A. S., & Schneider, B. (2003). Trust in schools: A core resource for school reform. *Educational Leadership, 60*(6), 40–44.

Bulkley, K. E., & Wohlstetter, P. (2004). *Taking account of charter schools.* New York: Teachers College Press.

Carnoy, M., & Loeb, S. (2003). Does external accountability affect student outcomes? *Educational Evaluation and Policy Analysis, 24,* 305–331.

Clement, N. I. (2002). Strengthen school culture using a customer service audit. *School Administrator, 59*(5), 39.

Cohen, D. K., & Hill, H. (2001). *Learning policy: When state education reform works.* New Haven, CT: Yale University Press.

Conyers, J. G. (2002). When status quo won't do. *School Administrator, 57*(6), 22–25.

Cuban, L. (1988). *The managerial imperative and the practice of leadership in schools.* Albany: State University of New York Press.

Datnow, A. (2002). Can we transplant educational reform, and does it last? *Journal of Educational Change, 3,* 215–239.

Earl, L., & Katz, S. (2002). Leading schools in a data-rich world. In K. Leithwood & P. Hallinger (Eds.), *Second international handbook of educational leadership and administration* (pp. 1003–1022).

Firestone, W. A., & Hirsch, L. S. (2006). *A formative evaluation of the implementation of New Jersey's professional development requirements for teachers: Year five.* New Brunswick, NJ: Rutgers University, Center for Educational Policy Analysis.

Fuhrman, S. H. (1993). The politics of coherence. In S. H. Fuhrman (Ed.), *Designing coherent education policy: Improving the system* (pp. 1–34). San Francisco: Jossey-Bass.

Fullan, M. (2005). *Leadership and sustainability.* Thousand Oaks, CA: Corwin Press.

Goertz, M. E., & Duffy, M. C. (2001). *Assessment and accountability systems in the 50 states: 1999–2000.* Philadelphia: Consortium for Policy Research in Education.

Gross, B., Kirst, M., Holland, D., & Luschei, T. (2005). Got you under my spell? How accountability policy is changing and not changing decision making in high schools. In B. Gross & M. Goertz, *Holding high hopes: How high schools respond to state accountability policies* (pp. 43–79). Philadelphia: Consortium for Policy Research in Education.

Gutmann, A. (1987). *Democratic education.* Princeton, NJ: Princeton University Press.

Herman, J. L., & Haertel, E. H. (2005). *Uses and misuses of data for educational accountability and improvement: 104th yearbook of the National Society for the Study of Education.* Malden, MA: Blackwell.

Kirst, M. (2002). *Mayoral influence, new regimes, and public school governance.* Philadelphia: Consortium for Policy Research in Education.

Miles, K. H., Odden, A., Fermanich, M., & Archibald, S. (2005). *Inside the black box: School district spending on professional development in education.* Retrieved April 12, 2006, from http://www.wallacefoundation.org/WF/ELAN/TR/KnowledgeCategories/Improving-Conditions/UseOfFinancialResources/inside_the_black_box.htm

National Center for Education Statistics. (2005). *The condition of education.* Retrieved October 13, 2005, from http://nces.ed.gov/programs/coe/

Olebe, M. G. et al. (1992). Consider the customer. *American School Board Journal, 179*(12), 52–55.

School Matters. (2005). *State and district information.* Retrived April 14, 2006, from http://www.schoolmatters.com/App/SES/SPSServlet/MenuLinksRequest?StateID=1036196&LocLevelID =162&StateLocLevelID=676&LocationID=1036195

Smith, P. S., Banilower, E. R. McMahon, K. C. & Weiss, I. R. (2002). *The National Survey of Science and Mathematics Education: Trends from 1977 to 2000.* Chapel Hill, NC: Horizon Research.

Spillane, J. (2004). *Standards deviation: How schools misunderstand education policy.* Cambridge, MA: Harvard University Press.

Supovitz, J. A., & Klein, V. (2003). *Mapping a course for improved student learning: How innovative schools systematically use student performance data to guide improvement.* Philadelphia: Consortium for Policy Research in Education.

Tyack, D. (1974). *The one best system.* Cambridge, MA: Harvard University Press.

Wayman, J. C., Stringfield, S., & Millard, M. O. (2004, April). *Software for disaggregating and reporting student data: Moving beyond "No Child Left Behind" to inform classroom practice.* Paper presented at the annual meeting of the American Educational Research Association, San Diego.

Weinbaum, E. H. (2005). Stuck in the middle with you: District response to state accountability. In B. Gross & M. Goertz (Eds.), *Holding high hopes: How high schools respond to state accountability policies* (pp. 95–119). Philadelphia: Consortium for Policy Research in Education.

CHAPTER 8

Black, P., Harrison, C., Lee, C., Marshall, B., & William, D. (2003). *Assessment for learning.* Berkshire, England: Open University Press.

Collins, J. (2001). *Good to great.* New York: HarperCollins.

Cuban, L. (1988). *The managerial imperative and the practice of leadership in schools.* Albany: State University of New York Press.

Darling-Hammond, L., Hightower, A. M., Husbands, J. L., LaFors, J. R., Young, V. M., & Christopher, C. (2005). *Instructional leadership for systemic change: The story of San Diego's reform.* Lanham, MD.: Scarecrow Education.

Elmore, R. F. (2002). *Bridging the gap between standards and achievement.* Washington, DC: Albert Shanker Institute.

Elmore, R. F., & Burney, D. (1997). *Investing in teacher learning: Staff development and instructional improvement in Community School District #2, New York City.* New York: National Commission on Teaching and America's Future.

Fullan, M. (1994). Coordinating top-down and bottom-up strategies for educational reform. In R. F. Elmore & S. H. Fuhrman (Eds.), *The governance of curriculum* (pp. 186–202). Alexandria, VA: Association for Supervision and Curriculum Development.

Herman, J. L., & Haertel, E. H. (Eds.). (2005). *Uses and misuses of data for educational accountability and improvement: The 104th yearbook of the National Society for the Study of Education.* Malden, MA: Blackwell.

Ladd, H. (1996). *Holding schools accountable: Performance based reform in education.* Washington, DC: Brookings Institution Press.

Lee, V. E., & Smith, J. B. (1996). Collective responsibility for learning and its effects on gains in achievement in early secondary school students. *American Journal of Education, 104,* 103–147.

McAdams, D. R. (2006). *What school boards can do: Reform governance for urban schools.* New York: Teachers College Press.

O'Day, J. (2003). Partnership, accountability, and standards-based reform: Reflections on the Baltimore city-state partnership. *Journal of Education for Students Placed at Risk, 8,* 149–163.

Rowan, B. (1990). Commitment and control: Alternative strategies for the organizational design of schools. *Review of Research in Education, 16,* 353–389.

Schein, E. H. (2004) *Organizational culture and leadership.* San Francisco: Jossey-Bass.

Snipes, J., Doolittle, F., & Herlihy, C. (2002). *Foundations for success: Case studies of how urban school systems improve student achievement.* Washington, DC: Council of Great City Schools.

Supovitz, J. A., & Klein, V. (2003). *Mapping a course for improved student learning: How innovative schools systematically use student performance data to guide improvement.* Philadelphia: Consortium for Policy Research in Education.

Togneri, W., & Anderson, S. E. (2003). *Beyond islands of excellence: What districts can do to improve instruction and achievement in all schools.* Washington, DC: Learning First Alliance.

Wiggins, G., & McTighe, J. (1998). *Understanding by design.* Alexandria, VA.: Association for Supervision and Curriculum Development.

About the Author

JONATHAN A. SUPOVITZ is an associate professor at the University of Pennsylvania and a senior researcher at the Consortium for Policy Research in Education. His mixed-method research and evaluation work focuses on educational policy and leadership issues in support of building and sustaining improvements in teaching and learning. He has published findings from numerous educational studies, including multiple studies of programmatic effectiveness; examinations of the relationships among teacher professional development, teaching practice, and student achievement; studies of educational leadership; efforts to develop communities of practice in schools; an examination of the equitability of different forms of student assessment; and investigations of the use of data and evidence for organizational improvement. He received his doctorate from the Harvard Graduate School of Education, his master's degree in public policy from Duke University, and his bachelor's degree in history from the University of California at Berkeley.

Index